W9-BCS-554

Sunset

BEST HOME PLANS

Starter & Retirement Homes

Compact plan of this elegant single-story house features large living spaces and a private master suite. See plan E-1435 on page 40.

Sunset Publishing Corporation ■ Menlo Park, California

SUNSET BOOKS
President and Publisher:
  Susan J. Maruyama
Director, Sales & Marketing:
  Richard A. Smeby
Director, New Business Development:
  Kenneth Winchester
Editorial Director:
  Bob Doyle
Production Director:
  Lory Day
Assistant Editor:
  Kevin Freeland
Contributing Editor:
  Don Vandervort

**SUNSET PUBLISHING
CORPORATION**
Chairman:
  Jim Nelson
**President/Chief Executive
  Officer:** Stephen J. Seabolt
Chief Financial Officer:
  James E. Mitchell
**Director, Finance & Business
  Affairs:** Lawrence J. Diamond
Publisher:
  Anthony P. Glaves
Vice President, Manufacturing:
  Lorinda Reichert
Circulation Director:
  Robert I. Gursha
Editor, Sunset Magazine:
  William R. Marken

Photographers: Mark Englund/
HomeStyles: 4, 5; Philip Harvey:
10 top, back cover; Stephen Marley:
11 top left and right; Russ Widstrand:
10 bottom; Tom Wyatt: 11 bottom.

Cover: Pictured is plan UDG-90009
on page 118. Cover design by
Naganuma Design & Direction.
Photography by Mark Englund/
HomeStyles.

First printing February 1996
Copyright © 1996, Sunset Publishing
Corporation, Menlo Park, CA 94025.
First edition. All rights reserved, including
the right of reproduction in whole or in part
in any form. ISBN 0-376-01143-2. Library of
Congress Catalog Card Number: 95-072508.
Printed in the United States.

♻ Printed on recycled paper

For more information on Sunset's *Best Home
Plans Starter & Retirement Homes* or any other
Sunset book, call (800) 634-3095. For special
sales, bulk orders, and premium sales infor-
mation, call Sunset Custom Publishing
Services at (415) 324-5577.

A Dream Come True

Planning and building a house is one of life's most creative and rewarding challenges. Whether you're seriously considering building a new home or you're just dreaming about it, this book offers a wealth of inspiration and information to help you get started.

On the following pages, you'll learn how to plan and manage a home-building project—and how to ensure its success. Then you'll discover more than 200 proven home plans, designed for families just like yours by architects and professional designers. Peruse the pages and study the floor plans; you're sure to find a home that's just right for you. When you're ready to order blueprints, you can simply call or mail in your order, and you'll receive the plans within days.

Enjoy the adventure!

Covered porch welcomes guests to this country-style charmer. For first-time buyers or empty-nesters, this home offers lots of extras in relatively little space. See plan VL-2069 on page 175.

Contents

When Less Is More

Whether you're a first-time home buyer who is anxious to enter the housing market or a retiree looking for a simpler style of living, a small, compact home may be the perfect answer, especially when that home is fitted with plenty of amenities. And as you'll see when you study the plans in this book, shared spaces, economical floor plans, and easy maintenance make these homes particularly desirable.

Best of all, these small homes don't scrimp on style. You'll discover a myriad of beautiful homes in a range of styles: traditional, contemporary, country, classic, even rustic. All are proven designs created by some of America's foremost residential architects and designers.

The two keys to success in building a home are capable project management and good design. The next few pages will walk you through some of the most important aspects of project management: you'll find an overview of the building process, directions for selecting the right plan and getting the most from it, and methods for working with a builder and other professionals.

The balance of this book presents professionally designed stock plans for homes in a wide range of styles and configurations. Once you find a plan that will work for you—perhaps with a few modifications made later to personalize it for your family—you can order construction blueprints for a fraction of the cost of a custom design, a savings of many thousands of dollars (see pages 12–15 for information on how to order).

Stylish two-story home designed for outdoor living features a spacious deck accessed through sliding glass doors in both the living room and master bedroom. There's even an optional greenhouse off the deck. Two more bedrooms and a bath are located upstairs. See plan AX-97144 on page 80.

Perfect for a small or narrow lot, this attractive two-story home offers traditional charm and modern amenities. The main floor boasts a relatively open floor plan. Three bedrooms and two baths are upstairs. See plan B-901 on page 45.

Easy-care, small-space home is ideal for retirees or families just starting out. The compact corner kitchen opens to a spacious family room on one side and a combination living/dining area on the other. See plan NW 864-J on page 48.

Setting the tone for this elegant retirement home is the spectacular entrance. Compactly contained in just a little more than 2,000 square feet are a generous master suite, an island kitchen, a central family room, formal living and dining rooms, and three additional bedrooms. See plan HDS-90-806 on page 50.

The Art of Building

As you embark on your home-building project, think of it as a trip—clearly not a vacation but rather an interesting, adventurous, at times difficult expedition. Meticulous planning will make your journey not only far more enjoyable but also much more successful. By careful planning, you can avoid—or at least minimize—some of the pitfalls along the way.

Start with realistic expectations of the road ahead. To do this, you'll want to gain an understanding of the basic house-building process, settle on a design that will work for you and your family, and make sure your project is actually doable. By taking those initial steps, you can gain a clear idea of how much time, money, and energy you'll need to invest to make your dream come true.

The Building Process

Your role in planning and managing a house-building project can be divided into two parts: prebuilding preparation and construction management.

■ **Prebuilding preparation.** This is where you should focus most of your attention. In the hands of a qualified contractor whose expertise you can rely on, the actual building process should go fairly smoothly. But during most of the prebuilding stage, you're generally on your own. Your job will be to launch the project and develop a talented team that can help you bring your new home to fruition.

When you work with stock plans, the prebuilding process usually goes as follows:

First, you research the general area where you want to live, selecting one or more possible home sites (unless you already own a suitable lot). Then you choose a basic house design, with the idea that it may require some modification. Finally, you analyze the site, the design, and your budget to determine if the project is actually attainable.

If you decide that it is, you purchase the land and order blueprints. If you want to modify them, you consult an architect, designer, or contractor. Once the plans are finalized, you request bids from contractors and arrange any necessary construction financing.

After selecting a builder and signing a contract, you (or your contractor) then file the plans with the building department. When the plans are approved, often several weeks—or even months—later, you're ready to begin construction.

■ **Construction management.** Unless you intend to act as your own contractor, your role during the building process is mostly one of quality control and time management. Even so, it's important to know the sequence of events and something about construction methods so you can discuss progress with your builder and prepare for any important decisions you may need to make along the way.

Decision-making is critical. Once construction begins, the builder must usually plunge ahead, keeping his carpenters and subcontractors progressing steadily. If you haven't made a key decision—which model bathtub or sink to install, for example—it can bring construction to a frustrating and expensive halt.

Usually, you'll make such decisions before the onset of building, but, inevitably, some issue or another will arise during construction. Being knowledgeable about the building process will help you anticipate and circumvent potential logjams.

Selecting a House Plan

Searching for the right plan can be a fun, interactive family experience—one of the most exciting parts of a house-building project. Gather the family around as you peruse the home plans in this book. Study the size, location, and configuration of each room; traffic patterns both inside the house and to the outdoors; exterior style; and how you'll use the available space. Discuss the pros and cons of the various plans.

Browse through pictures of homes in magazines to stimulate ideas. Clip the photos you like so you can think about your favorite options. When you visit the homes of friends, note special features that appeal to you. Also, look carefully at the homes in your neighborhood, noting their style and how they fit the site.

Mark those plans that most closely suit your ideals. Then, to narrow down your choices, critique each plan, using the following information as a guide.

■ **Overall size and budget.** How large a house do you want? Will the house you're considering fit your family's requirements? Look at the overall square footage and room sizes. If you have a hard time visualizing room sizes, measure some of the rooms in your present home and compare.

It's often better for the house to be a little too big than a little too small, but remember that every extra square foot will cost more money to build and maintain.

■ **Number and type of rooms.** Beyond thinking about the number of bedrooms and baths you want, consider your family's life-style and how you use space. Do you want both a family room and a living room? Do you need a formal dining space? Will you require some extra rooms, or "swing spaces," that can serve multiple purposes, such as a home office–guest room combination?

■ **Room placement and traffic patterns.** What are your preferences for locations of formal living areas, master bedroom, and children's rooms? Do you prefer a kitchen that's open to family areas or one that's private and out of the way? How much do you use exterior spaces and how should they relate to the interior?

Once you make those determinations, look carefully at the floor plan of the house you're considering to see if it meets your needs and if the traffic flow will be convenient for your family.

■ Architectural style. Have you always wanted to live in a Victorian farmhouse? Now is your chance to create a house that matches your idea of "home" (taking into account, of course, styles in your neighborhood). But don't let your preference for one particular architectural style dictate your home's floor plan. If the floor plan doesn't work for your family, keep looking.

■ Site considerations. Most people choose a site before selecting a plan—or at least they've zeroed in on the basic type of land where they'll situate their house. It sounds elementary, but choose a house that will fit the site.

When figuring the "footprint" of a house, you must know about any restrictions that will affect your home's height or proximity to the property lines. Call the local building department (look under city or county listings in the phone book) and get a very clear description of any restrictions, such as setbacks, height limits, and lot coverage, that will affect what you can build on the site (see "Working with City Hall," at right).

When you visit potential sites, note trees, rock outcroppings, slopes, views, winds, sun, neighboring homes, and other factors. All will impact on how your house works on a particular site.

Once you've narrowed down the choice of sites, consult an architect or building designer (see page 8) to help you evaluate how some potential houses will work on the sites you have in mind.

Is Your Project Doable?

Before you purchase land, make sure your project is doable. Although it's too early at this stage to pinpoint costs, making a few phone calls will help you determine whether your project is realistic. You'll be able to learn if you can afford to build the house, how long it will take, and what obstacles may stand in your way.

To get a ballpark estimate of cost, multiply a house's total square footage (of livable space) by the local average cost per square foot for new construction. (To obtain local averages, call a contractor, an architect, a realtor, or the local chapter of the National Association of Home Builders.) Some contractors may even be willing to give you a preliminary bid. Once you know approximate costs, speak to your lender to explore financing.

It's a good idea to discuss your project with several contractors (see page 8). They may be aware of problems in your area that could limit your options—bedrock that makes digging basements difficult, for example. These conversations are actually the first step in developing a list of contractors from which you'll choose the one who will build your home.

Working with City Hall ■

For any building project, even a minor one, it's essential to be familiar with building codes and other restrictions that can affect your project.

■ Building codes, generally implemented by the city or county building department, set the standards for safe, lasting construction. Codes specify minimum construction techniques and materials for foundations, framing, electrical wiring, plumbing, insulation, and all other aspects of a building. Although codes are adopted and enforced locally, most regional codes conform to the standards set by the national Uniform Building Code, Standard Building Code, or Basic Building Code. In some cases, local codes set more restrictive standards than national ones.

■ Building permits are required for home-building projects nearly everywhere. If you work with a contractor, the builder's firm should handle all necessary permits.

More than one permit may be needed; for example, one will cover the foundation, another the electrical wiring, and still another the heating equipment installation. Each will probably involve a fee and require inspections by building officials before work can proceed. (Inspections benefit *you*, as they ensure that the job is being done satisfactorily.) Permit fees are generally a percentage (1 to 1.5 percent) of the project's estimated value, often calculated on square footage.

It's important to file for the necessary permits. Failure to do so can result in fines or legal action against you. You can even be forced to undo the work performed. At the very least, your negligence may come back to haunt you later when you're ready to sell your house.

■ Zoning ordinances, particular to your community, restrict setbacks (how near to property lines you may build), your house's allowable height, lot coverage factors (how much of your property you can cover with structures), and other factors that impact design and building. If your plans don't conform to zoning ordinances, you can try to obtain a variance, an exception to the rules. But this legal work can be expensive and time-consuming. Even if you prove that your project won't negatively affect your neighbors, the building department can still refuse to grant the variance.

■ Deeds and covenants attach to the lot. Deeds set out property lines and easements; covenants may establish architectural standards in a neighborhood. Since both can seriously impact your project, make sure you have complete information on any deeds or covenants before you turn over a spadeful of soil.

Recruiting Your Home Team

A home-building project will inter-ject you and your family into the building business, an area that may be unfamiliar territory. Among the people you'll be working with are architects, designers, landscapers, contractors, and subcontractors.

Design Help

A qualified architect or designer can help you modify and personal-ize your home plan, taking into account your family's needs and budget and the house's style. In fact, you may want to consider consulting such a person while you're selecting a plan to help you articulate your needs.

Design professionals are capable of handling any or all aspects of the design process. For example, they can review your house plans, suggest options, and then provide rough sketches of the options on tracing paper. Many architects will even secure needed permits and negotiate with contractors or sub-contractors, as well as oversee the quality of the work.

Of course, you don't necessarily need an architect or designer to implement minor changes in a plan; although most contractors aren't trained in design, some can help you with modifications.

An open-ended, hourly-fee arrangement that you work out with your architect or designer allows for flexibility, but it often turns out to be more costly than working on a flat-fee basis. On a flat fee, you agree to pay a specific amount of money for a certain amount of work.

To find architects and designers, contact such trade associations as the American Institute of Architects (AIA), American Institute of Build-ing Designers (AIBD), American Society of Landscape Architects (ASLA), and American Society of Interior Designers (ASID). Although many professionals choose not to belong to trade associations, those who do have met the standards of their respective associations. For phone numbers of local branches, check the Yellow Pages.

■ **Architects** are licensed by the state and have degrees. They're trained in all facets of building design and construction. Although some can handle interior design and structural engineering, others hire specialists for those tasks.

■ **Building designers** are generally unlicensed but may be accredited by the American Institute of Building Designers. Their back-grounds are varied: some may be unlicensed architects in apprentice-ship; others are interior designers or contractors with design skills.

■ **Draftspersons** offer an economi-cal route to making simple changes on your drawings. Like building designers, these people may be unlicensed architect apprentices, engineers, or members of related trades. Most are accomplished at drawing up plans.

■ **Interior designers,** as their job title suggests, design interiors. They work with you to choose room fin-ishes, furnishings, appliances, and decorative elements. Part of their expertise is in arranging furnishings to create a workable space plan. Some interior designers are em-ployed by architectural firms; others work independently. Financial arrangements vary, depending on the designer's preference.

Related professionals are kitchen and bathroom designers, who con-centrate on fixtures, cabinetry, appliances, materials, and space planning for the kitchen and bath.

■ **Landscape architects, design-ers, and contractors** design out-door areas. Landscape architects are state-licensed to practice landscape design. A landscape designer usual-ly has a landscape architect's educa-tion and training but does not have a state license. Licensed landscape contractors specialize in garden construction, though some also have design skills and experience.

■ **Soils specialists and structural engineers** may be needed for proj-ects where unstable soils or uncom-mon wind loads or seismic forces must be taken into account. Any structural changes to a house re-quire the expertise of a structural engineer to verify that the house won't fall down.

Services of these specialists can be expensive, but they're impera-tive in certain conditions to ensure a safe, sturdy structure. Your build-ing department will probably let you know if their services are re-quired.

General Contractors

To build your house, hire a licensed general contractor. Most states re-quire a contractor to be licensed and insured for worker's compensa-tion in order to contract a building project and hire other subcontrac-tors. State licensing ensures that contractors have met minimum training standards and have a spec-ified level of experience. Licensing does not guarantee, however, that they're good at what they do.

When contractors hire subcon-tractors, they're responsible for overseeing the quality of work and materials of the subcontractors and for paying them.

■ **Finding a contractor.** How do you find a good contractor? Start by getting referrals from people you know who have built or remodeled their home. Nothing beats a personal recommendation. The best contractors are usually busily moving from one satisfied client to another prospect, adver-tised only by word of mouth.

You can also ask local real estate brokers and lenders or even your building inspector for names of qualified builders. Experienced lumber dealers are another good source of names.

In the Yellow Pages, look under "Contractors–Building, General"; or call the local chapter of the National Association of Home Builders.

■ **Choosing a contractor.** Once you have a list of names of pro-spective builders, call several of them. On the telephone, ask first whether they handle your type of job and can work within your schedule. If they can, arrange a meeting with each one and ask them to be prepared with references of former clients and photos of previous jobs. Better still, meet them at one of their current work sites so you can get a glimpse of the quality of their work and how organized and thorough they are.

Take your plan to the meeting and discuss it enough to request a rough estimate (some builders will comply, while others will be reluctant to offer a ballpark estimate, preferring to give you a hard bid based on complete drawings). Don't hesitate to probe for advice or suggestions that might make building your house less expensive.

Be especially aware of each contractor's personality and how well you communicate. Good chemistry between you and your builder is a key ingredient for success.

Narrow down the candidates to three or four. Ask each for a firm bid, based on the exact same set of plans and specifications. For the bids to be accurate, your plans need to be complete and the specifications as precise as possible, call-

ing out particular appliances, fixtures, floorings, roofing material, and so forth. (Some of these are specified in a stock-plan set; others are not.)

Call the contractors' references and ask about the quality of their work, their relationship with their clients, their promptness, and their readiness to follow up on problems. Visit former clients to check the contractor's work firsthand.

Be sure your final candidates are licensed, bonded, and insured for worker's compensation, public liability, and property damage. Also, try to determine how financially solvent they are (you can call their bank and credit references). Avoid contractors who are operating hand-to-mouth.

Don't automatically hire the contractor with the lowest bid if you don't think you'll get along well or if you have any doubts about the quality of the person's work. Instead, look for both the most reasonable bid and the contractor with the best credentials, references, terms, and compatibility with your family.

A word about bonds: You can request a performance bond that guarantees that your job will be finished by your contractor. If the job isn't completed, the bonding company will cover the cost of hiring another contractor to finish it. Bonds cost from 2 to 6 percent of the value of the project.

Your Building Contract

A building contract (see below) binds and protects both you and your contractor. It isn't just a legal document. It's also a list of the expectations of both parties. The best way to minimize the possibility of misunderstandings and costly changes later on is to write down every possible detail. Whether the contract is a standard form or one composed by you, have an attorney look it over before both you and the contractor sign it.

The contract should clearly specify all the work that needs to be done, including particular materials and work descriptions, the time schedule, and method of payment. It should be keyed to the working drawings.

A Sample Building Contract

Project and participants. Give a general description of the project, its address, and the names and addresses of both you and the builder.

Construction materials. Identify all construction materials by brand name, quality markings (species, grades, etc.), and model numbers where applicable. Avoid the clause "or equal," which allows the builder to substitute other materials for your choices. For materials you can't specify now, set down a budget figure.

Time schedule. Include both start and completion dates and specify that work will be "continuous." Although a contractor cannot be responsible for delays caused by strikes and material shortages, your builder should assume responsibility for completing the project within a reasonable period of time.

Work to be performed. State all work you expect the contractor to perform, from initial grading to finished painting.

Method and schedule of payment. Specify how and when payments are to be made. Typical agreements specify installment payments as particular phases of work are completed. Final payment is withheld until the job receives its final inspection and is cleared of all liens.

Waiver of liens. Protect yourself with a waiver of liens signed by the general contractor, the subcontractors, and all major suppliers. That way, subcontractors who are not paid for materials or services cannot place a lien on your property.

Personalizing Stock Plans

The beauty of buying stock plans for your new home is that they offer tested, well-conceived design at an affordable price. And stock plans dramatically reduce the time it takes to design a house, since the plans are ready when you are.

Because they were not created specifically for your family, stock plans may not reflect your personal taste. But it's not difficult to make revisions in stock plans that will turn your home into an expression of your family's personality. You'll surely want to add personal touches and choose your own finishes.

Ideally, the modifications you implement will be fairly minor. The more extensive the changes, the more expensive the plans. Major changes take valuable design time, and those that affect a house's structure may require a structural engineer's approval.

If you anticipate wholesale changes, such as moving a number of bearing walls or changing the roofline significantly, you may be better off selecting another plan. On the other hand, reconfiguring or changing the sizes of some rooms can probably be handled fairly easily.

Some structural changes may even be necessary to comply with local codes. Your area may have specific requirements for snow loads, energy codes, seismic or wind resistance, and so forth. Those types of modifications are likely to require the services of an architect or structural engineer.

Plan Modifications

Before you pencil in any changes, live with your plans for a while. Study them carefully—at your building site, if possible. Try to picture the finished house: how rooms will interrelate, where the sun will enter and at what angle, what the view will be from each window. Think about traffic patterns, access to rooms, room sizes, window and door locations, natural light, and kitchen and bathroom layouts.

Typical changes might involve adding windows or skylights to

bring in natural light or capture a view. Or you may want to widen a hallway or doorway for roomier access, extend a room, eliminate doors, or change window and door sizes. Perhaps you'd like to shorten a room, stealing the gained space for a large closet. Look closely at the kitchen; it's not difficult to reconfigure the layout if it makes the space more convenient for you.

Above all, take your time—this is your home and it should reflect your taste and needs. Make your changes now, during the planning stage. Once construction begins, it will take crowbars, hammers, saws, new materials, and, most significantly, time to alter the plans. Because changes are not part of your building contract, you can count on them being expensive extras once construction begins.

Specifying Finishes

One way to personalize a house without changing its structure is to substitute your favorite finishes for those specified on the plan.

Would you prefer a stuccoed exterior rather than the wood siding shown on the plan? In most cases, this is a relatively easy change. Do you like the look of a wood shingle roof rather than the composition shingles shown on the plan? This, too, is easy. Perhaps you would like to change the windows from sliders to casements, or upgrade to high-efficiency glazing. No problem. Many of those kinds of changes can be worked out with your contractor.

Inside, you may want hardwood where vinyl flooring is shown. In fact, you can—and should—choose types, colors, and styles of floorings, wall coverings, tile, plumbing fixtures, door hardware, cabinetry, appliances, lighting fixtures, and other interior details, for it's these materials that will personalize your home. For help in making selections, consult an architect or interior designer (see page 8).

Each material you select should be spelled out clearly and precisely in your building contract.

Finishing touches can transform a house built from stock plans into an expression of your family's taste and style. Clockwise, from far left: Colorful tilework and custom cabinetry enliven a bathroom (Design: Osburn Design); highly organized closet system maximizes storage space (Architect: David Jeremiah Hurley); low-level deck expands living space to outdoor areas (Landscape architects: The Runa Group, Inc.); built-ins convert the corner of a guest room into a home office (Design: Lynn Williams of The French Connection); French country cabinetry lends style and old-world charm to a kitchen (Design: Garry Bishop/Showcase Kitchens).

What the Plans Include

Complete construction blueprints are available for every house shown in this book. Clear and concise, these detailed blueprints are designed by licensed architects or members of the American Institute of Building Designers (AIBD). Each plan is designed to meet standards set down by nationally recognized building codes (the Uniform Building Code, Standard Building Code, or Basic Building Code) at the time and for the area where they were drawn.

Remember, however, that every state, county, and municipality has its own codes, zoning requirements, ordinances, and building regulations. Modifications may be necessary to comply with such local requirements as snow loads, energy codes, seismic zones, and flood areas.

Although blueprint sets vary depending on the size and complexity of the house and on the individual designer's style, each set may include the elements described below and shown at right.

■ **Exterior elevations** show the front, rear, and sides of the house, including exterior materials, details, and measurements.

■ **Foundation plans** include drawings for a full, partial, or daylight basement, crawlspace, pole, pier, or slab foundation. All necessary notations and dimensions are included. (Foundation options will vary for each plan. If the plan you choose doesn't have the type of foundation you desire, a generic conversion diagram is available.)

■ **Detailed floor plans** show the placement of interior walls and the dimensions of rooms, doors, windows, stairways, and similar elements for each level of the house.

■ **Cross sections** show details of the house as though it were cut in slices from the roof to the foundation. The cross sections give the home's construction, insulation, flooring, and roofing details.

■ **Interior elevations** show the specific details of cabinets (kitchen, bathroom, and utility room), fireplaces, built-in units, and other special interior features.

■ **Roof details** give the layout of rafters, dormers, gables, and other roof elements, including clerestory windows and skylights. These details may be shown on the elevation sheet or on a separate diagram.

■ **Schematic electrical layouts** show the suggested locations for switches, fixtures, and outlets. These details may be shown on the floor plan or on a separate diagram.

■ **General specifications** provide instructions and information regarding excavation and grading, masonry and concrete work, carpentry and woodwork, thermal and moisture protection, drywall, tile, flooring, glazing, and caulking and sealants.

Other Helpful Building Aids

In addition to the construction information on every set of plans, you can buy the following guides.

■ **Reproducible blueprints** are helpful if you'll be making changes to the stock plan you've chosen. These blueprints are original line drawings produced on erasable, reproducible paper for the purpose of modification. When alterations are complete, working copies can be made.

■ **Itemized materials list** details the quantity, type, and size of materials needed to build your home. (This list is extremely helpful in obtaining an accurate construction bid. It's not intended for use to order materials.)

■ **Mirror-reverse plans** are useful if you want to build your home in the reverse of the plan that's shown. Because the lettering and dimensions read backwards, be sure to buy at least one regular-reading set of blueprints.

■ **Description of materials** gives the type and quality of materials suggested for the home. This form may be required for obtaining FHA or VA financing.

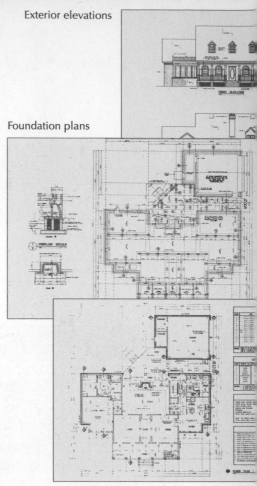

Exterior elevations

Foundation plans

Detailed floor plans

■ **How-to diagrams** for plumbing, wiring, solar heating, framing and foundation conversions show how to plumb, wire, install a solar heating system, convert plans with 2 by 4 exterior walls to 2 by 6 construction (or vice versa), and adapt a plan for a basement, crawlspace, or slab foundation. These diagrams are not specific to any one plan.

NOTE: Due to regional variations, local availability of materials, local codes, methods of installation, and individual preferences, detailed heating, plumbing, and electrical specifications are not included on plans. The duct work, venting, and other details will vary, depending on the heating and cooling system you use and the type of energy that operates it. These details and specifications are easily obtained from your builder or local supplier.

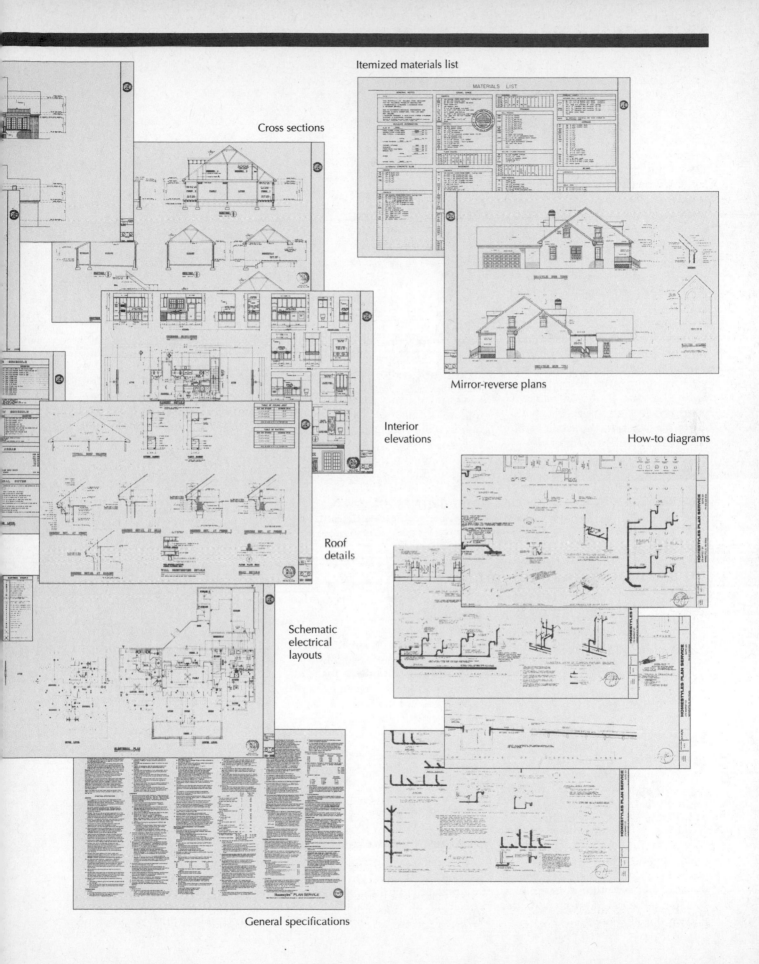

Itemized materials list

Cross sections

Mirror-reverse plans

Interior elevations

How-to diagrams

Roof details

Schematic electrical layouts

General specifications

Before You Order

Once you've chosen the one or two house plans that work best for you, you're ready to order blueprints. Before filling in the form on the facing page, note the information that follows.

How Many Blueprints Will You Need?

A single set of blueprints will allow you to study a home design in detail. You'll need more for obtaining bids and permits, as well as some to use as reference at the building site. If you'll be modifying your home plan, order a reproducible set (see page 12).

Figure you'll need at least one set each for yourself, your builder, the building department, and your lender. In addition, some subcontractors—foundation, plumber, electrician, and HVAC—may also need at least partial sets. If they do, ask them to return the sets when they're finished. The chart below can help you calculate how many sets you're likely to need.

Blueprint Checklist

____Owner's set(s)

____ **Builder usually requires at least three sets:** one for legal documentation, one for inspections, and a minimum of one set for subcontractors.

____ **Building department requires at least one set.** Check with your local department before ordering.

____ **Lending institution usually needs one set for a conventional mortgage,** three sets for FHA or VA loans.

____ TOTAL SETS NEEDED

Blueprint Prices

The cost of having an architect design a new custom home typically runs from 5 to 15 percent of the building cost, or from $5,000 to $15,000 for a $100,000 home. A single set of blueprints for the plans in this book ranges from $295 to $505, depending on the house's size. Working with these drawings, you can save enough on design fees to add a deck, a swimming pool, or a luxurious kitchen.

Pricing is based on "total finished living space." Garages, porches, decks, and unfinished basements are not included.

Price Code (Size)	1 Set	4 Sets	7 Sets	Reproducible Set
AAA (under 500 sq. ft.)	$245	$295	$330	$430
AA (500-999 sq. ft.)	$285	$335	$370	$470
A (1,000-1,499 sq. ft.)	$325	$375	$410	$510
B (1,500-1,999 sq. ft.)	$365	$415	$450	$550
C (2,000-2,499 sq. ft.)	$405	$455	$490	$590
D (2,500-2,999 sq. ft.)	$445	$495	$530	$630
E (3,000-3,499 sq. ft.)	$485	$535	$570	$670
F (3,500-3,999 sq. ft.)	$525	$575	$610	$710
G (4,000-4,499 sq. ft.)	$565	$615	$650	$750
H (4,500-4,999 sq. ft.)	$605	$655	$690	$790
I (5,000 sq. ft. and up)	$645	$695	$730	$830

Building Costs

Building costs vary widely, depending on a number of factors, including local material and labor costs and the finishing materials you select. For help estimating costs, see "Is Your Project Doable?" on page 7.

Foundation Options & Exterior Construction

Depending on your site and climate, your home will be built with a slab, pier, pole, crawlspace, or basement foundation. Exterior walls will be framed with either 2 by 4s or 2 by 6s, determined by structural and insulation standards in your area. Most contractors can easily adapt a home to meet the foundation and/or wall requirements for your area. Or ask for a conversion how-to diagram (see page 12).

Service & Blueprint Delivery

Service representatives are available to answer questions and assist you in placing your order. Every effort is made to process and ship orders within 48 hours.

Returns & Exchanges

Each set of blueprints is specially printed and shipped to you in response to your specific order; consequently, requests for refunds cannot be honored. However, if the prints you order cannot be used, you may exchange them for another plan from any Sunset home plan book. For an exchange, you must return all sets of plans within 30 days. A nonrefundable service charge will be assessed for all exchanges; for more information, call the toll-free number on the facing page. Note: Reproducible sets cannot be exchanged.

Compliance with Local Codes & Regulations

Because of climatic, geographic, and political variations, building codes and regulations vary from one area to another. These plans are authorized for your use expressly conditioned on your obligation and agreement to comply strictly with all local building codes, ordinances, regulations, and requirements, including permits and inspections at time of construction.

Architectural & Engineering Seals

With increased concern about energy costs and safety, many cities and states now require that an architect or engineer review and "seal" a blueprint prior to construction. To find out whether this is a requirement in your area, contact your local building department.

License Agreement, Copy Restrictions & Copyright

When you purchase your blueprints, you are granted the right to use those documents to construct a single unit. All the plans in this publication are protected under the Federal Copyright Act, Title XVII of the United States Code and Chapter 37 of the Code of Federal Regulations. Each designer retains title and ownership of the original documents. The blueprints licensed to you cannot be used by or resold to any other person, copied, or reproduced by any means. The copying restrictions do not apply to reproducible blueprints. When you buy a reproducible set, you may modify and reproduce it for your own use.

Blueprint Order Form

Complete this order form in just three easy steps. Then mail in your order or, for faster service, call toll-free.

1. Blueprints & Accessories

BLUEPRINT CHART

Price Code	1 Set	4 Sets	7 Sets	Reproducible Set*
AAA	$245	$295	$330	$430
AA	$285	$335	$370	$470
A	$325	$375	$410	$510
B	$365	$415	$450	$550
C	$405	$455	$490	$590
D	$445	$495	$530	$630
E	$485	$535	$570	$670
F	$525	$575	$610	$710
G	$565	$615	$650	$750
H	$605	$655	$690	$790
I	$645	$695	$730	$830

Prices subject to change

*A reproducible set is produced on erasable paper for the purpose of modification. It is only available for plans with prefixes A, AG, AGH, AH, AHP, APS, AX, B, C, CC, CPS, DCL, DD, DW, E, EOF, FB, GL, GML, GSA, H, HDS, HFL, J, K, KD, KLF, LMB, LRD, M, NW, OH, PH, PI, RD, S, SDG, THD, U, UDG, V

Mirror-Reverse Sets: $50 surcharge. From the total number of sets you ordered above, choose the number you want to be reversed. Pay only $50. *Note: All writing on mirror-reversed plans is backwards. Order at least one regular-reading set.*

Itemized Materials List : One set $50; each additional set $15. Details the quantity, type and size of materials needed to build your home.

Description of Materials: Sold only in a set of two for $50 (for use in obtaining FHA or VA financing).

Typical How-To Diagrams: One set $20; two sets $30; three sets $40; all four sets only $45. General guides on plumbing, wiring, and solar heating, plus information on how to convert from one foundation or exterior framing to another. *Note: These diagrams are not specific to any one plan.*

2. Sales Tax & Shipping

Determine your subtotal and add appropriate local state sales tax, plus shipping and handling (see chart below).

SHIPPING & HANDLING

	1-3 sets	4-6 sets	7 or More Sets	Reproducible Set
U.S. Regular (4-6 working days)	$17.50	$20.00	$22.50	$17.50
U.S. Express (2-3 working days)	$29.50	$32.50	$35.00	$29.50
Canada Regular (2-3 weeks)	$20.00	$22.50	$25.00	$20.00
Canada Express (4-6 working days)	$35.00	$40.00	$45.00	$35.00
Overseas/Airmail (7-10 working days)	$57.50	$67.50	$77.50	$57.50

3. Customer Information

Choose the method of payment you prefer. Include check, money order, or credit card information, complete name and address portion, and mail to:

Sunset/HomeStyles Plan Service
P.O. Box 50670
Minneapolis, MN 55405

FOR FASTER SERVICE CALL 1-800-820-1283

SS17

COMPLETE THIS FORM

Plan Number _____ **Price Code** _____

Foundation _____
(Review your plan carefully for foundation options—basement, pole, pier, crawlspace, or slab. Many plans offer several options; others offer only one.)

Number of Sets: $_____
- ☐ One Set   (See chart at left)
- ☐ Four Sets
- ☐ Seven Sets
- ☐ One Reproducible Set

Additional Sets _____ $_____
($40 each)

Mirror-Reverse Sets _____ $_____
($50 surcharge)

Itemized Materials List $_____
Only available for plans with prefixes AH, AHP, APS*, AX*, B*, C, CAR, CC, CDG*, CPS, DD*, DW, E, GSA, H, HFL, I*, J, K, LMB*, LRD, NW*, P, PH, R, S, THD, U, UDG, VL. *Not available on all plans. Please call before ordering.

Description of Materials $_____
Only available for plans with prefixes AHP, C, DW, H, HFL, J, K, LMB, P, PH, VL.

Typical How-To Diagrams $_____
☐ Plumbing   ☐ Wiring   ☐ Solar Heating   ☐ Foundation & Framing Conversion

SUBTOTAL	$_____
SALES TAX	$_____
SHIPPING & HANDLING	$_____
GRAND TOTAL	$_____

☐ Check/money order enclosed (in U.S. funds)
☐ VISA   ☐ MasterCard   ☐ AmEx   ☐ Discover

Credit Card # _____ **Exp. Date** _____

Signature _____

Name _____

Address _____

City _____ **State** ____ **Country** _____

Zip _____ **Daytime Phone** (_____) _____

☐ Please check if you are a contractor.

Mail form to: Sunset/HomeStyles Plan Service
P.O. Box 50670
Minneapolis, MN 55405

Or fax to: (612) 338-1626

FOR FASTER SERVICE CALL 1-800-820-1283

SS17

Covered Porch Invites Visitors

- This nice home welcomes visitors with its covered front porch and its wide-open living areas.
- Detailed columns, railings and shutters decorate the front porch that guides guests to the central entry.
- Just off the entry, the bright living room merges with the dining room. The side wall is lined with glass, including a glass door that opens to the yard.
- The angled kitchen features a serving counter facing the dining room. A handry laundry closet and access to a storage area and the garage is nearby.
- An angled hall leads to the bedroom wing. The master suite offers a private bath, a walk-in closet and a dressing area with a vanity. Two additional bedrooms and another full bath are located down the hall.

Plan E-1217

Bedrooms: 3	Baths: 2
Living Area:	
Main floor	1,266 sq. ft.
Total Living Area:	**1,266 sq. ft.**
Garage and storage	550 sq. ft.
Exterior Wall Framing:	2x6

Foundation Options:

Crawlspace
Slab
(All plans can be built with your choice of foundation and framing. A generic conversion diagram is available. See order form.)

BLUEPRINT PRICE CODE: A

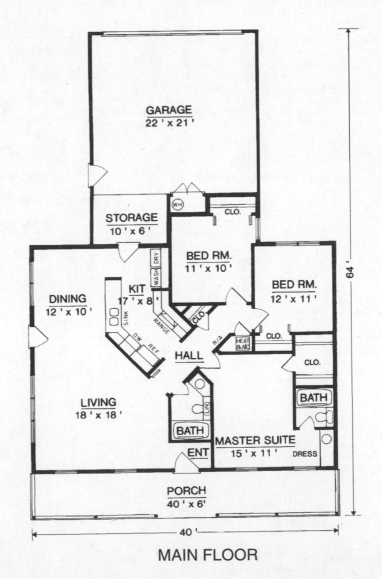

MAIN FLOOR

Plan E-1217

Economy with Style

A pleasantly efficient three-bedroom home with only 998 sq. ft. provides plenty of living space for empty nesters or for young families just starting out. Vertical and diagonal board siding combined with intersecting gable rooflines, add distinctive design interest.

Traffic flows easily, without cross-room traffic, from the front entry to the bedroom on the left or straight ahead into the living room, with fireplace, and the dining area. The large, open kitchen, with bay window and a breakfast counter, also is conveniently next to the garage door for bringing groceries in from the car. A patio or wood deck adjacent to the dining area and kitchen adds outdoor living and entertaining space.

The three bedrooms, all with generously sized closets, share the large hall bathroom. A daylight basement version of the plan, with stairs added along the garage wall, is available for larger or expanding families.

56'-0"
58'0" W/ BASEMENT

PATIO

BEDROOM-1
11/0 x 11/0

LIVING
13/0 x 16/0

DINING
9/0 x 10/0

FURN.
W.H.

GARAGE
21/8 x 21/4

BAR

TUB

W D

KITCHEN
9/0 x 11/6

ENTRY

38'-0"

LIN.

BEDRM.-2
9/0 x 10/0

BEDRM.-3
10/0 x 10/0

PLAN P-6552-A
WITHOUT BASEMENT

Total living area: 998 sq. ft.
(Not counting basement or garage)

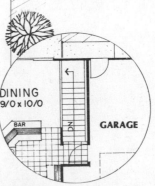

DINING
9/0 x 10/0

BAR

DN

GARAGE

PLAN P-6552-D
WITH DAYLIGHT BASEMENT

Blueprint Price Code A A

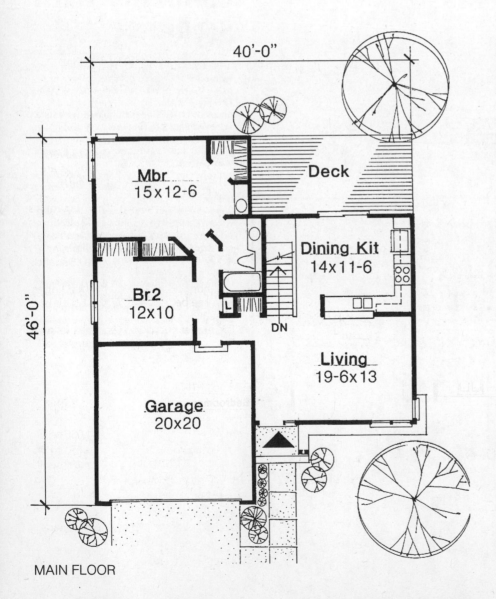

40'-0"

46'-0"

Mbr
15 x 12-6

Deck

Br2
12x10

Dining Kit
14 x 11-6

DN

Living
19-6 x 13

Garage
20x20

MAIN FLOOR

First-Home Features

- The first-time home buyer will be delighted with the features included in this 1,040-sq.-ft. ranch.
- The open entryway treats you to a view of the large living room, dining area and the rear deck and outdoors beyond.
- The L-shaped kitchen boasts a pass-through serving counter, making entertaining easy and convenient. Sliding glass doors bring in sunlight while providing access to the large deck.
- The master bedroom offers two closets, a lovely corner window, a personal dressing area and private entrance to the main bath.

Plan UDG-90015	
Bedrooms: 2	**Baths: 1**
Space:	
Main floor	1,040 sq. ft.
Total Living Area	**1,040 sq. ft.**
Basement	1,040 sq. ft.
Garage	400 sq. ft.
Exterior Wall Framing	2x4
Foundation options:	
Standard Basement	
(Foundation & framing conversion diagram	
available—see order form.)	
Blueprint Price Code	**A**

Plan UDG-90015

Country-Style Coziness

- Designed as a starter or retirement home, this delightful plan has a charming exterior and an open, airy interior.
- The spacious front porch gives guests a warm welcome and provides added space for relaxing or entertaining. The modified hip roof, half-round louver vent and decorative porch railings are other distinguishing features of the facade.
- Inside, the open dining and living rooms are heightened by dramatic vaulted ceilings. The streamlined kitchen has a snack counter joining it to the dining room. All three rooms reap the benefits of the fireplace.
- A laundry closet is in the hall leading to the three bedrooms. The main bath is close by.
- The master bedroom suite offers its own bath, plus a private patio sequestered behind the garage.

Plan APS-1002

Bedrooms: 3	Baths: 2
Space:	
Main floor	1,050 sq. ft.
Total Living Area	**1,050 sq. ft.**
Garage	288 sq. ft.
Exterior Wall Framing	2x4
Foundation options:	
Slab	
(Foundation & framing conversion diagram available—see order form.)	
Blueprint Price Code	A

Floor plan dimensions: 36 × 42

Rooms:
- MASTER BEDROOM 11 X 12
- BEDROOM 9 X 12
- PATIO
- BEDROOM 9 X 10
- KITCHEN 9 X 11
- GARAGE 12 x 24
- DINING 9 x 10
- LIVING 14 x 14
- VAULT

Cozy and Charming

- This compact two-bedroom home offers economical shelter and pleasant styling for a small family.
- A spacious kitchen/dining combination offers ample space for family dining and food preparation.
- Both bedrooms offer large closets plus convenient access to the bathroom.

- The large living room boasts large windows and an energy-efficient heat-circulating fireplace.
- The small but functional foyer is reached via an attractive oval-windowed front door.
- The basement doubles the size of the home.

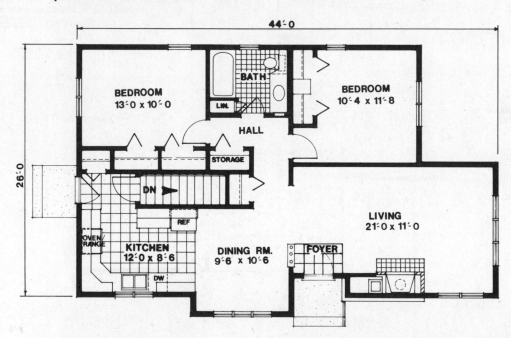

Plan CPS-1112-B

Bedrooms: 2	Baths: 1

Foundation options:
Standard basement only.
(Foundation & framing conversion diagram available — see order form.)

Total living area:	1,059 sq. ft.
Basement:	1,059 sq. ft.

Exterior Wall Framing:	2x6

Blueprint Price Code: A

Plan CPS-1112-B

PRICES AND DETAILS
ON PAGES 12-15

High Ceilings, Large Spaces!

- This affordable home is filled with large spaces that are further enhanced by high ceilings and lots of windows.
- The charming exterior is complemented by a combination of lap siding and brick, along with a columned front porch and a sidelighted entry door.
- Inside, the first area to come into view is the huge family room, which features a 15½-ft. vaulted ceiling and an efficient corner fireplace. Sliding glass doors open up the room to the backyard.

- The family room flows into the spacious breakfast room and kitchen. A picture window or an optional bay window brightens the breakfast room, while the kitchen offers a window above the sink and a convenient laundry closet that hides the clutter.
- The master suite leaves out nothing. An 11-ft. tray ceiling in the sleeping area gives way to the vaulted master bath, which is accented with a plant shelf above the entrance. A roomy walk-in closet is also included. The two smaller bedrooms share a hall bath.
- The optional basement doubles the home's size, providing ample expansion space.

Plan FB-1070	
Bedrooms: 3	**Baths:** 2
Living Area:	
Main floor	1,070 sq. ft.
Total Living Area:	**1,070 sq. ft.**
Daylight basement	1,070 sq. ft.
Garage	484 sq. ft.
Exterior Wall Framing:	2x4

Foundation Options:

Daylight basement
Crawlspace
Slab
(All plans can be built with your choice of foundation and framing. A generic conversion diagram is available. See order form.)

BLUEPRINT PRICE CODE: A

MAIN FLOOR

48'-0"

36'-0"

- OPT. BAY WINDOW
- Kitchen
- Breakfast
- Vaulted Family Room 13³ x 20¹⁰
- FPL.
- TUB
- Vaulted M. Bath
- W.i.c.
- PLANT SHELF
- TRAY CLG.
- Master Suite 14⁶ x 12⁰
- D.
- D.W.
- REF.
- W.
- Stor.
- OPT. STAIRS TO BSMT.
- VAULT
- W.H.
- LIN.
- Garage
- Covered Porch
- COATS
- Bedroom 2 10' x 10⁰
- Bedroom 3 11' x 10⁰

New Country Cottage

- This attractive, affordable one-story cottage is ideal for young families or empty-nesters.
- The charming exterior is accented by creative gabled rooflines, appealing window treatments and a railed porch that gives the plan its country flavor.
- Just past the entry, the spacious living room features a fireplace, built-in bookshelves and a rear window wall.
- The adjoining dining area shares an eating bar with the kitchen and includes sliding glass doors to a sunny patio.
- The modern kitchen is brightened by a big window over the sink and is easily accessible from the garage.
- The three bedrooms share a cleverly designed bath that allows private access from the largest, or master, bedroom. A laundry area and a linen closet are close by.
- The home also features energy-efficient 2x6 exterior walls.

Plans P-6616-2A & -2D

Bedrooms: 3	Baths: 1
Living Area:	
Main floor (crawlspace version)	1,088 sq. ft.
Main floor (basement version)	1,149 sq. ft.
Total Living Area:	**1,088/1,149 sq. ft.**
Daylight basement	1,174 sq. ft.
Garage	480 sq. ft.
Exterior Wall Framing:	2x6
Foundation Options:	**Plan #**
Daylight basement	P-6616-2D
Crawlspace	P-6616-2A

(All plans can be built with your choice of foundation and framing. A generic conversion diagram is available. See order form.)

BLUEPRINT PRICE CODE:	**A**

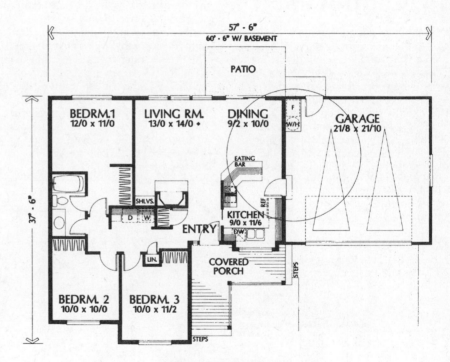

MAIN FLOOR

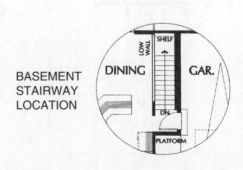

BASEMENT STAIRWAY LOCATION

City House, Country Home

- Gingerbread detailing and a covered front porch give this charming home a country-style feel, while its modest width makes it suitable for a city lot.
- The inviting entry leads directly into the spacious Great Room, which boasts a 14-ft. vaulted ceiling. An impressive brick fireplace adds warmth and atmosphere.

- A French door in the adjoining dining area opens to a covered back porch.
- The efficient L-shaped kitchen is open to the dining area and brightened by a window above the sink. The nearby laundry room also accesses the porch.
- The quiet master bedroom is furnished with a roomy walk-in closet. The central full bath is just steps away.
- An elegant open-railed stairway overlooks the entry and leads to the upper floor, where two additional bedrooms share a hallway linen closet and a second full bath.

Plan V-1098	
Bedrooms: 3	**Baths:** 2
Living Area:	
Upper floor	396 sq. ft.
Main floor	702 sq. ft.
Total Living Area:	**1,098 sq. ft.**
Exterior Wall Framing:	2x6

Foundation Options:

Crawlspace
(All plans can be built with your choice of foundation and framing. A generic conversion diagram is available. See order form.)

BLUEPRINT PRICE CODE: A

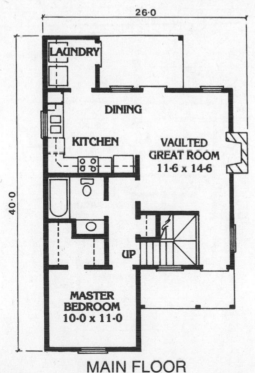

MAIN FLOOR

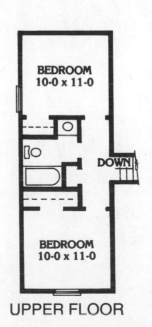

UPPER FLOOR

Casual, Cozy Retreat

- This cozy home is perfect as a weekend retreat, a summer home or a casual permanent residence.
- The living room, the kitchen and the dining area flow together, creating a huge space for relaxing or entertaining guests. A 23-ft.-high cathedral ceiling soars above a striking wall of glass that overlooks a nice front deck. Sliding glass doors access the deck.
- Two bedrooms and a full bath round out the main floor.
- The upstairs loft could serve as a private master bedroom or as a quiet study, den or studio. An open railing provides gorgeous views of both the living area below and the scenery beyond.
- Two outside storage areas offer plenty of space for tools and equipment.

Plan CPS-1095

Bedrooms: 2+	Baths: 1
Living Area:	
Upper floor	320 sq. ft.
Main floor	784 sq. ft.
Total Living Area:	**1,104 sq. ft.**
Standard basement	784 sq. ft.
Exterior Wall Framing:	2x6

Foundation Options:

Standard basement

(All plans can be built with your choice of foundation and framing. A generic conversion diagram is available. See order form.)

BLUEPRINT PRICE CODE:	**A**

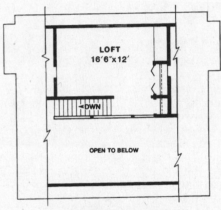

UPPER FLOOR

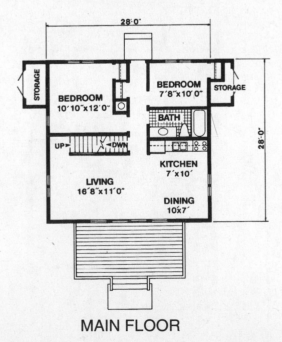

MAIN FLOOR

TO ORDER THIS BLUEPRINT, CALL TOLL-FREE 1-800-820-1283

Plan CPS-1095

PRICES AND DETAILS ON PAGES 12-15

Extra-Special Ranch-Style

- Repeating gables, wood siding and brick adorn this ranch-style home, which offers numerous amenities in its compact interior.
- The entry leads directly into a spectacular 21-ft.-high vaulted family room, an ideal entertainment area accented by a corner fireplace and a French door to the backyard.
- A serving bar connects the family room with the efficient kitchen, which has a handy pantry, ample counter space and a sunny breakfast room.
- The luxurious master suite boasts a 10½-ft. tray ceiling, a large bank of windows and a walk-in closet. The master bath features a garden tub.
- Two more bedrooms, one with a 14½-ft. vaulted ceiling, share another full bath.
- The two-car garage provides convenient access to the kitchen and laundry area.

Plan FB-1104

Bedrooms: 3	Baths: 2
Living Area:	
Main floor	1,104 sq. ft.
Total Living Area:	**1,104 sq. ft.**
Daylight basement	1,104 sq. ft.
Garage	400 sq. ft.
Exterior Wall Framing:	2x4

Foundation Options:

Daylight basement

Crawlspace

(All plans can be built with your choice of foundation and framing. A generic conversion diagram is available. See order form.)

BLUEPRINT PRICE CODE: **A**

46'-6"

41'-0"

M. Bath

W.i.c

Bath

LIN.

TRAY CLG.

Master Suite
14⁰ x 12⁰

FPL.

Vaulted
Family Room
16⁰ x 16⁵

VAULT VAULT

COAT

Vaulted
Bedroom
10⁰ x 10³

VAULT VAULT

Bedroom
10⁰ x 10⁰

FRENCH
DOOR

Breakfast

SERVING
BAR

Kit.

RANGE

D.

REF.

W.

PAN.

Storage

OPT. STAIRS
TO BASEMENT

Garage

MAIN FLOOR

FRONT VIEW

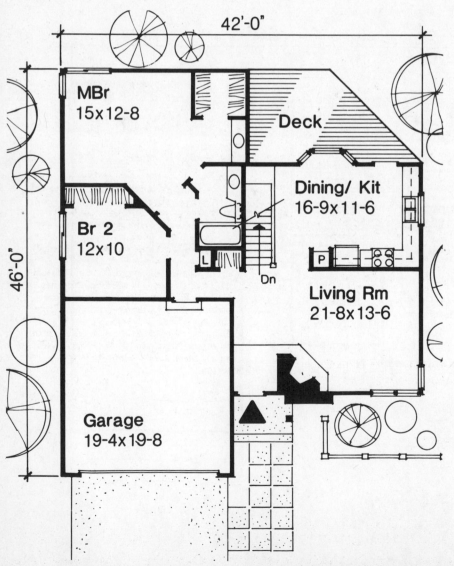

42'-0"

MBr
15x12-8

Deck

Dining/ Kit
16-9x11-6

Br 2
12x10

46'-0"

Dn

Living Rm
21-8x13-6

Garage
19-4x19-8

Compact Plan Features Large Master Bedroom

This affordable 1,123 sq. ft. plan adds interior excitement with vaulted ceiling, through views and a large master bedroom.

Note how well furniture can be placed to give a natural conversation area in the living room focusing on the fireplace. The dining/kitchen area has a bay window and access to a backyard deck.

The basement opens further potential for individual customizing. In the non-basement (slab) version, the stairwell area is used for a laundry and utility space. Design features 2x4 single-wall construction.

Total living area: 1,123 sq. ft.
(Not counting basement or garage)

PLAN B-116-8506
WITH BASEMENT

Blueprint Price Code A

Plan B-116-8506

*TO ORDER THIS BLUEPRINT,
CALL TOLL-FREE 1-800-820-1283*

*PRICES AND DETAILS
ON PAGES 12-15*

For Singles or Starting Couples

The simple roof line and double-car garage effectively complement and enhance this 1,169 sq. ft., one-level home. The entry provides easy access to every room of the dwelling. The homemaker will love the kitchen built-ins and the separate laundry room.

This home also features the Great Room with a dining area. In addition, there is a nice den and two bedrooms. The master bedroom boasts a private bath and a large closet.

Perfect as a starter home, this floor plan arrangement will also be the ideal answer for the lifestyle of a the single working person.

Total living area: 1,169 sq. ft.
(Not counting garage)

PLAN R-1075
WITHOUT BASEMENT
(CRAWLSPACE FOUNDATION)

Floor Plan

48'-0"

47'-0"

PATIO

DINING

GREAT RM.
25/0x14/0

MASTER
14/0x10/4

KITCH

ENTRY

wh | furn | W | D

DEN
9/0x11/0

BEDRM.2
11/6x9/0

lin

GARAGE
19/4x26/4

Blueprint Price Code A

Plan R-1075

TO ORDER THIS BLUEPRINT,
CALL TOLL-FREE 1-800-820-1283

*PRICES AND DETAILS
ON PAGES 12-15*

27

An Answer to Rising Costs

As an answer to rising land and construction costs, this plan carefully combines three bedrooms and family living spaces into only 1,180 sq. ft.

A covered entry opens into the generously sized living room and then into the adjacent family room, offering ample space for daily activities and entertaining. A sliding glass door in the family room leads to the yard — for outdoor meals, gardening, or just relaxing.

Dining space is available in the family room, next to the fully equipped, U-shaped kitchen. The adjacent laundry room has a service door into the two-car garage.

At the other end of the house, the master bedroom has a sunny window seat and its own full bathroom. The other two bedrooms, with large six-foot closets, share the bathroom in the hall.

Designed to meet Uniform Building Code requirements, this home also is energy efficient. Exterior walls are 2x6 construction, for R-19 insulation. Ceilings and floors allow space for plenty of insulation, depending on your climate. All windows are double-glazed. Roof is framed with trusses.

Total living area: 1,180 sq. ft.
(Not counting garage)

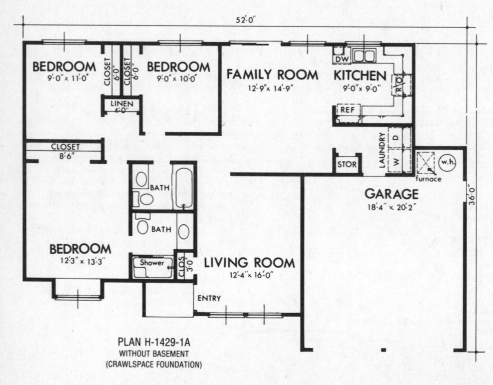

PLAN H-1429-1A
WITHOUT BASEMENT
(CRAWLSPACE FOUNDATION)

(Exterior walls are 2x6 construction).

**TO ORDER THIS BLUEPRINT,
CALL TOLL-FREE 1-800-820-1283**

Blueprint Price Code A
Plan H-1429-1A

*PRICES AND DETAILS
ON PAGES 12-15*

Cottage with Country Charm

- This charming country cottage makes the most of its living space, with an open room arrangement, vaulted ceilings and modern window treatments.
- The covered front porch is 7 ft. deep, providing plenty of room for outdoor relaxation.
- Once inside the entry, guests are greeted by a dynamite Great Room with a 12-ft. vaulted ceiling and a warm

energy-efficient woodstove. Lots of windows, plus sliding glass doors to the side yard, brighten the room.
- Expanding the area is a spacious dining room, which has easy access to the uniquely shaped kitchen. A breakfast bar, a garden window above the sink and a pantry closet are highlights here.
- The master bedroom is enhanced by a 12-ft.-high vaulted ceiling and a large picture window. The master bath offers a spa tub, a skylighted dressing area and a walk-in closet.
- The secondary bedroom is enviable in its own right, boasting a beautiful bay window and a roomy wardrobe closet.

Plan LMB-1211	
Bedrooms: 2	**Baths:** 2
Living Area:	
Main floor	1,186 sq. ft.
Total Living Area:	**1,186 sq. ft.**
Garage	494 sq. ft.
Exterior Wall Framing:	2x6

Foundation Options:

Crawlspace
(All plans can be built with your choice of foundation and framing. A generic conversion diagram is available. See order form.)

BLUEPRINT PRICE CODE: A

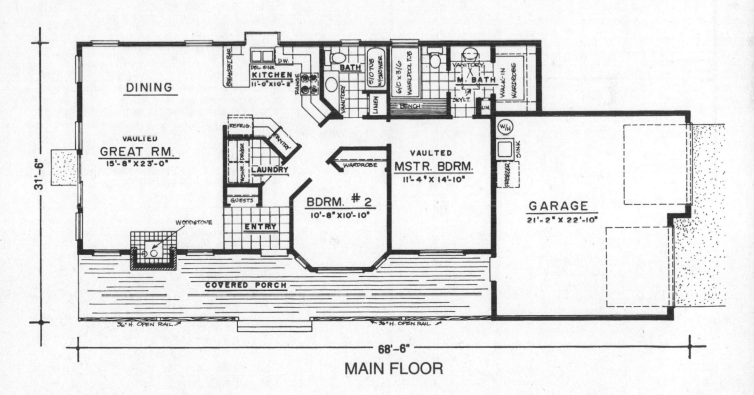

MAIN FLOOR

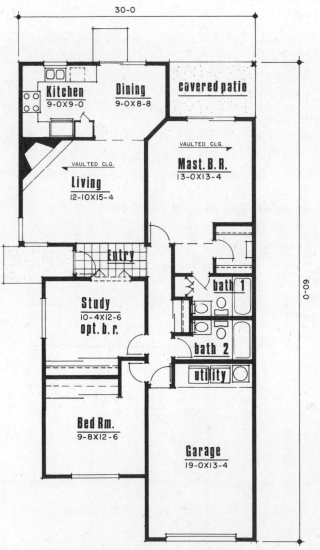

Vaulted Ceilings in Long, Low Plan

- Both the living room and master suite feature vaulted ceilings.
- Living room focuses on distinctive corner fireplace.
- Living and dining rooms flow together to make big space for entertaining.
- Master suite includes private bath and large walk-in closet.
- Study off the entry could be an office, if not needed as a third bedroom.
- Kitchen opens to the dining area to eliminate the confined feeling often experienced in many kitchens.

Plan Q-1190-1A

Bedrooms: 2-3	Baths: 2
Total living area:	1,190 sq. ft.
Garage:	253 sq. ft.
Exterior Wall Framing:	2x4

Foundation options:
Slab only.
(Foundation & framing conversion diagram available — see order form.)

Blueprint Price Code:	A

Affordable Amenities

- Affordably-sized, yet filled with exciting features, this charming one-story is the perfect choice for young families or "empty-nest" couples.
- The foyer flows directly into the impressive living room, which boasts a 10-ft., 10-in.-high vaulted ceiling and a handsome window-flanked fireplace. The adjoining dining room offers sliding glass doors to a backyard patio.
- The good-sized kitchen includes a windowed sink, a pantry and a sunny bayed breakfast nook.
- The master bedroom features a walk-in closet and a private bath.
- Double doors off the foyer lead into the den or third bedroom, which would also make an ideal home office.
- Another bedroom, a second full bath and a space-saving laundry closet complete the plan.

Plan CDG-1001

Bedrooms: 2+	Baths: 2

Living Area:	
Main floor	1,199 sq. ft.
Total Living Area:	**1,199 sq. ft.**
Garage	494 sq. ft.
Exterior Wall Framing:	2x6

Foundation Options:

Crawlspace

(All plans can be built with your choice of foundation and framing. A generic conversion diagram is available. See order form.)

BLUEPRINT PRICE CODE:	**A**

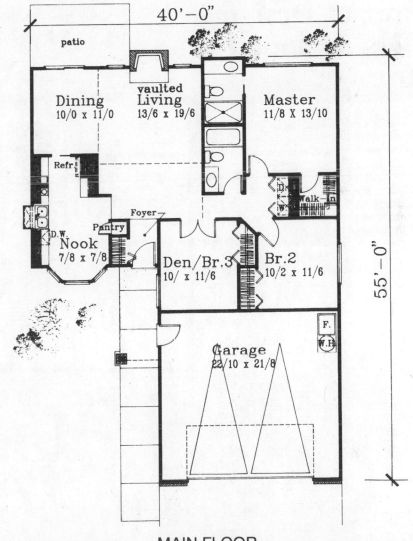

MAIN FLOOR

Compact Design Offers Secluded Entry

- This efficient and economical design offers a stylish exterior and an interior that provides for comfortable living.
- The living and dining area is huge for a home of this size, and the corner fireplace is a real eye-catcher.
- The efficient U-shaped kitchen is open to the dining room and includes a floor-to-ceiling pantry as well as abundant cabinet space.
- The master suite boasts a private bath and a large walk-in closet. Two other bedrooms share another full bath.
- A small side porch accesses the dining room as well as a large utility and storage area.

Plan E-1214

Bedrooms: 3	Baths: 2
Space:	
Main floor	1,200 sq. ft.
Total Living Area	**1,200 sq. ft.**
Porches	60 sq. ft.
Utility & Storage	100 sq. ft.
Exterior Wall Framing	2x6

Foundation options:

Crawlspace

Slab

(Foundation & framing conversion diagram available—see order form.)

Blueprint Price Code	A

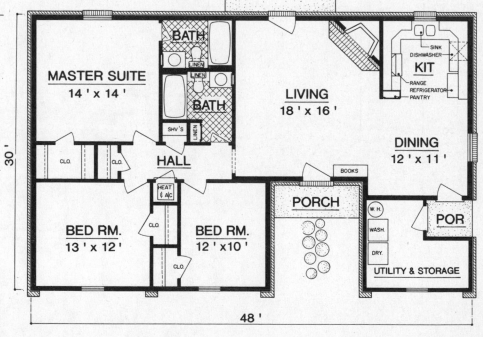

Plan E-1214

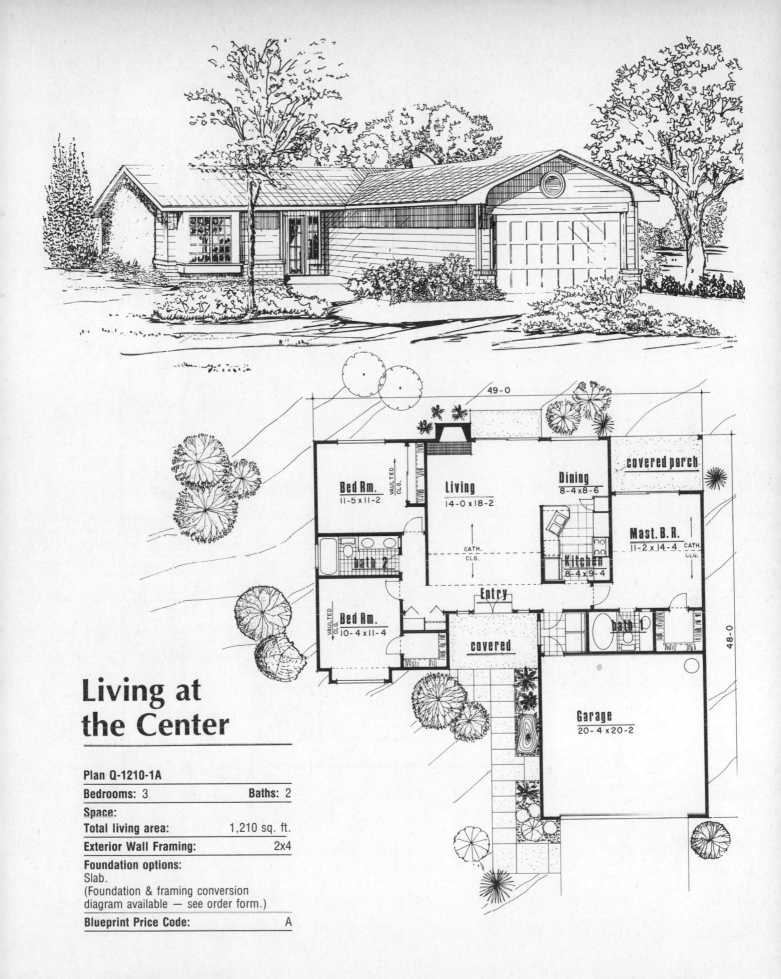

Living at the Center

Plan Q-1210-1A

Bedrooms: 3	Baths: 2

Space:

Total living area:	1,210 sq. ft.
Exterior Wall Framing:	2x4

Foundation options:
Slab.
(Foundation & framing conversion
diagram available — see order form.)

Blueprint Price Code:	A

Plan Q-1210-1A

Ritzy Rambler

- This inviting one-story home is full of fancy touches not usually associated with such an economical floor plan!
- A quaint, covered porch adorns the entry, which leads first to two secondary bedrooms and the well-placed laundry facilities between them.
- The laundry room has convenient access to the two-car garage, where you'll find plenty of room to assemble that soapbox derby car.
- At the back of the home, the family room faces a warm fireplace, offering peaceful surroundings for loved ones to share the day's events.
- With a versatile center island, the adjoining kitchen and breakfast nook promise easy food preparation and convenience for meals on the go!
- From the nook, sliding glass doors lead to a backyard patio, a perfect escape during large parties. In the summer, the patio and backyard may host a happy family barbecue, complete with lawn darts, badminton and your favorite aunt's famous potato salad!
- Occupying a secluded corner, the master bedroom boasts a roomy walk-in closet and a private bath with a handy linen cupboard.

Plan NW-531

Bedrooms: 3	Baths: 2
Living Area:	
Main floor	1,214 sq. ft.
Total Living Area:	**1,214 sq. ft.**
Garage	380 sq. ft.
Exterior Wall Framing:	2x6

Foundation Options:

Crawlspace
(All plans can be built with your choice of foundation and framing. A generic conversion diagram is available. See order form.)

BLUEPRINT PRICE CODE: A

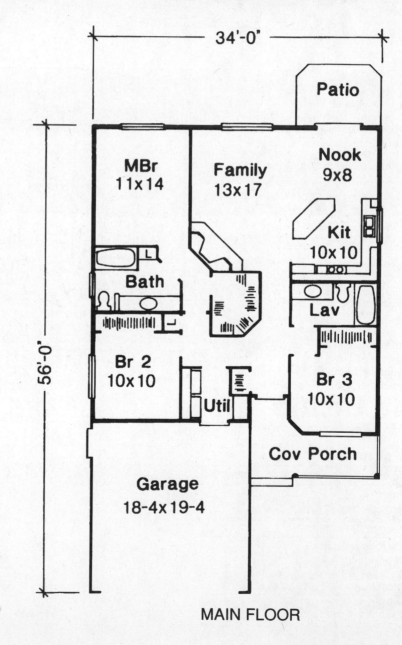

MAIN FLOOR

Plan NW-531

PRICES AND DETAILS ON PAGES 12-15

Affordable Comfort

- This cozy home makes comfortable living available at an affordable price.
- Nestled into a cozy covered porch, the bright, sidelighted front door opens into a welcoming tiled foyer.
- To the left of the foyer, a striking 11-ft. cathedral ceiling soars over the inviting living room, where your family will enjoy countless fun-filled nights. The living room features a warm fireplace.
- Nearby, two bright skylights cheer up the combined kitchen and dining area. The spacious eating area boasts sliding glass doors that open to an expansive backyard deck.
- In the master suite, a great 9-ft. tray ceiling lends a touch of style, while the handy private bath adds convenience.
- A second bedroom across the hall is serviced by a full hall bath.
- A bay window adds a splash of sunlight to the quiet den, which may also serve as an additional bedroom.
- The centrally located laundry facilities make daily chores a snap.

Plan GL-1226

Bedrooms: 2+	Baths: 2
Living Area:	
Main floor	1,226 sq. ft.
Total Living Area:	**1,226 sq. ft.**
Standard basement	1,204 sq. ft.
Garage	450 sq. ft.
Exterior Wall Framing:	2x4

Foundation Options:

Standard basement

(All plans can be built with your choice of foundation and framing. A generic conversion diagram is available. See order form.)

BLUEPRINT PRICE CODE: A

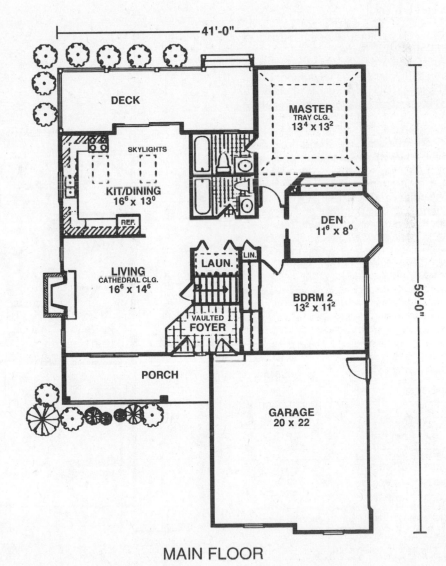

MAIN FLOOR

Affordable Charm

- An inviting columned porch introduces this affordable home.
- Inside, soaring ceilings and attention to detail highlight the efficient floor plan.
- The foyer leads to an eat-in kitchen, which includes a handy built-in pantry. A great 10-ft. ceiling enhances this sunny space.
- A convenient serving counter connects the kitchen to the open dining room. A beautiful bay window is topped by a half-round transom.
- The adjacent living room features an energy-efficient fireplace and French-door access to an inviting rear deck.
- A dramatic 14-ft. vaulted ceiling soars above the living and dining rooms.
- The spacious master bedroom boasts a striking 11-ft. vaulted ceiling, a large walk-in closet and private access to the hall bath.
- Two additional bedrooms and a linen closet round out the floor plan.

Plan B-93015

Bedrooms: 3	Baths: 1
Living Area:	
Main floor	1,227 sq. ft.
Total Living Area:	**1,227 sq. ft.**
Standard basement	1,217 sq. ft.
Garage	385 sq. ft.
Exterior Wall Framing:	2x6

Foundation Options:

Standard basement

(All plans can be built with your choice of foundation and framing. A generic conversion diagram is available. See order form.)

BLUEPRINT PRICE CODE: **A**

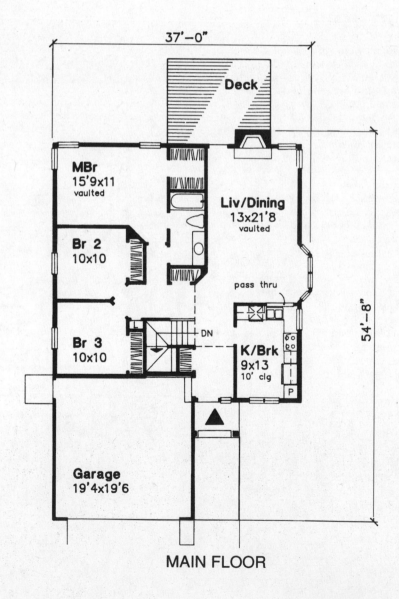

MAIN FLOOR

TO ORDER THIS BLUEPRINT, CALL TOLL-FREE 1-800-820-1283

Plan B-93015

PRICES AND DETAILS ON PAGES 12-15

Classic Country

- This country home features a classic exterior and a luxurious interior design in an economical floor plan.
- A covered front porch leads through a sidelighted entry directly to the living room. A coat closet is close by.
- Stylish windows brighten the spacious living room, where a handsome recessed fireplace crackles. A marvelous 12-ft., 3-in. vaulted ceiling soars overhead and extends to the dining room and kitchen.

- Stately columns set off the entry to the dining room, which offers French-door access to a backyard terrace that is perfect for summertime entertainment.
- The dining room and the efficient kitchen share a stylish serving bar.
- The secluded master suite is graced by a 12-ft. cathedral ceiling. A French door opens to a private terrace.
- The master bath flaunts a refreshing whirlpool tub and a separate shower.
- Lovely windows bring natural light into two more bedrooms. A hall bath easily services both rooms.

Plan AHP-9507	
Bedrooms: 3	**Baths:** 2
Living Area:	
Main floor	1,232 sq. ft.
Total Living Area:	**1,232 sq. ft.**
Standard basement	1,183 sq. ft.
Garage and storage	324 sq. ft.
Exterior Wall Framing:	2x4 or 2x6
Foundation Options:	
Standard basement	
Crawlspace	
Slab	

(All plans can be built with your choice of foundation and framing. A generic conversion diagram is available. See order form.)

BLUEPRINT PRICE CODE: A

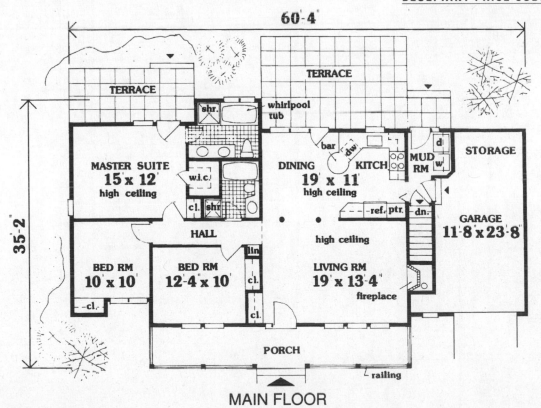

MAIN FLOOR

Modest-Sized Home Offers
Large Dining/ Living Area

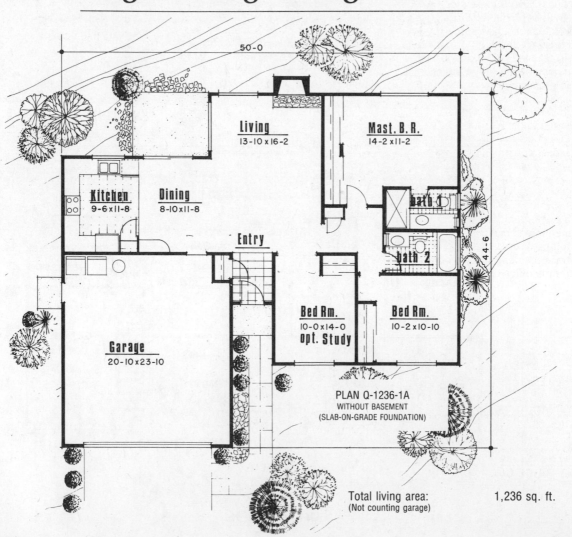

50-0

Living
13-10 x 16-2

Mast. B.R.
14-2 x 11-2

Kitchen
9-6 x 11-8

Dining
8-10 x 11-8

bath 1

Entry

bath 2

44-6

Bed Rm.
10-0 x 14-0
opt. Study

Bed Rm.
10-2 x 10-10

Garage
20-10 x 23-10

PLAN Q-1236-1A
WITHOUT BASEMENT
(SLAB-ON-GRADE FOUNDATION)

Total living area:
(Not counting garage)

1,236 sq. ft.

Blueprint Price Code A

Plan Q-1236-1A

Attractive and Affordable

- This attractive, up-to-date design offers lots of extras in an affordable square footage. The stone chimney, striking windows and gable louver make the facade irresistible.

- The sidelighted, raised entry introduces the open living room, which boasts a corner fireplace and a lovely window arrangement. The living room shares a 13-ft.-high vaulted ceiling with the dining room and the kitchen.

- Sliding glass doors in the dining room provide access to a nice patio. The galley-style kitchen offers an angled sink and a pantry closet, with a plant shelf high above.

- The spacious and quiet master suite features a corner window and a private, compartmentalized bath.

- Another full bath serves the second bedroom and the den, which would be a perfect home office or third bedroom.

Plan B-88021

Bedrooms: 2+	Baths: 2
Living Area:	
Main floor	1,231 sq. ft.
Total Living Area:	**1,231 sq. ft.**
Standard basement	1,231 sq. ft.
Garage	400 sq. ft.
Exterior Wall Framing:	2x4

Foundation Options:

Standard basement

(All plans can be built with your choice of foundation and framing. A generic conversion diagram is available. See order form.)

BLUEPRINT PRICE CODE: A

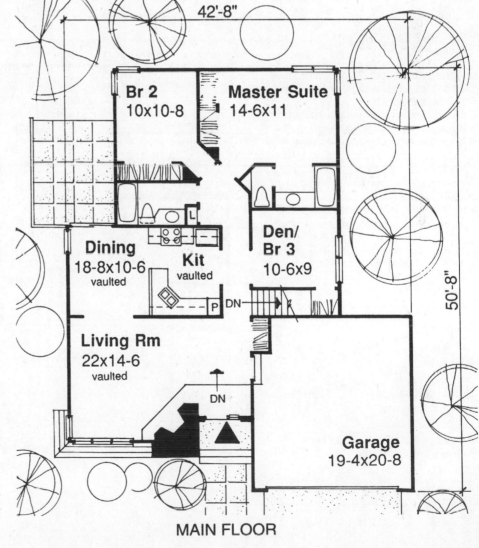

MAIN FLOOR

Quality Details Inside and Out

- A sparkling stucco finish, an eye-catching roofline and elegant window treatments hint at the quality features found inside this exquisite home.
- The airy entry opens to a large, central living room, which is embellished with a 10-ft. ceiling and a dramatic fireplace.
- The living room flows into a nice-sized dining area. A covered side porch expands the entertaining area.
- A functional eating bar and pantry are featured in the adjoining U-shaped kitchen. The nearby hallway to the garage neatly stores a washer, a dryer and a laundry sink.
- Secluded to the back of the home is a private master suite with a romantic sitting area and a large walk-in closet. The master bath offers dual sinks and an exciting oval tub.
- Two secondary bedrooms and another bath are located on the other side of the living room and entry.

Plan E-1435

Bedrooms: 3	Baths: 2
Living Area:	
Main floor	1,442 sq. ft.
Total Living Area:	**1,442 sq. ft.**
Garage and storage	516 sq. ft.
Exterior Wall Framing:	2x4

Foundation Options:

Crawlspace

Slab

(All plans can be built with your choice of foundation and framing. A generic conversion diagram is available. See order form.)

BLUEPRINT PRICE CODE: A

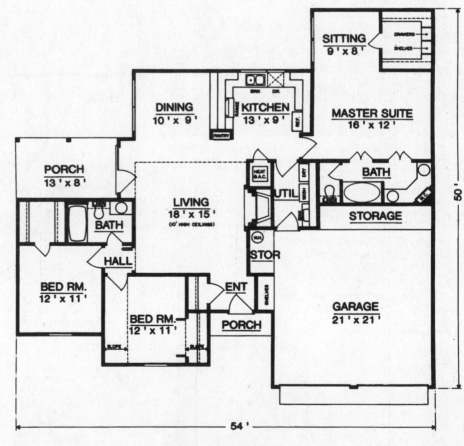

MAIN FLOOR

Plan E-1435

PRICES AND DETAILS ON PAGES 12-15

Simple, Stylish and Affordable

- This affordable three-bedroom, single-story home is perfect for the young family or for retirees.
- Vaulted ceilings in the living room and dining room create drama and volume. The big fireplace and rear windows bring in light and warmth.
- The efficient design of the kitchen includes a corner sink framed by windows and a breakfast bar open to the dining room.
- The adjoining screen porch could serve as expansion space.
- A main-floor laundry closet is conveniently located in the bedroom wing. The large master bedroom features a vaulted ceiling, a walk-in closet and a private bath. The two secondary bedrooms show off lovely window seats and share a second bath.

Plan B-91016

Bedrooms: 3	Baths: 2
Living Area:	
Main floor	1,263 sq. ft.
Total Living Area:	**1,263 sq. ft.**
Standard basement	1,263 sq. ft.
Garage	441 sq. ft.
Screen porch	126 sq. ft.
Exterior Wall Framing:	2x6

Foundation Options:

Standard basement

(Typical foundation & framing conversion diagram available—see order form.)

BLUEPRINT PRICE CODE:	**A**

Floor Plan

53'-4"

46'-0"

Kitchen 10x10

Living 12x16 vaulted

MBr 13x14—8 vaulted

Screen Porch

Dining 10—4x9—6 vaulted

wood storage

W D

DN

Garage 21—4x20—8

Br 3 10x10—4

seat

Br 2 11—4x10—4

seat

L

MAIN FLOOR

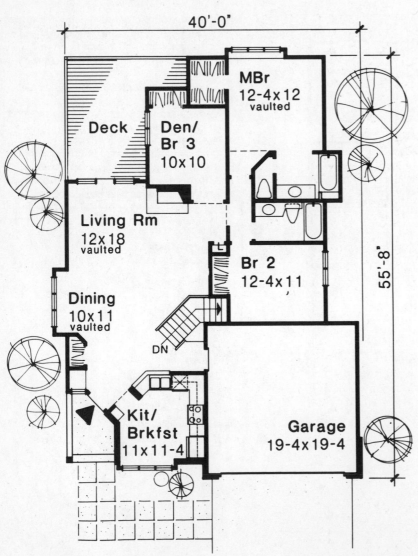

Deck

Den/
Br 3
10x10

MBr
12-4x12
vaulted

Living Rm
12x18
vaulted

Dining
10x11
vaulted

DN

Br 2
12-4x11

Kit/
Brkfst
11x11-4

Garage
19-4x19-4

40'-0"

55'-8"

Compact,
Efficient Design

PLAN B-87116
WITH BASEMENT

Total living area: 1,270 sq. ft.
(Not counting basement or garage)

Blueprint Price Code A

Plan B-87116

TO ORDER THIS BLUEPRINT,
CALL TOLL-FREE 1-800-820-1283

PRICES AND DETAILS
ON PAGES 12-15

Spacious Living/Dining Area

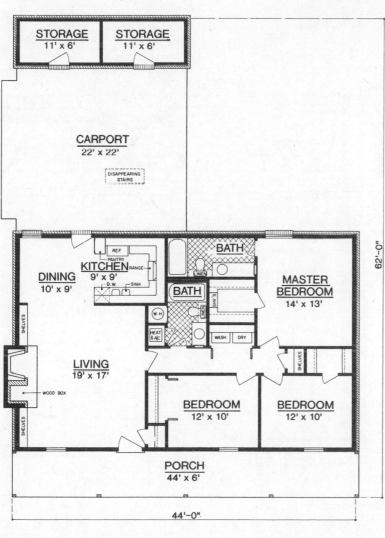

AREAS	
Living	1244 sq. ft.
Porches	269 sq. ft.
Carport	484 sq. ft.
Storage	132 sq. ft.
Total	2129 sq. ft.

Exterior walls are 2x6 construction.
Specify crawlspace or slab foundation.

Floor plan labels:
STORAGE 11' x 6'
STORAGE 11' x 6'
CARPORT 22' x 22'
DISAPPEARING STAIRS
REF. PANTRY
KITCHEN 9' x 9' RANGE
D.W. SINK
DINING 10' x 9'
BATH
LINEN
BATH
MASTER BEDROOM 14' x 13'
W H
HEAT & A/C
WASH DRY
SHELVES
LIVING 19' x 17'
WOOD BOX
SHELVES
BEDROOM 12' x 10'
BEDROOM 12' x 10'
PORCH 44' x 6'
44'-0"
62'-0"

Blueprint Price Code A
Plan E-1219

**TO ORDER THIS BLUEPRINT,
CALL TOLL-FREE 1-800-820-1283**

*PRICES AND DETAILS
ON PAGES 12-15*

43

Big Impact!

- The luxurious features of this affordably-sized one-story home give it extra impact.
- The inviting covered porch leads into the central foyer, which neatly channels traffic to all areas of the home.
- Just ahead, the living room adjoins the dining room, forming a spacious formal area. A 12-ft.-high sloped ceiling enhances both rooms. The living room features a glass-flanked fireplace, while the dining room offers sliding glass doors to a rear terrace.
- The L-shaped kitchen includes an eating bar and merges with the family room to create a casual family atmosphere. A laundry/mudroom and a half-bath are conveniently nearby.
- The sleeping wing contains three bedrooms. The master bedroom features two wardrobe closets and a private skylighted bath.
- The remaining bedrooms are serviced by a hallway linen closet and a second skylighted bath.

Plan K-696-T

Bedrooms: 3	Baths: 2½
Living Area:	
Main floor	1,272 sq. ft.
Total Living Area:	**1,272 sq. ft.**
Standard basement	1,232 sq. ft.
Garage	509 sq. ft.
Exterior Wall Framing:	2x4 or 2x6

Foundation Options:

Standard basement
Slab
(All plans can be built with your choice of foundation and framing. A generic conversion diagram is available. See order form.)

BLUEPRINT PRICE CODE: A

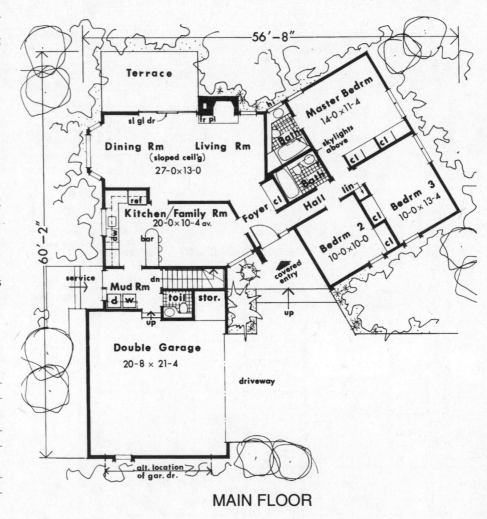

MAIN FLOOR

Traditional Flavor for Modern Plan

First floor:	817 sq. ft.
Second floor:	699 sq. ft.
Total living area:	1,516 sq. ft.
(Not counting basement or garage)	

PLAN B-901
WITH BASEMENT

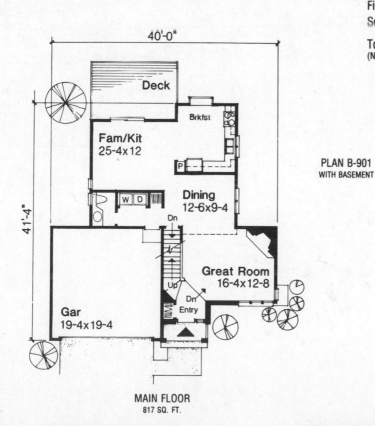

MAIN FLOOR
817 SQ. FT.

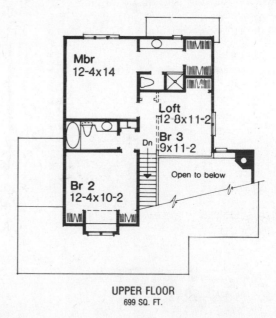

UPPER FLOOR
699 SQ. FT.

Blueprint Price Code B
Plan B-901

TO ORDER THIS BLUEPRINT,
CALL TOLL-FREE 1-800-820-1283

PRICES AND DETAILS
ON PAGES 12-15

45

Charming Accents

- Traditional accents add warmth and charm to the facade of this affordable one-story home.
- Decorative, beveled oval glass adorns the elegant entry, which is flanked by sidelights.
- The tiled foyer introduces the spacious family room, which is enhanced by a 12-ft. vaulted ceiling and a nice fireplace. A French door provides easy access to the backyard.
- The galley-style kitchen flows into the sunny dining area, which can be extended with an optional bay window.
- The secluded master bedroom features plenty of closet space. The private master bath boasts a corner garden tub, a separate shower and two sinks. The bath may be expanded with a 13-ft. vaulted ceiling.
- Two additional bedrooms share a hall bath in the opposite wing. A nice-sized laundry room is centrally located.

Plan APS-1205

Bedrooms: 3	Baths: 2
Living Area:	
Main floor	1,296 sq. ft.
Total Living Area:	**1,296 sq. ft.**
Garage	380 sq. ft.
Exterior Wall Framing:	2x4

Foundation Options:

Crawlspace
Slab
(All plans can be built with your choice of foundation and framing. A generic conversion diagram is available. See order form.)

BLUEPRINT PRICE CODE:	**A**

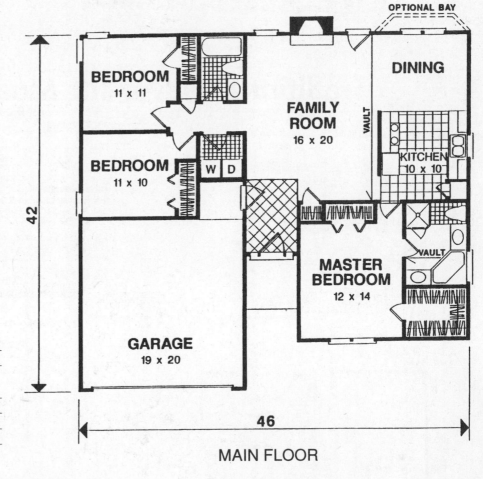

MAIN FLOOR

Plan APS-1205

PRICES AND DETAILS
ON PAGES 12-15

Easy Living on Sloping Lot

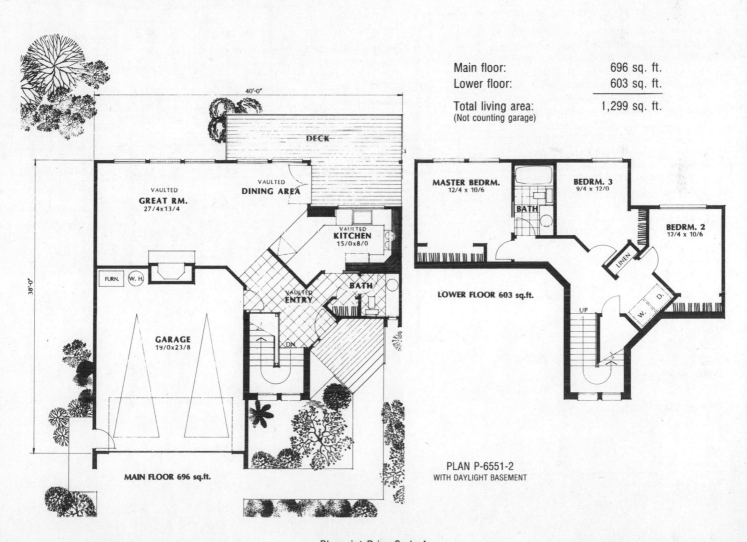

Main floor: 696 sq. ft.
Lower floor: 603 sq. ft.

Total living area: 1,299 sq. ft.
(Not counting garage)

40'-0"

DECK

VAULTED
GREAT RM.
27/4 x 13/4

VAULTED
DINING AREA

VAULTED
KITCHEN
15/0 x 8/0

FURN. W. H.

BATH

VAULTED
ENTRY

DN

GARAGE
19/0 x 23/8

38'-0"

MAIN FLOOR 696 sq. ft.

MASTER BEDRM.
12/4 x 10/6

BATH

BEDRM. 3
9/4 x 12/0

LINEN

BEDRM. 2
12/4 x 10/6

LOWER FLOOR 603 sq. ft.

UP

W. D.

PLAN P-6551-2
WITH DAYLIGHT BASEMENT

Blueprint Price Code A

Plan P-6551-2

Creatively Compact

- The living space of this stylish and compact home is maximized with the creative use of angles.
- The facade is accented by an attractive boxed window and unique round-bottom shingles above the garage door.
- Inside, a spacious formal living expanse unfolds from the entry. The openness of the living room to the dining room allows plenty of space for your entertaining needs.
- The dining room adjoins the kitchen, which is neatly cornered for easy service to both the formal and the informal living areas. A convenient snack bar and a cozy fireplace are angled to face the merging family room. A covered deck behind the kitchen is accessible from the family room.
- The master bedroom is strategically buffered from the living areas with a large walk-in closet and a private bath.
- The two secondary bedrooms share another bath off the hallway. The bedroom wing also houses a centrally located laundry room.

Plan NW-864-J

Bedrooms: 3	Baths: 2
Living Area:	
Main floor	1,552 sq. ft.
Total Living Area:	**1,552 sq. ft.**
Garage	410 sq. ft.
Exterior Wall Framing:	2x6

Foundation Options:

Crawlspace
(All plans can be built with your choice of foundation and framing. A generic conversion diagram is available. See order form.)

BLUEPRINT PRICE CODE:	B

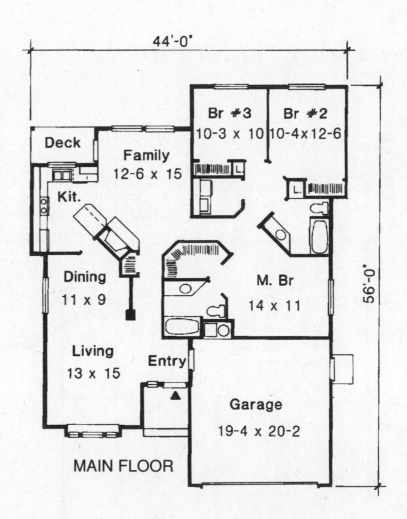

MAIN FLOOR

Plan NW-864-J

PRICES AND DETAILS
ON PAGES 12-15

Space-Saving Floor Plan

- Easy, affordable living is the basis for this great town and country design.
- The welcoming porch and the graceful arched window give the home its curb appeal. Inside, the floor plan provides large, highly livable spaces rather than several specialized rooms.
- The foyer opens to the spacious living room. A column separates the foyer from the formal dining room, which features a bay window and an alcove that is perfect for a china hutch. The country kitchen is large enough to accommodate family and guests alike.
- A beautiful open staircase leads to the second floor, where there are three bedrooms and two baths. The master bedroom offers a tray ceiling and a luxurious bath with a sloped ceiling and a corner shower.

Photo by Mark Englund/HomeStyles

Plan AX-92320

Bedrooms: 3	Baths: 2½
Living Area:	
Upper floor	706 sq. ft.
Main floor	830 sq. ft.
Total Living Area:	**1,536 sq. ft.**
Standard basement	754 sq. ft.
Garage	510 sq. ft.
Exterior Wall Framing:	2x6
Foundation Options:	
Standard basement	
Slab	
(Typical foundation & framing conversion diagram available—see order form.)	
BLUEPRINT PRICE CODE:	B

**NOTE:
The above photographed home may have been modified by the homeowner. Please refer to floor plan and/or drawn elevation shown for actual blueprint details.

FRONT VIEW

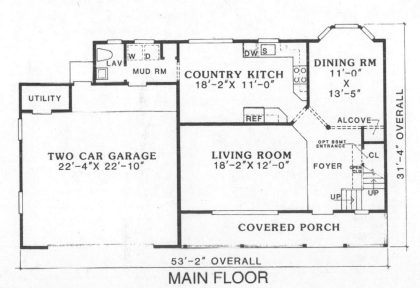

MAIN FLOOR

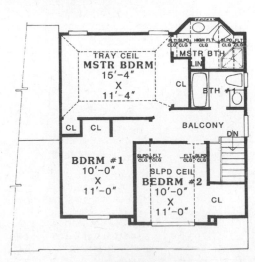

UPPER FLOOR

Elaborate Entry

- This home's important-looking covered entry greets guests with heavy, banded support columns, sunburst transom windows and dual sidelights.
- Once inside the home, the 15-ft.-high foyer is flanked by the formal living and dining rooms, which have 10½-ft. vaulted ceilings. Straight ahead and beyond five decorative columns lies the spacious family room.
- Surrounded by 8-ft.-high walls, the family room features a 13-ft. vaulted ceiling, a fireplace and sliding doors to a covered patio. A neat plant shelf above the fireplace adds style.
- The bright and airy kitchen has a 13-ft. ceiling and serves the family room and the breakfast area, which is enhanced by a corner window and a French door.
- The master suite enjoys a 13-ft. vaulted ceiling and features French-door patio access, a large walk-in closet and a private bath with a corner platform tub and a separate shower.
- Across the home, three secondary bedrooms share a hall bath, which boasts private access to the patio.

Plan HDS-90-806

Bedrooms: 4	Baths: 2
Living Area:	
Main floor	2,041 sq. ft.
Total Living Area:	**2,041 sq. ft.**
Garage	452 sq. ft.

Exterior Wall Framing:
2x4 or 8-in. concrete block

Foundation Options:
Slab
(All plans can be built with your choice of foundation and framing. A generic conversion diagram is available. See order form.)

BLUEPRINT PRICE CODE:	C

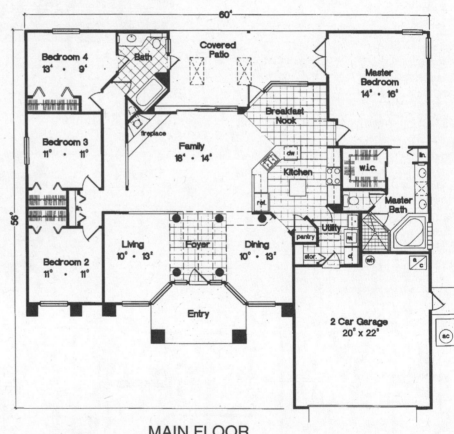

MAIN FLOOR

NOTE:
The above photographed home may have been modified by the homeowner. Please refer to floor plan and/or drawn elevation shown for actual blueprint details.

TO ORDER THIS BLUEPRINT, CALL TOLL-FREE 1-800-820-1283

Plan HDS-90-806

PRICES AND DETAILS ON PAGES 12-15

Traditional Heritage

- A distinctive roofline and a covered wraparound porch reflect this charming home's traditional heritage.
- The roomy entry flows directly into the spacious, open living area. Enhanced by a cathedral ceiling, the living room is warmed by a fireplace and offers a French door to a backyard patio. A good-sized laundry room is nearby.

- The adjoining dining area shares porch access with the stylish gourmet kitchen, which includes an eating bar and a garden window over the sink.
- The master bedroom suite features a lavish private bath with a garden spa tub, a separate shower, a dual-sink vanity and a big walk-in closet.
- A second full bath, located at the end of the bedroom hallway, is convenient to the two remaining bedrooms.
- The double carport includes a separate lockable storage area.

Plan J-86142

Bedrooms: 3	Baths: 2
Living Area:	
Main floor	1,536 sq. ft.
Total Living Area:	**1,536 sq. ft.**
Standard basement	1,536 sq. ft.
Carport and storage	520 sq. ft.
Exterior Wall Framing:	2x4

Foundation Options:

Standard basement
Crawlspace
Slab
(All plans can be built with your choice of foundation and framing. A generic conversion diagram is available. See order form.)

BLUEPRINT PRICE CODE: B

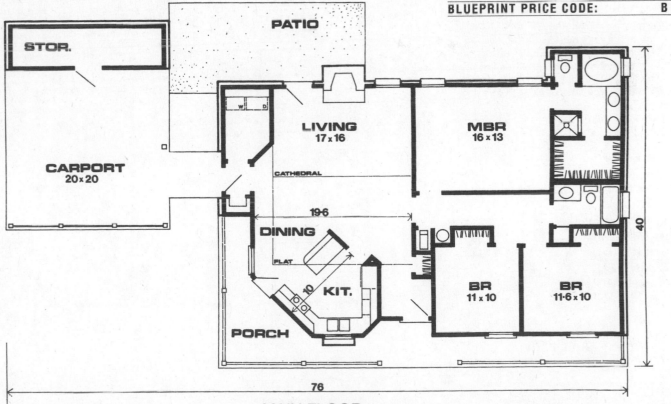

MAIN FLOOR

Cozy, Rustic Country Home

- This cozy, rustic home offers a modern, open interior that efficiently maximizes the square footage.
- The large living room features a 13-ft. sloped ceiling accented by rustic beams and an eye-catching corner fireplace.
- The living room flows into the adjoining dining room and the efficient U-shaped kitchen for a spacious, open feel.
- The master and secondary bedrooms are separated by the activity areas. The master suite includes a private bath and a separate dressing area with a dual-sink vanity.
- The secondary bedrooms share another full bath.

Plan E-1109

Bedrooms: 3	Baths: 2
Living Area:	
Main floor	1,191 sq. ft.
Total Living Area:	**1,191 sq. ft.**
Garage	462 sq. ft.
Storage & utility	55 sq. ft.
Exterior Wall Framing:	2x6

Foundation Options:
Crawlspace
Slab
(All plans can be built with your choice of foundation and framing. A generic conversion diagram is available. See order form.)

BLUEPRINT PRICE CODE: A

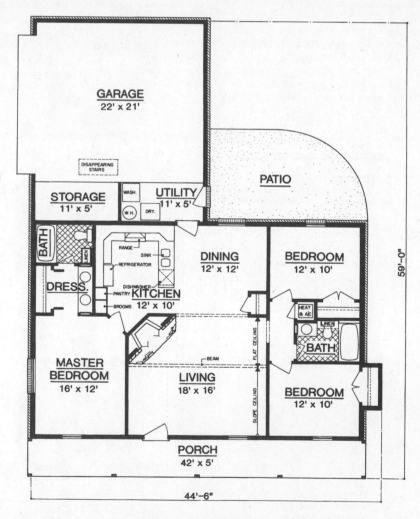

MAIN FLOOR

Plan E-1109

Making the Most of a Small Lot

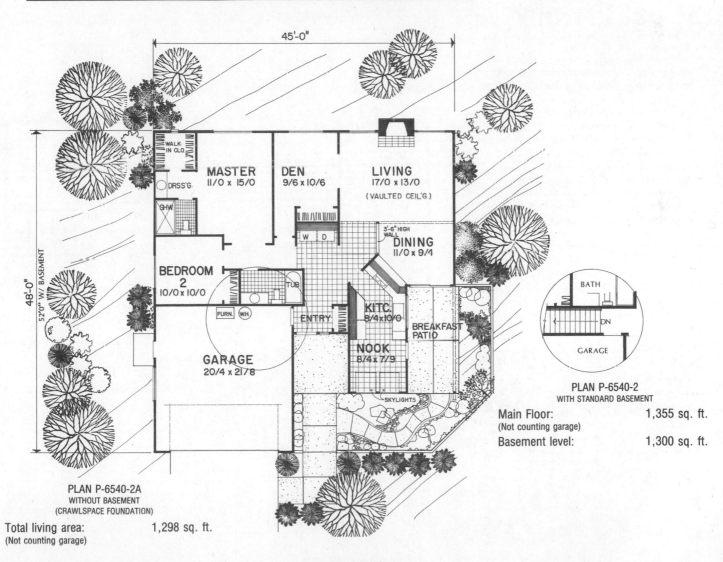

MASTER
11/0 x 15/0

DEN
9/6 x 10/6

LIVING
17/0 x 13/0
(VAULTED CEIL'G.)

WALK-IN CLO.

DRSS'G.

SHW

DINING
11/0 x 9/4

3'-6" HIGH WALL

W   D

BEDROOM 2
10/0 x 10/0

TUB

FURN. W.H.

ENTRY

KITC.
8/4 x 10/0

BREAKFAST PATIO

GARAGE
20/4 x 21/8

NOOK
8/4 x 7/9

SKYLIGHTS

45'-0"

48'-0"

52'0" W/ BASEMENT

BATH

DN

GARAGE

PLAN P-6540-2
WITH STANDARD BASEMENT

Main Floor: 1,355 sq. ft.
(Not counting garage)

Basement level: 1,300 sq. ft.

PLAN P-6540-2A
WITHOUT BASEMENT
(CRAWLSPACE FOUNDATION)

Total living area: 1,298 sq. ft.
(Not counting garage)

Blueprint Price Code A

TO ORDER THIS BLUEPRINT,
CALL TOLL-FREE 1-800-820-1283

Plans P-6540-2 & -2A

PRICES AND DETAILS
ON PAGES 12-15

53

Street Privacy

- If privacy from street traffic or noise is a concern, this unique home design will fit the bill. The views are oriented to the rear, leaving the front of the home quiet and protected.
- The covered entry porch opens to a spacious living room that overlooks a back porch and patio area. A dramatic corner fireplace is an inviting feature.
- A functional snack bar separates the kitchen from the adjoining dining room, which boasts a lovely bay window.
- Just off the kitchen, a deluxe utility room doubles as a mudroom. The area includes a pantry, a broom closet, a storage closet and laundry facilities.
- The private master suite has an angled window wall, a large walk-in closet and a nice-sized bath with twin sinks.
- Two more bedrooms share another full bath on the opposite end of the home.

Plan E-1424

Bedrooms: 3	Baths: 2
Living Area:	
Main floor	1,415 sq. ft.
Total Living Area:	**1,415 sq. ft.**
Garage	484 sq. ft.
Storage	60 sq. ft.
Exterior Wall Framing:	2x6

Foundation Options:
Crawlspace
Slab
(All plans can be built with your choice of foundation and framing. A generic conversion diagram is available. See order form.)

BLUEPRINT PRICE CODE: A

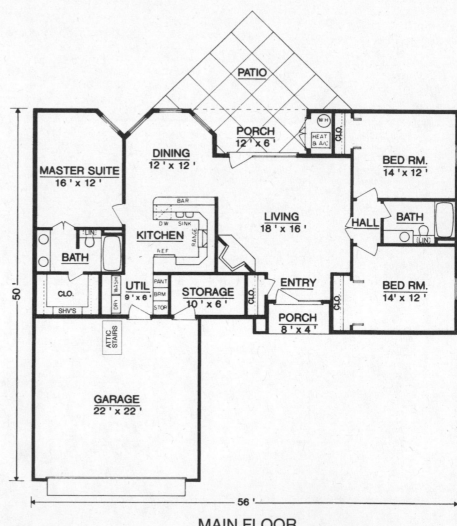

MAIN FLOOR

Plan E-1424

PRICES AND DETAILS ON PAGES 12-15

FRONT VIEW

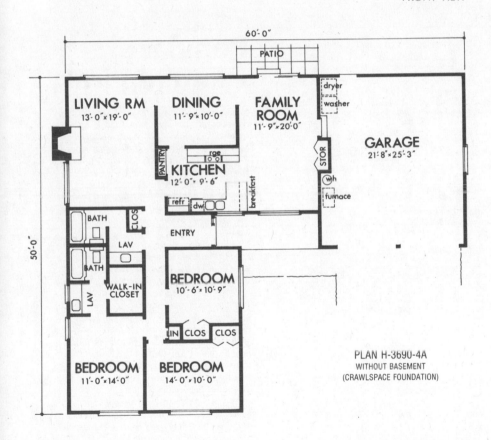

LIVING RM
13'-0"×19'-0"

DINING
11'-9"×10'-0"

FAMILY ROOM
11'-9"×20'-0"

dryer
washer

GARAGE
21'-8"×25'-3"

PANTRY

rge

STOR

KITCHEN
12'-0"×9'-6"

breakfast

w.h.

refr

furnace

dw

ENTRY

BATH

CLOS

LAV

BEDROOM
10'-6"×10'-9"

BATH

WALK-IN CLOSET

LAV

LIN

CLOS

CLOS

BEDROOM
11'-0"×14'-0"

BEDROOM
14'-0"×10'-0"

60'-0"

50'-0"

PATIO

PLAN H-3690-4A
WITHOUT BASEMENT
(CRAWLSPACE FOUNDATION)

L-Shaped Ranch Style for Livability and Economical Construction

Here is a home design in keeping with the times — to offer you the maximum in livable features within a very functional floor plan. One may pass from one room to another without being involved in unnecessary crossroom traffic.

A generous-sized entry is tucked into the alcove leading off the protected front porch, and a central hallway leads down to the interior of the three bedroom wing. Notice the linen and guest closet that flank both sides of the walkway and the access to the centrally located full bathroom.

An additional bathroom is also located adjacent to the walk-in closet that serves the master bedroom.

In addition to an 11'-9" x 10'-0" dining room, a house-spanning family room is next to the kitchen and separated by a breakfast bar.

Total living area: 1,529 sq. ft.
(Not counting garage)

*TO ORDER THIS BLUEPRINT,
CALL TOLL-FREE 1-800-820-1283*

Blueprint Price Code B
Plan H-3690-4A

*PRICES AND DETAILS
ON PAGES 12-15*

55

Popular Contemporary

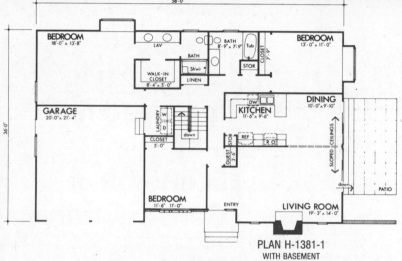

PLAN H-1381-1
WITH BASEMENT

Total living area: 1,596 sq. ft.
(Not counting basement or garage)

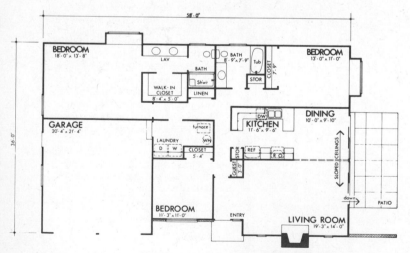

PLAN H-1381-1A
WITHOUT BASEMENT
(CRAWLSPACE FOUNDATION)

Total living area: 1,587 sq. ft.
(Not counting garage)

This low-slung contemporary design contains a lot more space than is apparent from the outside. Oriented towards the outdoor sideyard, it features a pair of sliding glass doors offering outside access from both the living and dining room.

Effective zoning is the rule here: Bedrooms are secluded on one side to the rear; living areas and active kitchen space are grouped on the opposite side of the home.

All of these rooms are easily reached from a central hallway that provides excellent traffic flow, precluding unnecessary cross-room traffic.

Note the convenient location of the laundry room and staircase to the basement. Access to the garage is also available from the interior of the home. A generous assortment of plumbing facilities is grouped at the rear of the home. One bath serves the master bedroom privately. Another complete unit serves the balance of the house.

The attractive low silhouette is embellished with architectural touches such as the interesting window seats, the extension of the masonry wall that shields the side patio, and the low pitched roof.

Overall width of the home is 58' and greatest depth measures 36'. Exterior walls are 2x6 construction.

Blueprint Price Code B

Plans H-1381-1 & -1A

TO ORDER THIS BLUEPRINT, CALL TOLL-FREE 1-800-820-1283

PRICES AND DETAILS ON PAGES 12-15

Classic Country-Style

- The classic covered front porch with decorative railings and columns make this home reminiscent of an early 20th-century farmhouse.
- Dormers give the home the appearance of a two-story, even though it is designed for single-level living.
- The huge living room features a ceiling that slopes up to 13 feet. A corner fireplace radiates warmth to both the living room and the dining room.
- The dining room overlooks a backyard patio and shares a versatile serving bar with the open kitchen. A large utility room is just steps away.
- The master bedroom boasts a roomy bath with a dual-sink vanity. The two smaller bedrooms at the other end of the home share a full bath.

Plan E-1412

Bedrooms: 3	Baths: 2
Living Area:	
Main floor	1,484 sq. ft.
Total Living Area:	**1,484 sq. ft.**
Garage	440 sq. ft.
Exterior Wall Framing:	2x6

Foundation Options:

Crawlspace

Slab

(All plans can be built with your choice of foundation and framing. A generic conversion diagram is available. See order form.)

BLUEPRINT PRICE CODE: **A**

MAIN FLOOR

Functional, Nostalgic Home Offers Choices in Floor Plans

- Your choice of first- and second-floor room arrangements and foundation plans is required when ordering this design.
- Pick from a family room/kitchen combination with a separate living room, or an expansive living/dining room adjoining a kitchen and nook with either two or three bedrooms.
- In both cases, front entry parlor has an open stairway brightened by a round glass window.
- 8' wide front porch connects with a covered walk to a detached double-car garage.

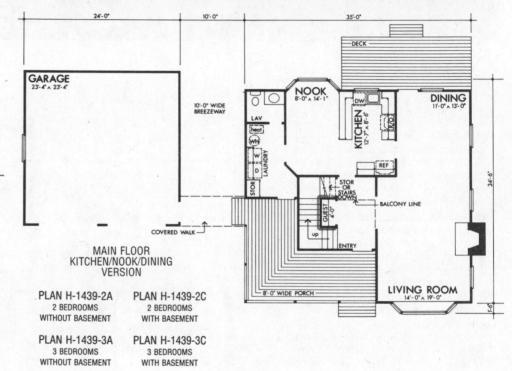

MAIN FLOOR
KITCHEN/NOOK/DINING VERSION

PLAN H-1439-2A
2 BEDROOMS
WITHOUT BASEMENT

PLAN H-1439-2C
2 BEDROOMS
WITH BASEMENT

PLAN H-1439-3A
3 BEDROOMS
WITHOUT BASEMENT

PLAN H-1439-3C
3 BEDROOMS
WITH BASEMENT

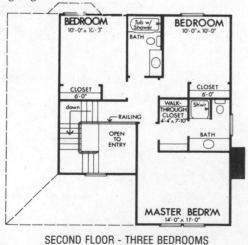

SECOND FLOOR - THREE BEDROOMS
678 SQUARE FEET

SECOND FLOOR - TWO BEDROOMS
678 SQUARE FEET

TO ORDER THIS BLUEPRINT, CALL TOLL-FREE 1-800-820-1283 Plans H-1439-2A, -2C, -3A & -3C **PRICES AND DETAILS ON PAGES 12-15**

Design Fits Narrow Lot

- This compact, cozy and dignified plan makes great use of a small lot, while also offering an exciting interior design.
- In from the covered front porch, the living room features a warm fireplace and a 13-ft., 6-in. cathedral ceiling.
- The bay-windowed dining room joins the living room to provide a spacious area for entertaining.
- The galley-style kitchen has easy access to a large pantry closet, the utility room and the carport.
- The master suite includes a deluxe bath and a roomy walk-in closet.
- Two secondary bedrooms share another bath off the hallway.
- A lockable storage area is located off the rear patio.

Plan J-86161

Bedrooms: 3	Baths: 2
Living Area:	
Main floor	1,626 sq. ft.
Total Living Area:	**1,626 sq. ft.**
Standard basement	1,626 sq. ft.
Carport	410 sq. ft.
Storage	104 sq. ft.
Exterior Wall Framing:	2x4

Foundation Options:

Standard basement

Crawlspace

Slab

(All plans can be built with your choice of foundation and framing. A generic conversion diagram is available. See order form.)

BLUEPRINT PRICE CODE: B

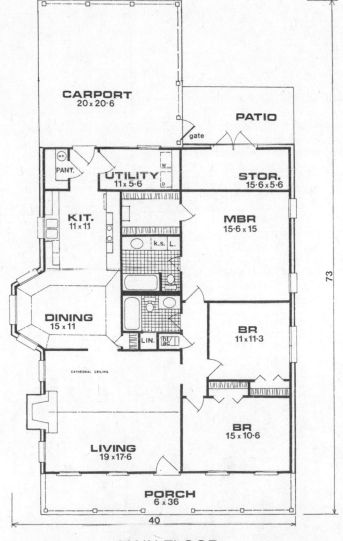

MAIN FLOOR

Instant Impact

- Bold rooflines, interesting angles and unusual window treatments give this stylish home lots of impact.
- Inside, high ceilings and an open floor plan maximize the home's square footage. At only 28 ft. wide, the home also is ideal for a narrow lot.
- A covered deck leads to the main entry, which features a sidelighted door, angled glass walls and a view of the striking open staircase.
- The Great Room is stunning, with its 16-ft. vaulted ceiling, energy-efficient woodstove and access to a large deck.
- A flat ceiling distinguishes the dining area, which shares an angled snack bar/cooktop with the step-saving kitchen. A laundry/mudroom is nearby.
- Upstairs, the master suite offers a sloped 13-ft. ceiling and a clerestory window. A walk-through closet leads to the private bath, which is enhanced by a skylighted, sloped ceiling.
- Another full bath and plenty of storage serve the other bedrooms, one of which has a sloped ceiling and a dual closet.

Plans H-1427-3A & -3B

Bedrooms: 3	Baths: 2½
Living Area:	
Upper floor	880 sq. ft.
Main floor	810 sq. ft.
Total Living Area:	**1,690 sq. ft.**
Daylight basement	810 sq. ft.
Garage	409 sq. ft.
Exterior Wall Framing:	2x4
Foundation Options:	**Plan #**
Daylight basement	H-1427-3B
Crawlspace	H-1427-3A

(All plans can be built with your choice of foundation and framing. A generic conversion diagram is available. See order form.)

BLUEPRINT PRICE CODE:	B

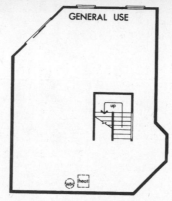

DAYLIGHT BASEMENT

UPPER FLOOR

STAIRWAY AREA IN CRAWLSPACE VERSION

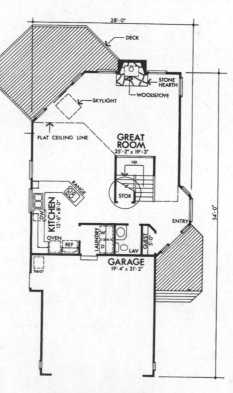

MAIN FLOOR

TO ORDER THIS BLUEPRINT, CALL TOLL-FREE 1-800-820-1283

Plans H-1427-3A & -3B

PRICES AND DETAILS ON PAGES 12-15

Friendly Farmhouse

- Reminiscent of a turn-of-the-century farmhouse, this warm, friendly home is characterized by an authentic front porch with fine post-and-rail detailing.
- The open entry provides a sweeping view of the dining room and the adjoining living room. Three columns function as an elegant divider between the two rooms. The living room features a 12-ft.-high sloped ceiling with exposed beams, an inviting fireplace, built-in bookshelves and windows overlooking the rear patio.
- A nice-sized eating area opens to the airy kitchen, which offers a snack bar, a pantry and a lazy Susan. Double doors conceal a utility room with extra storage space.
- Another set of double doors opens to the bedroom wing, where all three bedrooms have walk-in closets. The master bedroom has a private bath with a dual-sink vanity. The secondary bedrooms share another full bath.

Plan E-1813

Bedrooms: 3	Baths: 2
Living Area:	
Main floor	1,892 sq. ft.
Total Living Area:	**1,892 sq. ft.**
Carport	440 sq. ft.
Storage	120 sq. ft.
Exterior Wall Framing:	2x6

Foundation Options:

Crawlspace
Slab
(All plans can be built with your choice of foundation and framing. A generic conversion diagram is available. See order form.)

BLUEPRINT PRICE CODE: **B**

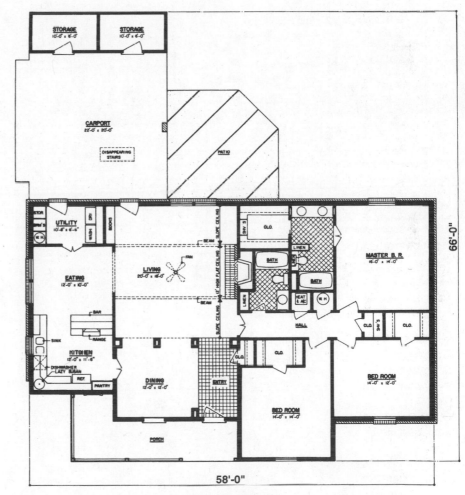

MAIN FLOOR

FRONT VIEW

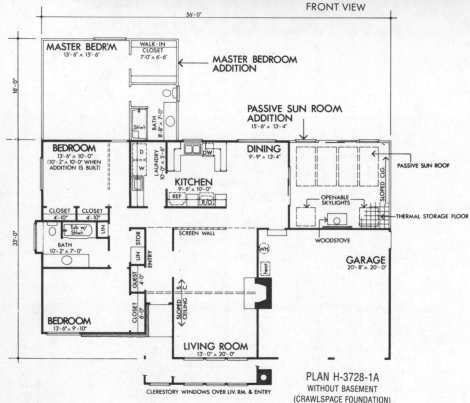

MASTER BEDR'M
13'-6" x 15'-6"

WALK-IN
CLOSET
7'-0" x 6'-6"

MASTER BEDROOM
ADDITION

PASSIVE SUN ROOM
ADDITION
15'-6" x 13'-4"

BATH
8'-8" x 7'-0"

Shw'r

BEDROOM
13'-6" x 10'-0"
(10'-2" x 10'-0" WHEN
ADDITION IS BUILT)

DINING
9'-9" x 13'-4"

PASSIVE SUN ROOF

D   DW

W

LAUNDRY
10'-0" x 5'-0"

KITCHEN
9'-6" x 10'-0"

REF

R/O

SLOPED CLG.

OPENABLE
SKYLIGHTS

THERMAL STORAGE FLOOR

WOODSTOVE

CLOSET
4'-10"

CLOSET
4'-10"

LIN

SCREEN WALL

BATH
10'-2" x 7'-0"

Tub w/
Shw'r

GUEST   LIN STOR

ENTRY

CLOSET
6'-0"

4'-0"

WH

heat

GARAGE
20'-8" x 20'-0"

SLOPED
CEILING

S.
C.

BEDROOM
13'-6" x 9'-10"

LIVING ROOM
13'-0" x 20'-0"

PLAN H-3728-1A
WITHOUT BASEMENT
(CRAWLSPACE FOUNDATION)

CLERESTORY WINDOWS OVER LIV. RM. & ENTRY

Starter House Designed for Expansion

For young couples just getting started, or for retirees searching for a smaller home, this plan provides plenty of livability and two bedrooms in just 1,189 sq. ft. And the same set of plans also includes options for adding a third bedroom, with bath, and a passive solar family room to provide for a growing family or to enhance resale value.

The basic house has an easy traffic flow from the front entry into a central hallway or into the comfortable living room, with its sloped ceiling and large fireplace. The hallway turns left to the two bedrooms, which flank a full bathroom, or right to the kitchen and adjacent dining/family room area. There is a laundry/utility room next to the kitchen, and plenty of storage space in the bedrooms and hallway.

Part of the original second bedroom is taken to add the hallway to the optional third bedroom, and a door is cut through the back wall. Plumbing already is stubbed in at the utility room to ease the cost of new plumbing.

The passive sun room is added by laying brick pavers over the original concrete patio slab, framing the room and adding a glass-panel roof and openable skylights. The masonry floor acts as a heat collector and sliding glass doors are used to regulate the flow of sun-warmed air into the home.

Exterior walls are framed with 2x6 studs.

Two-bedroom starter house:	1,189 sq. ft.
Master bedroom addition:	286 sq. ft.
Passive sun room addition:	224 sq. ft.
Total living area: (Not counting garage)	1,699 sq. ft.

REAR VIEW-PLAN H-3728-1A
TWO-BEDROOM STARTER HOUSE

REAR VIEW-PLAN H-3728-1A
TWO-BEDROOM STARTER HOUSE
WITH MASTER BEDROOM AND
PASSIVE SUN ROOM ADDITIONS

Blueprint Price Code B

Plan H-3728-1A

62   *TO ORDER THIS BLUEPRINT,*
CALL TOLL-FREE 1-800-820-1283

PRICES AND DETAILS
ON PAGES 12-15

Skylights Bring in Outdoors

- Skylights brighten the interior of this three bedroom ranch.
- Cathedral ceilings hover above the spacious family room, central living room, bayed breakfast room and dining room.
- Only a half-wall separates the breakfast area from the family room, which features a fireplace and sliders to the patio.
- A roomy master bedroom is secluded to the rear; it offers a generous walk-in closet and a private bath with twin vanities and a skylit tub.
- Two additional bedrooms share a second full bath.

Plan AX-91311

Bedrooms: 3	Baths: 2
Space:	
Main floor	1,915 sq. ft.
Total Living Area	**1,915 sq. ft.**
Basement	1,915 sq. ft.
Garage	387 sq. ft.
Exterior Wall Framing	2x4

Foundation options:
Standard Basement
Slab
(Foundation & framing conversion diagram available—see order form.)

Blueprint Price Code	B

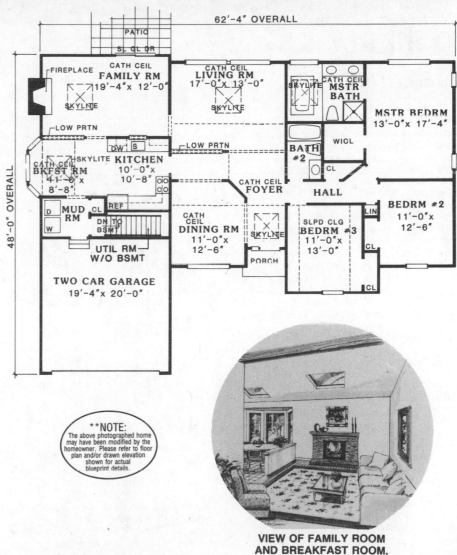

**NOTE: The above photographed home may have been modified by the homeowner. Please refer to floor plan and/or drawn elevation shown for actual blueprint details.

VIEW OF FAMILY ROOM AND BREAKFAST ROOM.

Traditional Elegance

This home represents the best of both worlds. It relies on the past for such fine architectural details as fishscale siding and arched windows, but it also utilizes modern, energy-efficient construction techniques. The plan calls for 2X6 exterior wall construction, specifying R-19 insulation in the walls and R-38 in the ceilings.

By looking at the floor plan, one would think this three-bedroom house is larger than 1,979 sq. ft. The sheltered front entry leads to an open foyer with vaulted ceilings. A guest closet is between the foyer and living room. More storage is behind the stairwell, and a pantry closet serves the kitchen. A half-bath is conveniently located in the center of the first floor.

There are virtually no hallways, with the foyer opening onto all the major areas of the house. To the left is the large living room with fireplace and stone hearth. To the right is the dining room with traditional bay windows that jut out onto the front porch. There's also space in the dining room for built-in shelves or a custom-made china hutch.

A popular feature of this house is the open combination of kitchen, nook, and family room. The U-shaped kitchen is off the laundry room, which can be entered through the garage. The nook faces a backyard patio, accessible by French doors in the family room.

The second floor is just as impressive. The master suite features a dressing room area with vanity opposite the walk-in

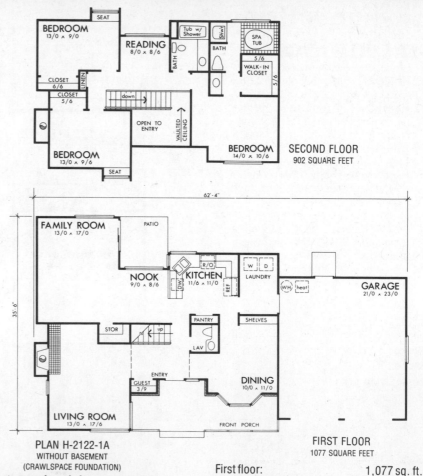

SECOND FLOOR
902 SQUARE FEET

PLAN H-2122-1A
WITHOUT BASEMENT
(CRAWLSPACE FOUNDATION)

FIRST FLOOR
1077 SQUARE FEET

closet. A spa tub and shower complete the master bath. Another full bath serves the remaining two bedrooms, each of which has a window seat, and a reading room overlooks the downstairs foyer.

First floor:	1,077 sq. ft.
Second floor:	902 sq. ft.
Total living area: (Not counting garage)	1,979 sq. ft.

Blueprint Price Code B

Plan H-2122-1A

Downstairs Master Suite

- One of the appealing features of this economical home is the separation of the master and secondary bedrooms.
- The master bedroom is secluded on the main floor, offering privacy and accessibility. Corner windows add light, style and a sense of spaciousness. The walk-in closet and direct entrance to the main-floor bath are other extras.
- The two secondary bedrooms share another full bath on the upper floor.

- The easy traffic flow and openness of the living areas create a large space for family activities and entertaining.
- Adjacent to the foyer, the living room flaunts a handsome fireplace, a dramatic half-round transom window and a 16-ft. vaulted ceiling.
- The adjoining dining room expands to a good-sized rear deck through sliding glass doors.
- A neat pantry and a functional snack counter are featured in the kitchen, which is oriented to interact with the living and dining rooms.
- The two-car garage is accessed through a side door in the foyer.

Plan B-89031

Bedrooms: 3	Baths: 2
Living Area:	
Upper floor	446 sq. ft.
Main floor	857 sq. ft.
Total Living Area:	**1,303 sq. ft.**
Standard basement	857 sq. ft.
Garage	400 sq. ft.
Exterior Wall Framing:	2x4

Foundation Options:

Standard basement
(All plans can be built with your choice of foundation and framing. A generic conversion diagram is available. See order form.)

BLUEPRINT PRICE CODE: A

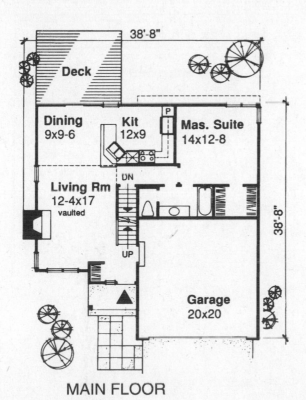

MAIN FLOOR

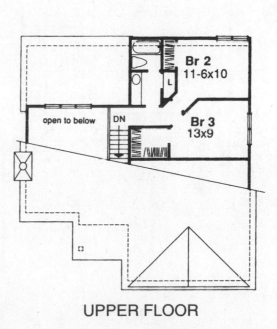

UPPER FLOOR

Off to a Great Start!

- Perfectly sized for families starting out, this charming, feature-filled home is a great choice!
- The entry, which flows directly into the Great Room, is graced by overhead plant shelves and a high 10-ft. ceiling.
- The central Great Room boasts a handsome fireplace under a 14-ft. vaulted ceiling. The right side of the room has a 17-ft. flat ceiling and sliding French doors to a nice backyard patio.
- The dining room is easily served from the open kitchen, which includes a handy pass-through, a bayed breakfast area, a pantry and a laundry closet. The two-car garage is conveniently nearby.
- Upstairs, a railed balcony provides a dramatic view of the Great Room.
- The secluded master suite features a 10-ft., 5-in. vaulted ceiling, a roomy walk-in closet and a private bath.
- Two additional bedrooms and a hallway bath complete the upper floor.

Plan AG-1301-A	
Bedrooms: 3	**Baths:** 2½
Living Area:	
Upper floor	652 sq. ft.
Main floor	673 sq. ft.
Total Living Area:	**1,325 sq. ft.**
Standard basement	620 sq. ft.
Garage	406 sq. ft.
Exterior Wall Framing:	2x4
Foundation Options:	

Standard basement
Crawlspace
(All plans can be built with your choice of foundation and framing. A generic conversion diagram is available. See order form.)

BLUEPRINT PRICE CODE:	A

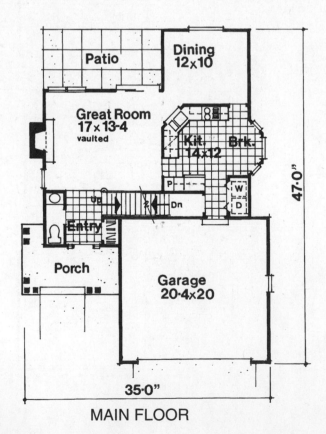

MAIN FLOOR

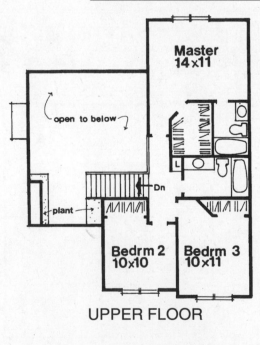

UPPER FLOOR

Plan AG-1301-A

Pleasant Facade

- The pleasant facade of this two-story home boasts a columned front porch and a sidelighted entry.
- The home's modest width makes it ideal for a narrow lot.
- Inside, overhead plant shelves preside over the entry foyer, which includes a coat closet and a handy powder room.
- Straight ahead, the central Great Room is enhanced by a 15-ft. vaulted ceiling and a striking fireplace. Sliding French doors provide access to a lovely patio.
- The well-organized kitchen features a bayed breakfast nook, a convenient pantry and a pass-through to the Great Room. A laundry closet is nearby.
- The secluded dining room offers a quiet setting for formal entertaining.
- Three bedrooms and two baths are found upstairs. The hall balcony offers a view of the Great Room below.
- The master suite includes a private bath and a good-sized walk-in closet.

Plan AG-1301-B

Bedrooms: 3	**Baths:** 2½
Living Area:	
Upper floor	652 sq. ft.
Main floor	673 sq. ft.
Total Living Area:	**1,325 sq. ft.**
Standard basement	620 sq. ft.
Garage	406 sq. ft.
Exterior Wall Framing:	2x4

Foundation Options:

Standard basement
Crawlspace
(All plans can be built with your choice of foundation and framing. A generic conversion diagram is available. See order form.)

BLUEPRINT PRICE CODE: A

UPPER FLOOR

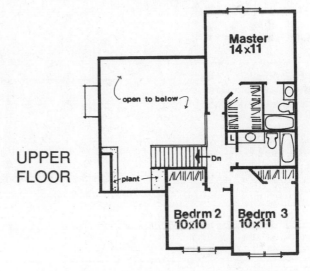

MAIN FLOOR

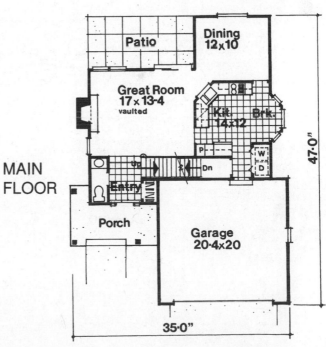

Intriguing Great Room

- The focal point of this open, economical home is its comfortable Great Room and dining area. An inviting fireplace, a dramatic arched window and a 13-ft. vaulted ceiling spark conversation.
- The roomy kitchen incorporates a sunny breakfast room with a 10-ft. vaulted ceiling. Sliding glass doors open to the backyard deck. The kitchen also has a pantry and a handy pass-through to the dining room.
- The bedroom wing includes a lovely master suite and two secondary bedrooms. The master suite boasts a private bath with a separate tub and shower, while the secondary bedrooms share another full bath.
- The washer and dryer are conveniently located near the bedroom wing and the entrance from the garage.

Plan B-90008

Bedrooms: 3	Baths: 2
Living Area:	
Main floor	1,325 sq. ft.
Total Living Area:	**1,325 sq. ft.**
Standard basement	1,325 sq. ft.
Garage	390 sq. ft.
Exterior Wall Framing:	2x6

Foundation Options:

Standard basement

(All plans can be built with your choice of foundation and framing. A generic conversion diagram is available. See order form.)

BLUEPRINT PRICE CODE: A

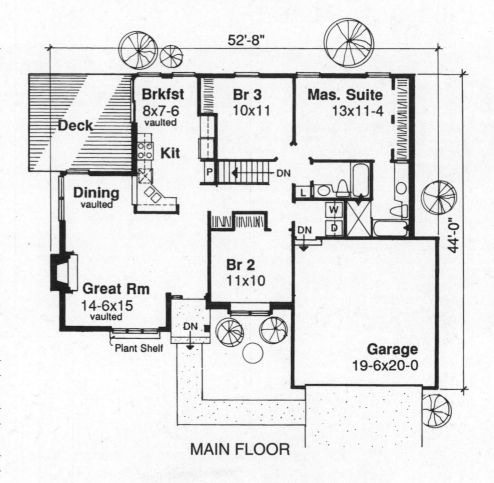

MAIN FLOOR

TO ORDER THIS BLUEPRINT, CALL TOLL-FREE 1-800-820-1283

Plan B-90008

PRICES AND DETAILS ON PAGES 12-15

Practical and Cozy

This three-bedroom, two-bath eye-catcher blends plenty of practicality with a hideaway coziness. Its multi-level design places two bedrooms and one bath upstairs, ideal as the separate children's area that many parents prize. They will also enjoy the lavish master suite that awaits on the main floor, complete with its pass-through walk-in wardrobe and over-sized vanity counter.

Within outside dimensions of 34' wide by 48' deep, this home appears to far exceed its 1,346 sq. ft. Vaulted ceilings sweep up to meet an exposed beam that spans the entire diagonal length of the immense Great Room and dining areas. Another exposed beam merges with the first to extend its vaulted ceilings over a sunny morning room that opens to an intimate private patio. Note the stylish kitchen design, with its convenient access to the two adjacent eating areas.

Main floor:	963 sq. ft.
Upper floor:	383 sq. ft.
Total living area: (Not counting garage)	1,346 sq. ft.

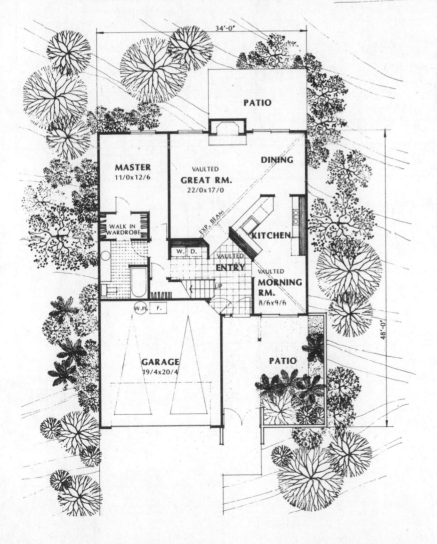

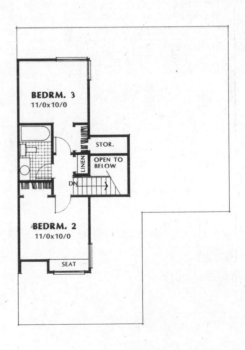

PLAN P-6564-3A
WITHOUT BASEMENT

Blueprint Price Code A

Plan P-6564-3A

TO ORDER THIS BLUEPRINT,
CALL TOLL-FREE 1-800-820-1283

PRICES AND DETAILS
ON PAGES 12-15

69

Enticing Ranch

- This enticing one-story offers a broad range of features; yet its modest width makes it perfect for a narrow lot.
- An attractive garden area to the right of the front door is bathed in sunlight through an opening in the roof.
- The 10-ft., 4-in.-high vaulted entry unfolds directly into the living room, where a cozy woodstove is the center of attention. A bay window and a 13-ft. vaulted ceiling add further interest.
- A wide arched opening introduces the 14-ft.-high dining room.
- The kitchen features a pantry closet, a lazy Susan, a breakfast bar and an 11-ft. ceiling. A pass-through to the backyard deck makes outdoor meals a breeze.
- The spacious family room is expanded by a 13-ft., 4-in. vaulted ceiling. Sliding glass doors provide easy deck access.
- The quiet master suite offers a walk-in wardrobe and a private bath with a dual-sink vanity.
- A skylighted hall bath serves the other two bedrooms, one of which boasts a window seat. The linen closet is also accessible from the hallway.
- The skylighted laundry room is conveniently located near the bedrooms and the two-car garage.

Plan LMB-3713-T

Bedrooms: 3	Baths: 2

Living Area:

Main floor	1,352 sq. ft.
Total Living Area:	**1,352 sq. ft.**
Garage	380 sq. ft.
Exterior Wall Framing:	2x4

Foundation Options:

Crawlspace

(All plans can be built with your choice of foundation and framing. A generic conversion diagram is available. See order form.)

BLUEPRINT PRICE CODE: A

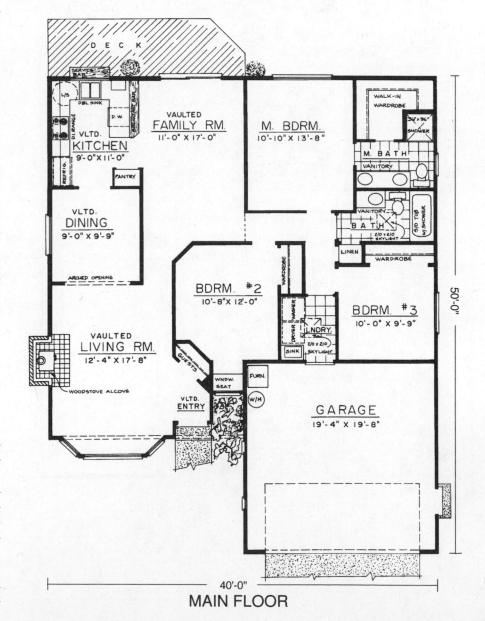

MAIN FLOOR

Plan LMB-3713-T

Spacious Great Room Featured

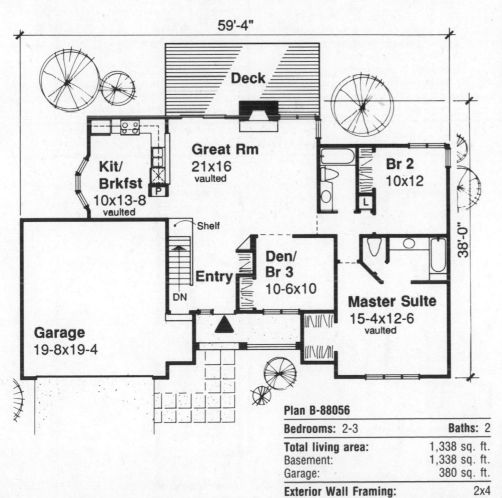

59'-4"

Deck

Great Rm
21x16
vaulted

Kit/ Brkfst
10x13-8
vaulted

Br 2
10x12

L

Shelf

Entry

Den/ Br 3
10-6x10

Master Suite
15-4x12-6
vaulted

DN

Garage
19-8x19-4

38'-0"

- A spacious Great Room takes this modest-sized home out of the ordinary.
- Great Room includes an impressive fireplace and easy access — both physically and visually — to a large deck.
- The kitchen/breakfast area includes sunny bay windows and a vaulted ceiling.
- The master suite also features a vaulted ceiling, and has a private, compartmentalized bath and large walk-in closet.
- The optional third bedroom would make an attractive and convenient home office.
- Basement stairs are convenient to both the front entry and garage door.

Plan B-88056

Bedrooms: 2-3	Baths: 2
Total living area:	1,338 sq. ft.
Basement:	1,338 sq. ft.
Garage:	380 sq. ft.
Exterior Wall Framing:	2x4

Foundation options:
Standard basement only.
(Foundation & framing conversion diagram available — see order form.)

Blueprint Price Code: A

Adorable and Affordable

- Traditional country style and a hint of Victorian design combine to give this charming home lasting appeal.
- The inviting covered porch leads directly into the spacious Great Room, which is warmed by a handsome fireplace. A back door provides easy outdoor access.

- The adjoining dining area is open to the efficient L-shaped kitchen, which includes a pantry and a windowed sink. A laundry room with backyard access is conveniently close by.
- The master bedroom features a roomy walk-in closet and is serviced by a nearby hallway bath.
- A railed staircase overlooks the Great Room on its way to the upper floor.
- Two mirror-image secondary bedrooms share a hallway linen closet and a second full bath.

Plan V-1366

Bedrooms: 3	Baths: 2
Living Area:	
Upper floor	480 sq. ft.
Main floor	886 sq. ft.
Total Living Area:	**1,366 sq. ft.**
Exterior Wall Framing:	2x6

Foundation Options:

Crawlspace
(All plans can be built with your choice of foundation and framing. A generic conversion diagram is available. See order form.)

BLUEPRINT PRICE CODE: **A**

MAIN FLOOR

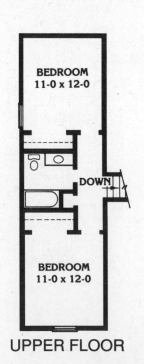

UPPER FLOOR

Plan V-1366

Attention to Detail

- Attention to detail allows this modest-sized, affordable home to maintain an open, roomy feel.
- A peaceful covered porch opens into the inviting tiled foyer. To the left, the huge living room features a soaring 10-ft., 3-in. ceiling. A cozy fireplace warms the room on winter nights.
- The living room embraces the versatile dining room, which serves well for both formal and casual meals. A beautiful French door opens to a covered backyard porch.
- The family cook will love the well-planned kitchen. The adjacent utility room provides access to a two-car garage with a storage area.
- Beyond the living room, the master suite features a walk-in closet and a private bath with a dual-sink vanity.
- Two secluded secondary bedrooms with good-sized closets share a centrally located hall bath.

Plan VL-1372

Bedrooms: 3	Baths: 2
Living Area:	
Main floor	1,372 sq. ft.
Total Living Area:	**1,372 sq. ft.**
Garage and storage	465 sq. ft.
Exterior Wall Framing:	2x4

Foundation Options:

Crawlspace

Slab

(All plans can be built with your choice of foundation and framing. A generic conversion diagram is available. See order form.)

BLUEPRINT PRICE CODE:	**A**

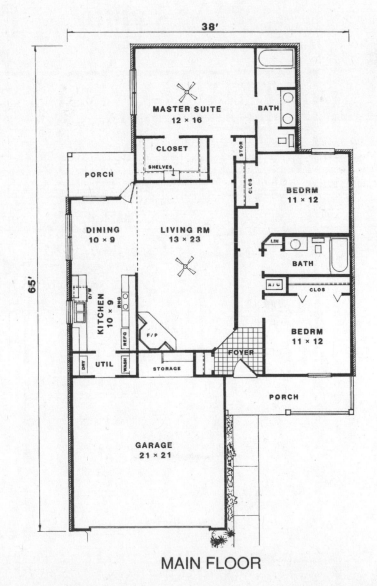

MAIN FLOOR

Great Room Features Cathedral Ceiling

clo.

clo.

Mast. B. R.
14-2X13-0

Bed Rm.
11-6X10-6

ATTIC ACCESS

CLO.

Great Rm.
14-8X17-10

CATH. CLG.

covered

Dining
8-8X10-0

bath 1

Entry

Bed Rm.
10-0X10-8

stor.

bath 2

utility

Kitchen
11-5X9-3

D.W.

GREENHOUSE WDW.

WASH

DRYER   REF.

covered porch

Garage
20-4X19-8

PLAN Q-1380-1A
WITHOUT BASEMENT
(CRAWLSPACE FOUNDATION)

Total living area: 1,380 sq. ft.
(Not counting garage)

48 - 0

51 - 0

Blueprint Price Code A

Plan Q-1380-1A

TO ORDER THIS BLUEPRINT,
CALL TOLL-FREE 1-800-820-1283

PRICES AND DETAILS
ON PAGES 12-15

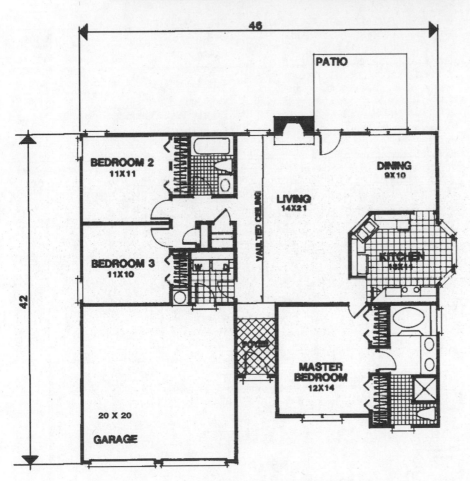

MAIN FLOOR

Versatile Ranch

- A choice of exterior siding treatments (included with the blueprints) and an open floor plan give this attractive ranch its versatility and its affordability.
- The large living room features a vaulted ceiling, a fireplace and access to a rear patio. The dining room is open to the living room and offers a view to the patio.
- The octagonal kitchen is truly unique. The bay-windowed nook is large enough for a breakfast table, and a cutout over the sink overlooks the living area.
- The master bedroom suite is isolated from the other bedrooms. It includes twin closets and a private bath with a step-up garden tub, a separate shower and a double-bowl vanity. The two smaller bedrooms share a hall bath.
- A laundry room is located just off the garage, where it doubles as a mud room.

Plan APS-1303

Bedrooms 3	Baths 2
Living Area:	
Main floor	1,387 sq. ft.
Total Living Area:	**1,387 sq. ft.**
Garage	400 sq. ft.
Exterior Wall Framing:	2x4

Foundation Options:

Slab

(Typical foundation & framing conversion diagram available—see order form.)

BLUEPRINT PRICE CODE: A

TO ORDER THIS BLUEPRINT,
CALL TOLL-FREE 1-800-820-1283

Plan APS-1303

PRICES AND DETAILS
ON PAGES 12-15

75

Inviting Country Porch

- A columned porch with double doors invites you into the rustic living areas of this ranch-style home.
- Inside, the entry allows views back to the expansive, central living room and the backyard beyond.
- The living room boasts an exposed-beam ceiling and a massive fireplace

with a wide stone hearth, a wood box and built-in bookshelves. A sunny patio offers additional entertaining space.
- The dining room and the efficient kitchen combine for easy meal service, with a serving bar separating the two.
- The main hallway leads to the sleeping wing, which offers a large master bedroom with a walk-in closet and a private bath.
- Two additional bedrooms share another full bath, and a laundry closet is accessible to the entire bedroom wing.

Plan E-1304

Bedrooms: 3	**Baths:** 2

Living Area:	
Main floor	1,395 sq. ft.
Total Living Area:	**1,395 sq. ft.**
Garage & storage	481 sq. ft.
Exterior Wall Framing:	2x4

Foundation Options:

Crawlspace
Slab
(All plans can be built with your choice of foundation and framing. A generic conversion diagram is available. See order form.)

BLUEPRINT PRICE CODE: **A**

MAIN FLOOR

TO ORDER THIS BLUEPRINT,
CALL TOLL-FREE 1-800-820-1283

Plan E-1304

PRICES AND DETAILS
ON PAGES 12-15

Affordable Two-Story

- Designed with affordability in mind, this charming two-story home makes the most of its modest square footage.
- The home's lovely exterior features shuttered windows, a decorative sunburst and a covered front porch.
- Beyond the covered porch, the welcoming foyer includes garage access. A coat closet and a half-bath are located conveniently close by.

- The open kitchen merges with a sun-drenched dinette that features a boxed-out window bay. The dinette is a great spot for casual family meals.
- The formal dining room nearby flows into the living room to create a spacious entertaining expanse. Bright sliding glass doors in the living room open to the yard.
- A wraparound railed staircase overlooks the living room on its way to the upper floor. Three good-sized bedrooms with ample closets are serviced by an efficient full bath located off the hall.

Plan GL-1397	
Bedrooms: 3	**Baths: 1½**
Living Area:	
Upper floor	681 sq. ft.
Main floor	716 sq. ft.
Total Living Area:	**1,397 sq. ft.**
Standard basement	716 sq. ft.
Garage	420 sq. ft.
Exterior Wall Framing:	2x4

Foundation Options:

Standard basement
(All plans can be built with your choice of foundation and framing. A generic conversion diagram is available. See order form.)

BLUEPRINT PRICE CODE: **A**

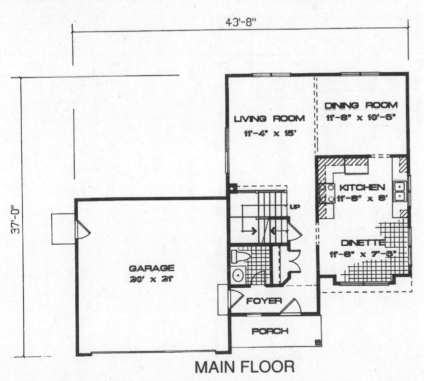

MAIN FLOOR

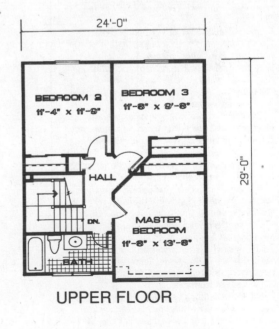

UPPER FLOOR

FRONT VIEW

An Affordable Home for a Narrow Lot

Economy is the designer's primary consideration in this compact three-bedroom home with two full baths, at 1,399 sq. ft. The overall width of 38' meets side setback requirements for most 50' lots.

Several economical yet distinctive features are evident throughout this plan. An attractive Dutch hipped facade gives way to a gable in the rear of the home. Standard truss rafter design is used throughout, except for cut rafters over the covered entryway.

Centralized plumbing enables laundry, kitchen and both baths to share a common corner and thus eliminate undesirable long hot water runs.

On the plan with basement, the laundry is directly below this plumbing core. A linen, guest and two storage closets all located in the hall provide abundant storage space in this functional design.

The modern kitchen is U-shaped, allowing all appliances to be only a step away. A dishwasher and built-in range/oven with side tray storage to accommodate oversized, unusual shaped kitchen utensils are standard features.

Exterior studding is 2x6 with R-19 insulation in the walls and under the floor. The basement plan shows an R-11 with furring at the concrete walls. Plans call for R-30 in the ceiling.

Two large skylights permit natural lighting to the entry hall — another of the unusual features of this cost-conscious home design.

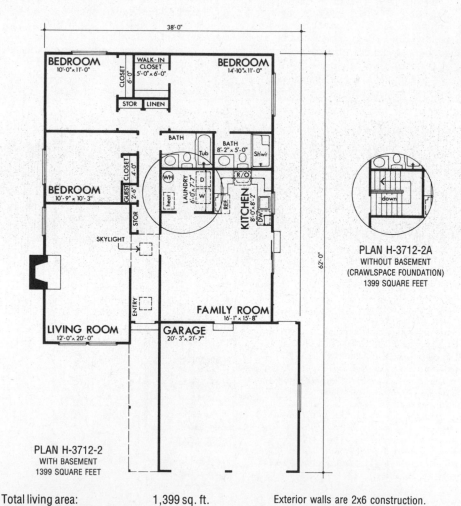

PLAN H-3712-2A
WITHOUT BASEMENT
(CRAWLSPACE FOUNDATION)
1399 SQUARE FEET

PLAN H-3712-2
WITH BASEMENT
1399 SQUARE FEET

Total living area: 1,399 sq. ft.
(Not counting basement or garage)

Exterior walls are 2x6 construction.

Blueprint Price Code A

Plans H-3712-2 & -2A

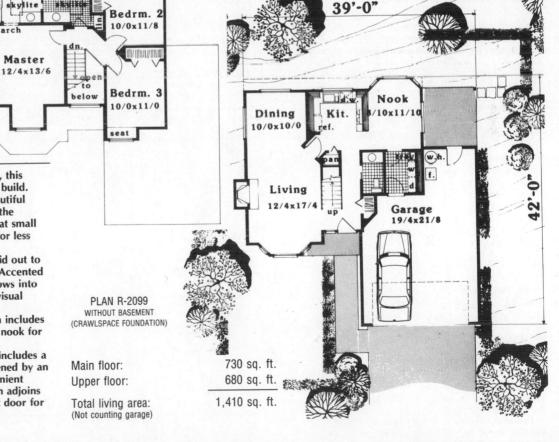

Economy and Beauty

Measuring in at only 1,410 sq. ft., this home will be very economical to build. What you'll also discover are beautiful arched windows which highlight the exterior, underscoring the fact that small doesn't mean you have to settle for less design quality.

The traffic plan is efficiently laid out to maximize the usable living area. Accented by a fireplace, the living room flows into the dining room to increase the visual feeling of spaciousness.

The practical U-shaped kitchen includes a handy pantry and opens to the nook for informal dining.

Upstairs, the master bedroom includes a convenient walk-in closet brightened by an illuminating skylight and a convenient vanity. Notice how the main bath adjoins the master bedroom via a pocket door for easy accessibility.

PLAN R-2099
WITHOUT BASEMENT
(CRAWLSPACE FOUNDATION)

Main floor: 730 sq. ft.
Upper floor: 680 sq. ft.

Total living area: 1,410 sq. ft.
(Not counting garage)

Blueprint Price Code A

Plan R-2099

TO ORDER THIS BLUEPRINT,
CALL TOLL-FREE 1-800-820-1283

PRICES AND DETAILS
ON PAGES 12-15

79

Stylish Brick and Windows

- This home features rich-looking brick, stylish windows and a space-saving L-shaped design.
- The foyer flows toward the living room, which boasts a 16-ft. cathedral ceiling and a fireplace flanked by sliding glass doors that open to an optional deck.
- The gourmet kitchen offers a built-in desk, a snack bar to the breakfast area and easy service to the dining room. A handy laundry/mudroom opens to the garage and the side yard.
- An optional glass-enclosed greenhouse is ideally located off the deck and the breakfast area.
- Sliding glass doors provide outdoor access from the secluded main-floor master suite, which includes a private bath with an 11-ft. cathedral ceiling, a garden tub and a separate shower.
- A tall window brightens the stairway to the upper floor, where a balcony hall bridges two bedrooms that share another full bath.

Plan AX-97144

Bedrooms: 3	Baths: 2½
Living Area:	
Upper floor	529 sq. ft.
Main floor	1,491 sq. ft.
Total Living Area:	**2,020 sq. ft.**
Optional greenhouse	204 sq. ft.
Standard basement	1,412 sq. ft.
Garage	440 sq. ft.
Exterior Wall Framing:	2x4

Foundation Options:

Standard basement
Crawlspace
Slab
(All plans can be built with your choice of foundation and framing. A generic conversion diagram is available. See order form.)

BLUEPRINT PRICE CODE: C

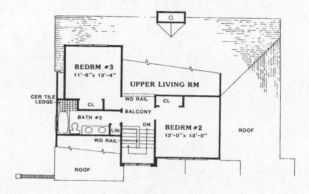

UPPER FLOOR

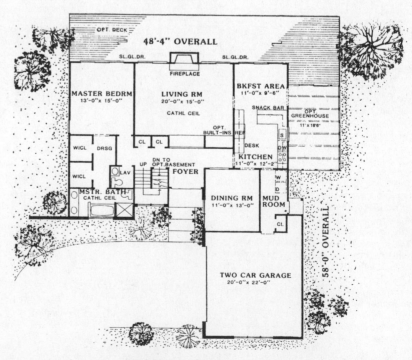

MAIN FLOOR

Plan AX-97144

PRICES AND DETAILS ON PAGES 12-15

Practical Narrow-Lot Design

This plan features good use of space for a narrow lot. At 655 sq. ft. of living space and 404 sq. ft. of garage on the main floor, it requires only a 40x100' lot — even narrower in some jurisdictions. The second floor adds 755 sq. ft., for a total living area of 1,410 sq. ft.

The entry hall provides access to all parts of the home, including the second floor, without crossing any other room. A convenient lavatory is off this entry hall.

The living room features a vaulted ceiling. The family room adjoining the living room adds extra entertaining space for parties or family gatherings.

A U-shaped kitchen is directly accessible from the garage. Laundry facilities are concealed behind louvered doors in the kitchen.

A winding balcony stairway leads to the second floor. The large master suite includes a balcony bedroom, large walk-through wardrobe, and a spacious private bathroom. Two additional bedrooms share a second full-sized bath.

First floor:	655 sq. ft.
Second floor:	755 sq. ft.
Total living area:	1,410 sq. ft.
Garage:	404 sq. ft.

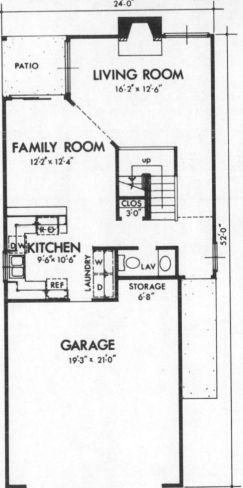

FIRST FLOOR

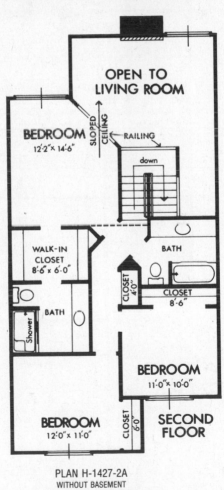

PLAN H-1427-2A
WITHOUT BASEMENT
(CRAWLSPACE FOUNDATION)

Attractive Alternatives

- This affordable one-story home is available with two attractive facades. Elevation A offers a gable roof for that clean-lined look. Elevation B sports a handsome hipped roof. (Please specify your elevation choice when ordering.)
- In either case, the home is given a warm welcome look by the covered front porch.
- The focal point of the home is the inviting fireplace in the vaulted living room. The adjoining dining room is also vaulted, and features access to a rear patio via sliding glass doors.
- A serving counter is conveniently placed between the dining area and the well-planned kitchen.
- The secluded master suite boasts a walk-in closet and a private bath.
- A hall bath is shared by the two remaining bedrooms.
- A large laundry room is located just off the garage entrance.

ELEVATION A

ELEVATION B

Plan U-91-104

Bedrooms: 3	**Baths:** 2

Living Area:

Main floor	1,410 sq. ft.
Total Living Area:	**1,410 sq. ft.**
Garage	462 sq. ft.
Exterior Wall Framing:	2x6

Foundation Options:
Crawlspace
Slab
(Typical foundation & framing conversion diagram available—see order form.)

BLUEPRINT PRICE CODE:	**A**

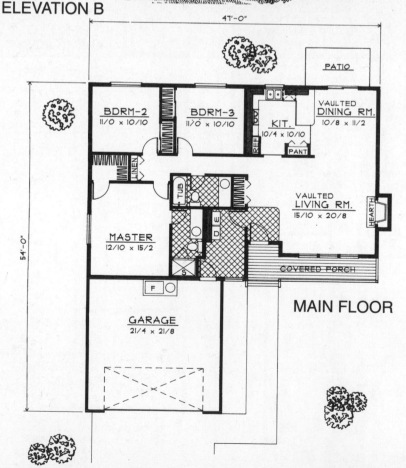

MAIN FLOOR

Plan U-91-104

PRICES AND DETAILS ON PAGES 12-15

Two-Bedroom Country Cottage

A covered veranda and screened rear porch provide extra living spaces in this modest-sized ranch design. The large all-purpose family room has a built-in fireplace and bright dining corner.

Two roomy bedrooms and two full baths make up the sleeping wing.

An efficient galley kitchen is adjacent to utility room (with pantry) and side-entry garage.

Total living area: 1,420 sq. ft.
(Not counting basement or garage)

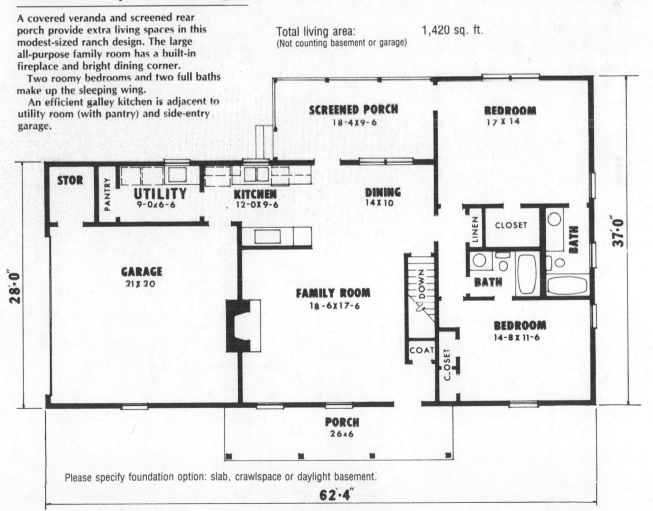

Please specify foundation option: slab, crawlspace or daylight basement.

Blueprint Price Code A

Plan C-7520

TO ORDER THIS BLUEPRINT,
CALL TOLL-FREE 1-800-820-1283

PRICES AND DETAILS
ON PAGES 12-15

83

Simple, but Dramatic

- A dramatic sloped roof exterior and interior living room with sloped ceiling, floor-to-ceiling windows, an adjoining deck and wood stove give this home an interesting, but easy and affordable structure under 1,500 square feet.
- The attached kitchen and dining area also has access to the deck, for an outdoor dining alternative; a pantry and convenient laundry room is secluded to the rear.
- The main-level bedroom could ideally be used as the master; it offers dual closets and nearby bath.
- Off the two-story foyer is the stairway to the second level which ends in a balcony area that overlooks the living room. Two good-sized bedrooms, one with unique dressing vanity, share the upper level with a second bath.

Plan HFL-1382

Bedrooms: 3	Baths: 2
Living Area:	
Upper floor	465 sq. ft.
Main floor	963 sq. ft.
Total Living Area:	**1,428 sq. ft.**
Standard basement	811 sq. ft.
Garage	220 sq. ft.
Exterior Wall Framing:	2x6

Foundation Options:

Standard basement
Slab
(Typical foundation & framing conversion diagram available—see order form.)

BLUEPRINT PRICE CODE: A

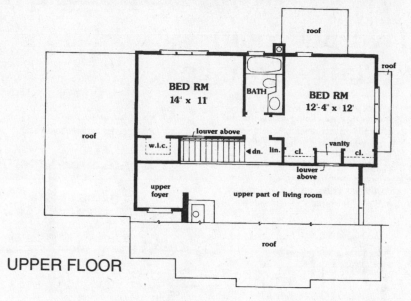

UPPER FLOOR

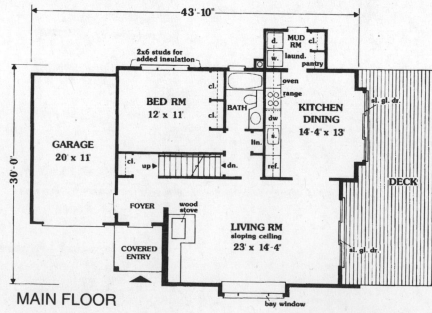

MAIN FLOOR

Plan HFL-1382

PRICES AND DETAILS ON PAGES 12-15

Cottage-Sized Classic

- Foyer opens into large Great Room.
- Master bedroom suite includes deluxe private bath.
- Exterior design reflects quiet dignity of gracious living.
- Great Room features fireplace.

Plan V-1428

Bedrooms: 3		Baths: 2
Total living area:		1,428 sq. ft.
Dimensions:		
Width		40'
Depth		47'
Exterior Wall Framing:		2x6
Ceiling Height:		9'

Foundation options:
Crawlspace only.
(Foundation & framing conversion diagram available — see order form.)

Blueprint Price Code: A

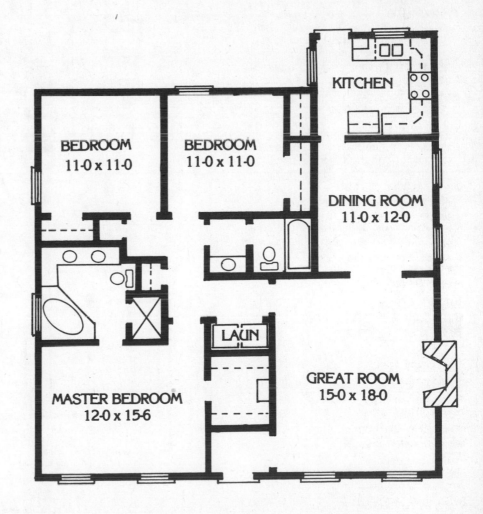

BEDROOM
11-0 x 11-0

BEDROOM
11-0 x 11-0

KITCHEN

DINING ROOM
11-0 x 12-0

MASTER BEDROOM
12-0 x 15-6

LAUN

GREAT ROOM
15-0 x 18-0

Starter Home Offers Options

- Country styling adds to the appeal of this two-story, ideal as a starter home.
- Beyond the wide front porch, the foyer flows to both the living room and the kitchen. Limited hall space maximizes the living area of the home.
- The large living room enjoys a view of the porch through a pair of shuttered windows. Sliding glass doors in the adjoining dining area offer a view of the backyard from either location.
- The open and efficient kitchen has easy access to the one-car garage and the main-floor laundry room. Closed off by a pocket door, the generous-sized laundry area has a convenient folding counter that can also serve as a work desk or planning center.
- Three bedrooms and two baths are located on the upper floor. An alternate one-bathroom version is included with the blueprints.
- An optional two-car garage adds four feet to the overall width of the home.

Plan GL-1430-P

Bedrooms: 3	Baths: 1½-2½
Living Area:	
Upper floor	720 sq. ft.
Main floor	710 sq. ft.
Total Living Area:	**1,430 sq. ft.**
Standard basement	710 sq. ft.
One-car garage	341 sq. ft.
Optional two-car garage	427 sq. ft.
Exterior Wall Framing:	2x4

Foundation Options:

Standard basement

(All plans can be built with your choice of foundation and framing. A generic conversion diagram is available. See order form.)

BLUEPRINT PRICE CODE: A

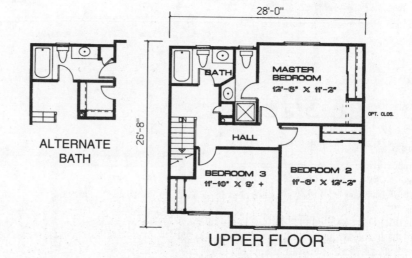

ALTERNATE BATH

UPPER FLOOR

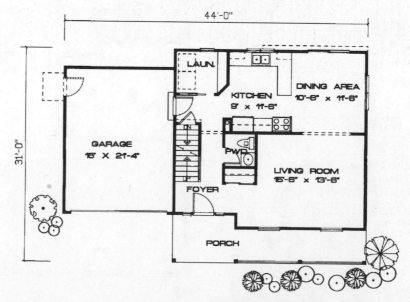

MAIN FLOOR

TO ORDER THIS BLUEPRINT, CALL TOLL-FREE 1-800-820-1283

Plan GL-1430-P

PRICES AND DETAILS ON PAGES 12-15

Economical One-Level Comfort

- This charming one-level home was designed with economy in mind.
- The plan is based on the Great Room concept, which makes the most of available square footage and creates an open feeling throughout the house.
- A dining area is defined by the sunny bay windows in the Great Room near the kitchen.
- The open-plan kitchen is combined with a sunny nook for an open, airy feeling.
- The private area of the home features a master suite which is impressive for a home of this size. It features two walk-in closets as well as a private bath with double-bowl vanity.
- Two secondary bedrooms share another full bath.
- A utility area in the garage entryway includes space for a washer and dryer.

Plan S-52191

Bedrooms: 3	Baths: 2
Space:	
Main floor	1,441 sq. ft.
Total Living Area	**1,441 sq. ft.**
Basement	1,441 sq. ft.
Garage	473 sq. ft.
Exterior Wall Framing	2x6

Foundation options:

Standard Basement

Crawlspace

(Foundation & framing conversion diagram available—see order form.)

Blueprint Price Code	A

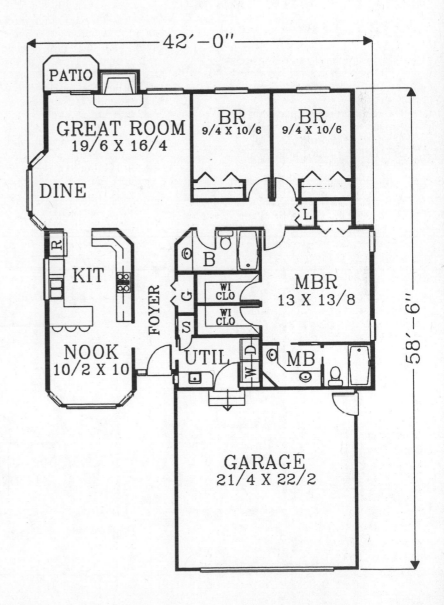

Extraordinary Split-Level

- This design boasts a striking arched window in an inviting facade that introduces an extraordinary split-level floor plan.
- The recessed entry opens into the expansive living room, with its fabulous windows, nice fireplace and breathtaking 12-ft. vaulted ceiling.
- The dining room, which features a 14-ft. vaulted ceiling, expands the open living area and lends an air of spaciousness to the entire main floor.
- The kitchen is a gourmet's dream, offering a wraparound counter, a double sink and a pass-through to the dining room. A 12-ft. vaulted ceiling is shared with the sunny breakfast room, which shows off a built-in desk and sliding-door access to a backyard deck.
- The sizable master bedroom, a second bedroom and a shared bath are several steps up from the main level, creating a sense of privacy.
- The third bedroom makes a great den, playroom, office or guest room.

Plan B-87112	
Bedrooms: 2+	**Baths:** 2
Living Area:	
Main floor	1,452 sq. ft.
Total Living Area:	**1,452 sq. ft.**
Standard basement	1,452 sq. ft.
Garage	448 sq. ft.
Exterior Wall Framing:	2x4

Foundation Options:

Standard basement
(All plans can be built with your choice of foundation and framing. A generic conversion diagram is available. See order form.)

BLUEPRINT PRICE CODE:	**A**

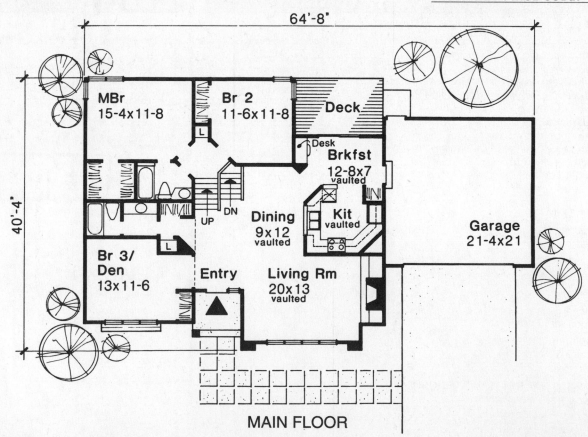

MAIN FLOOR

TO ORDER THIS BLUEPRINT, CALL TOLL-FREE 1-800-820-1283

Plan B-87112

PRICES AND DETAILS ON PAGES 12-15

Comfortable and Affordable

- This plan proves that comfort and affordability can go hand in hand.
- The home's square shape and simple lines make it easier to build, but it's far from plain. In fact, the optional elevations shown here are just two examples of the customizing touches that are possible.
- The gabled roofline and covered front porch with decorative railings render a warm, appealing look. Inside, the floor plan is generous without being wasteful.
- The large living room with fireplace is open to the dining room, maximizing space. The dining room, in turn, flows into the kitchen and dinette. A pocket door leads to a mud room, half-bath and laundry area, all of which are also accessible from the garage.

Elevation A

- The three bedrooms on the second floor share a full bath that has a private entrance from the master bedroom.
- Please specify Elevation A or Elevation B when ordering.

Elevation B

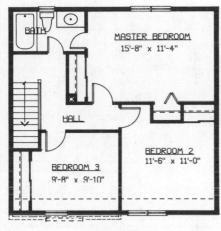

UPPER FLOOR

Plan GL-1473

Bedrooms: 3	Baths: 1 ½
Space:	
Upper floor	676 sq. ft.
Main floor	797 sq. ft.
Total Living Area	**1,473 sq. ft.**
Basement	797 sq. ft.
Garage	440 sq. ft.
Exterior Wall Framing	**2x6**
Foundation options:	

Standard Basement

(Foundation & framing conversion diagram available—see order form.)

Blueprint Price Code	**A**

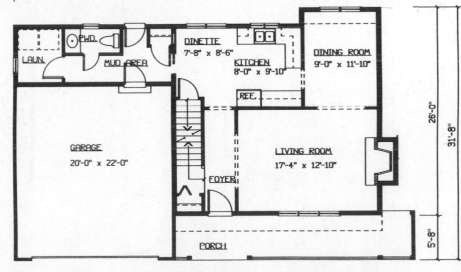

MAIN FLOOR

Perfect for a Growing Family

- Central living areas with shared views, along with a bonus room and an optional two-car garage, make this attractive two-story the perfect choice for a growing family.
- Inside, the tiled foyer unfolds nicely to the open living areas. The spacious living room boasts a lovely front-facing bay window and a handsome fireplace.
- The adjoining dining room features triple French doors, opening to an inviting backyard patio.
- The roomy kitchen showcases an angled countertop with a double sink and a serving bar for easy entertaining. A half-bath and garage access are just steps away.
- Upstairs, the nice-sized master bedroom flaunts a 10-ft. vaulted ceiling, a deep walk-in closet and a private bath.
- Two additional bedrooms, another full bath and a bright bonus room complete this smart design.

Plan B-93013

Bedrooms: 3+	Baths: 2½
Living Area:	
Upper floor	650 sq. ft.
Main floor	649 sq. ft.
Bonus room	168 sq. ft.
Total Living Area:	**1,467 sq. ft.**
Standard basement	649 sq. ft.
Garage	226 sq. ft.
Exterior Wall Framing:	2x6

Foundation Options:

Standard basement
(All plans can be built with your choice of foundation and framing. A generic conversion diagram is available. See order form.)

BLUEPRINT PRICE CODE: A

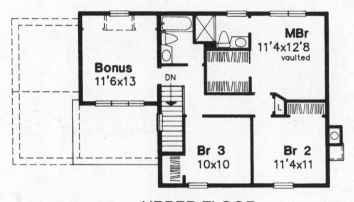

UPPER FLOOR

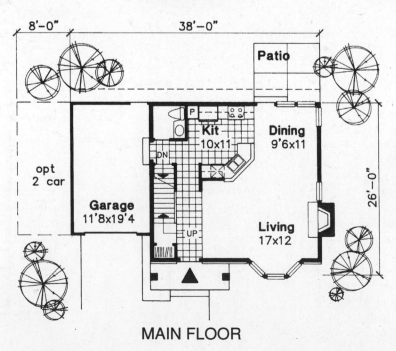

MAIN FLOOR

Plan B-93013

Design Harmony

- This home combines several distinct architectural styles to achieve a design harmony all its own.
- The front columns are reminiscent of ancient Greece, while the Palladian window in the master bedroom originated in the Renaissance period. The sleek rectangular shape of the home gives it an updated, contemporary look.
- The portico columns are repeated inside, where they are used to visually separate the foyer from the living room and to dramatize the 18-ft. cathedral ceiling. Columns also frame the handsome fireplace.
- Straight ahead, the dining room and kitchen share a high 10-ft. ceiling. The entire area basks in natural light from two skylights, a large bow window and sliding glass doors that open to a sizable backyard terrace.
- The master bedroom boasts a 10-ft. ceiling, a gorgeous Palladian window and a private whirlpool bath.

Plan HFL-1200-FH

Bedrooms: 3	Baths: 2
Living Area:	
Main floor	1,530 sq. ft.
Total Living Area:	**1,530 sq. ft.**
Standard basement	1,434 sq. ft.
Garage and storage	463 sq. ft.
Exterior Wall Framing:	2x6

Foundation Options:

Standard basement

Slab

(All plans can be built with your choice of foundation and framing. A generic conversion diagram is available. See order form.)

BLUEPRINT PRICE CODE: B

VIEW INTO LIVING ROOM

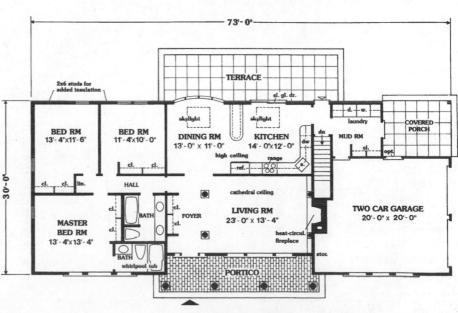

MAIN FLOOR

Basic Pleasures

- This eye-pleasing two-story recalls the days when comfort and conversation were high on our list of basic pleasures.
- The quaint covered porch shields your guests from the elements, while inspiring friendly chitchat. The sidelighted, 17-ft.-high entry ushers them into the formal living spaces.
- Perfect placement of the island kitchen allows service to both the formal dining room and the family room. The laundry facilities and the two-car garage are also reached easily.
- Friends and family alike will be enthralled by the handsome, central fireplace in the family room. On balmy nights, you can savor the aroma wafting from the patio barbecue!
- After a long day, imagine what a relief the master retreat will be, with its airy 10½-ft. vaulted ceiling. A warm shower in the well-appointed private bath will help to sweep you into slumber.
- Tuck in the kids in their bedrooms just down the hall. The balcony rail allows one last-minute check on your home before turning in for the night.

Plan AG-1508

Bedrooms: 3	Baths: 2½
Living Area:	
Upper floor	737 sq. ft.
Main floor	794 sq. ft.
Total Living Area:	**1,531 sq. ft.**
Standard basement	761 sq. ft.
Garage	400 sq. ft.
Exterior Wall Framing:	2x4

Foundation Options:

Standard basement
(All plans can be built with your choice of foundation and framing. A generic conversion diagram is available. See order form.)

BLUEPRINT PRICE CODE:	B

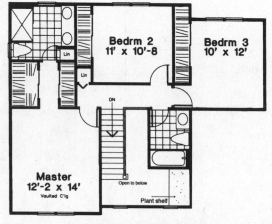

UPPER FLOOR

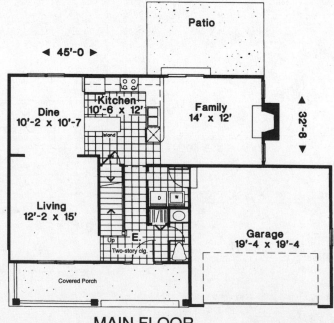

MAIN FLOOR

TO ORDER THIS BLUEPRINT,
CALL TOLL-FREE 1-800-820-1283

Plan AG-1508

PRICES AND DETAILS
ON PAGES 12-15

CONTEMPORARY

Split-Level with Flexibility

TRADITIONAL

- Choose a contemporary or a traditional facade for this roomy split-level plan. Both popular options are included in the blueprints.
- The covered front entry opens into the Great Room, which boasts a 13-ft. vaulted ceiling, a warm fireplace and access to a rear deck.
- The open kitchen offers a snack counter and a handy pantry. The windowed sink overlooks an outdoor plant shelf.
- Upstairs, the master bedroom features built-in shelves, a walk-in closet and a private bath.
- Two more bedrooms share another full bath. The third bedroom could double as a den.
- The bonus space on the lower floor would make a great playroom, study, office or entertainment area. A convenient half-bath is nearby.

Plan B-8321

Bedrooms: 2+	Baths: 2½
Living Area:	
Main floor	1,096 sq. ft.
Lower floor	400 sq. ft.
Total Living Area:	**1,496 sq. ft.**
Partial basement	405 sq. ft.
Garage	400 sq. ft.
Exterior Wall Framing:	2x4

Foundation Options:

Partial basement

(All plans can be built with your choice of foundation and framing. A generic conversion diagram is available. See order form.)

BLUEPRINT PRICE CODE: A

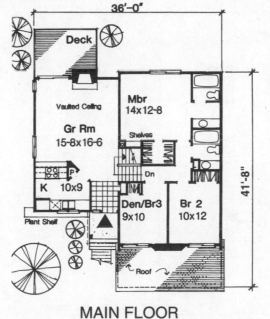

MAIN FLOOR

LOWER FLOOR

 labels: 36'-0", Deck, Vaulted Ceiling, Mbr 14x12-8, Shelves, Gr Rm 15-8x16-6, Dn, K 10x9, Den/Br3 9x10, Br 2 10x12, 41'-8", Plant Shelf, Roof

 labels: Bonus Space, Shelves, Basement, Up, W D, Dn, Garage 20x20, Planter

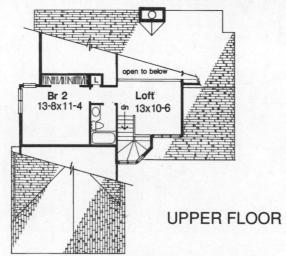

UPPER FLOOR

Smart Look, Smart Price

- Smart in looks, function and cost, this design is filled with flexible spaces and all the best in features.
- The exterior has a natural look, with its clean roofline, wood siding and stone veneer.
- The high-impact foyer has views of the winding stair tower brightened by a clerestory window.
- Straight ahead, the Great Room and the open kitchen serve as one huge, flexible living space. The Great Room features a cathedral ceiling, a built-in wet bar, a cozy fireplace and lots of glass overlooking the backyard deck. The kitchen is highlighted by a clever pass-through to the Great Room.
- The main-floor master suite offers all of today's amenities, including a window seat facing the backyard, a walk-in closet and a private bath.
- Another full bathroom, a roomy bedroom and a multipurpose loft are on the upper floor.

Plan B-711

Bedrooms: 2-3	Baths: 2½
Living Area:	
Upper floor	454 sq. ft.
Main floor	1,044 sq. ft.
Total Living Area:	**1,498 sq. ft.**
Standard basement	1,044 sq. ft.
Garage	380 sq. ft.
Exterior Wall Framing:	2x6
Foundation Options:	
Standard basement	
(Typical foundation & framing conversion diagram available—see order form.)	
BLUEPRINT PRICE CODE:	A

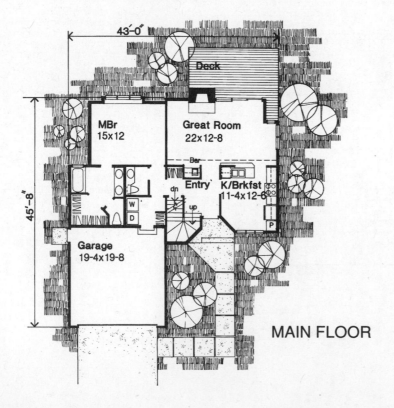

MAIN FLOOR

Plan B-711

Great Room Features Cathedral Ceiling

Total living area:
(Not counting garage)

1,559 sq. ft.

PLAN Q-1559-1A
WITHOUT BASEMENT
(SLAB-ON-GRADE FOUNDATION)

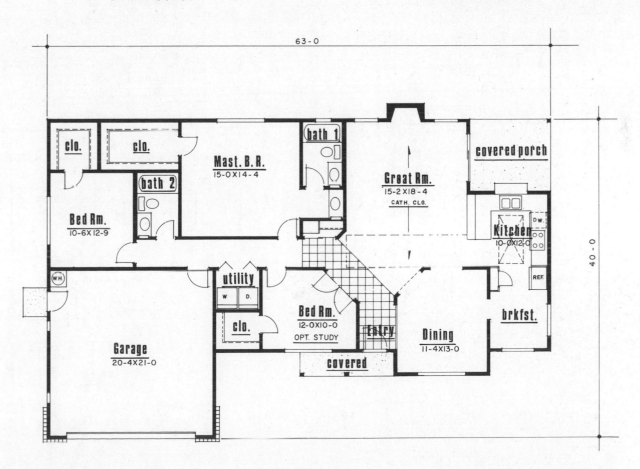

Blueprint Price Code B

Plan Q-1559-1A

TO ORDER THIS BLUEPRINT,
CALL TOLL-FREE 1-800-820-1283

PRICES AND DETAILS
ON PAGES 12-15

95

REAR VIEW

A Natural Complement

- Its rustic facade and woodsy appeal make this home a wonderful complement to nature's backdrop.
- A wide entry deck leads past a handy ski storage area to the 17-ft.-high foyer.
- To the right, the walk-through kitchen offers outdoor access.
- The adjoining dining room is brightened by a large window. A handsome fireplace warms the enormous living room, where two sets of sliding glass doors open to a sprawling deck in the backyard.
- Two large bedrooms down the hall share a full bath.
- On the upper floor, the luxurious master bedroom boasts sliding glass doors to a romantic balcony.
- Past a dressing area, the master bath is enhanced by a refreshing whirlpool tub and a separate shower. A balcony offers beautiful morning views.
- An unfinished attic space flaunts lots of natural light and could be used as a future bedroom, if desired.

Plan AX-8382	
Bedrooms: 3+	**Baths:** 2
Living Area:	
Upper floor	419 sq. ft.
Main floor	1,144 sq. ft.
Total Living Area:	**1,563 sq. ft.**
Unfinished attic (future bedroom)	235 sq. ft.
Standard basement	1,144 sq. ft.
Exterior Wall Framing:	2x4
Foundation Options:	

Standard basement
Crawlspace
Slab
(All plans can be built with your choice of foundation and framing. A generic conversion diagram is available. See order form.)

BLUEPRINT PRICE CODE: B

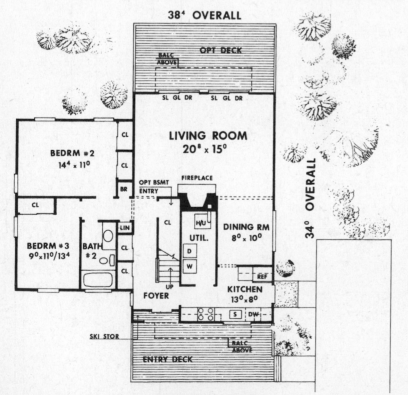

MAIN FLOOR

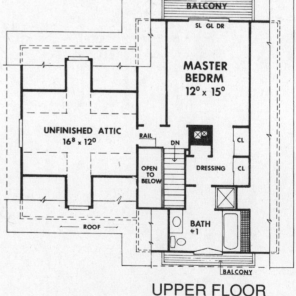

UPPER FLOOR

Affordable and Stylish

- While highly fashionable today, this plan is also affordable due to its moderate size and relative simplicity of construction.
- The large Great Room displays a vaulted ceiling and impressive fireplace.
- A cozy breakfast nook adjoins the Great Room on one side and the efficient galley-type kitchen on the other.
- The master bedroom boasts a huge walk-in closet and a private bath with two sinks and separate tub and shower.
- Two secondary bedrooms share a second full bath.

Plan B-89018

Bedrooms: 3	Baths: 2
Total living area:	1,587 sq. ft.
Basement:	1,587 sq. ft.
Garage:	484 sq. ft.
Exterior Wall Framing:	2x4

Foundation options:
Standard basement only.
(Foundation & framing conversion diagram available — see order form.)

Blueprint Price Code:	B

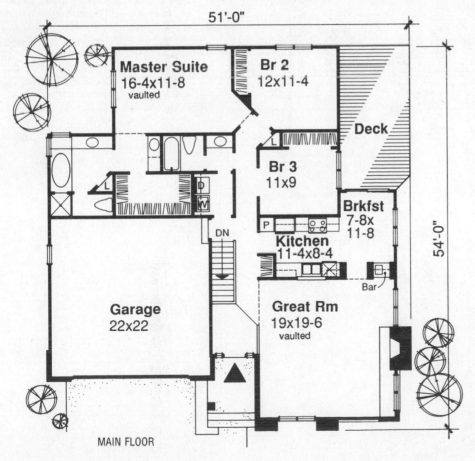

51'-0"

54'-0"

Master Suite
16-4x11-8
vaulted

Br 2
12x11-4

Deck

Br 3
11x9

Brkfst
7-8x
11-8

DN

Kitchen
11-4x8-4

Bar

Garage
22x22

Great Rm
19x19-6
vaulted

MAIN FLOOR

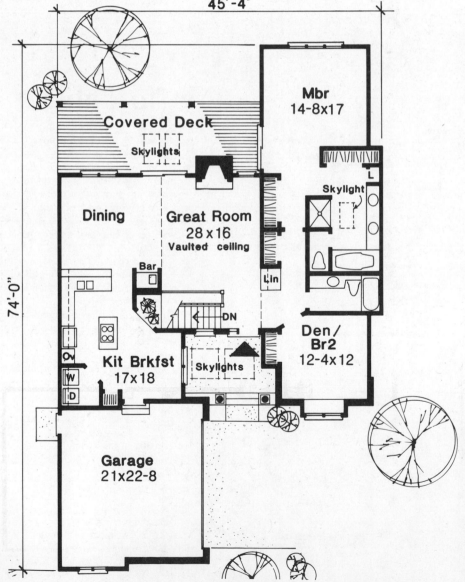

45'-4"

74'-0"

Covered Deck
Skylights

Mbr
14-8x17

Skylight

Dining

Great Room
28 x 16
Vaulted ceiling

Bar

Lin

DN

Den/
Br2
12-4x12

Kit Brkfst
17x18

Skylights

Garage
21x22-8

Refined Ranch

- Multiple gables, brick veneer, half-round transom window, and columned front porch with skylights all give this exciting ranch plan a refined exterior appeal.
- The interior gives a feeling of spaciousness beyond its size with vaulted ceilings, open stair rails to the basement, and a long view from the entry to the rear covered deck with skylights.
- The island kitchen serves the large formal dining room and sunny breakfast eating area and has a view of the Great Room's fireplace.
- The master suite features access through sliders to the covered deck, plenty of closet hanging space, and a large skylit private bath.

Plan UDG-90007

Bedrooms: 2	Baths: 2
Space:	
Total living area:	1,596 sq. ft.
Basement:	1,596 sq. ft.
Garage:	476 sq. ft.
Exterior Wall Framing:	2x4

Foundation options:
Standard basement.
(Foundation & framing conversion diagram available — see order form.)

Blueprint Price Code:	B

Friendly Facade

- Charming shuttered windows and a friendly front porch adorn the facade of this updated two-story home.
- The long foyer is embraced by the formal living spaces. The living room is extended with a lovely boxed-out window. The dining room is large enough for special occasions.
- The family room, dinette and kitchen are oriented to the back of the home. The family room shows off a handsome fireplace and a dramatic 12-ft.-high skylighted area at the rear.
- An open railing sets off the sunny dinette, which opens to the outdoors through sliding glass doors.
- The U-shaped kitchen features a functional lazy Susan and a windowed sink. A half bath and a laundry room are located between the kitchen and the entrance to the garage.
- Three generous-sized bedrooms and a large bath occupy the upper floor.

Plan A-2237-DS

Bedrooms: 3	Baths: 1½
Living Area:	
Upper floor	672 sq. ft.
Main floor	972 sq. ft.
Total Living Area:	**1,644 sq. ft.**
Standard basement	972 sq. ft.
Garage	484 sq. ft.
Exterior Wall Framing:	2x6

Foundation Options:

Standard basement

(All plans can be built with your choice of foundation and framing. A generic conversion diagram is available. See order form.)

BLUEPRINT PRICE CODE:	B

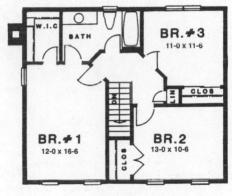

UPPER FLOOR

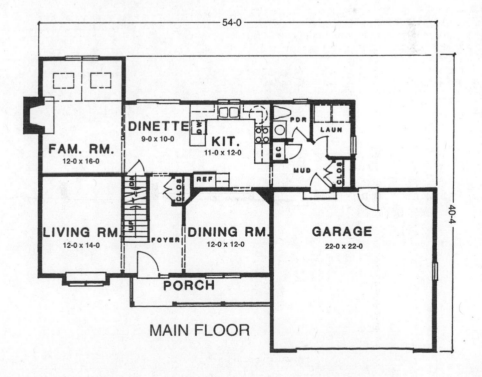

MAIN FLOOR

Striking Modern Ranch

- Captivating angles and bright living spaces are two distinguishing features of this unique ranch design.
- The living and dining areas combine to create an expansive activity or entertaining area that boasts a cathedral ceiling, a lovely bay window, a dramatic angled fireplace and sliding glass doors to a backyard terrace.
- The kitchen is centrally located and offers ample counter space and a handy snack bar. The adjoining dinette and family room are illuminated by glass roof panels with adjustable louvered shades.
- The sleeping wing includes a spacious master bedroom with a sloped ceiling, a private terrace, a large walk-in closet and its own bath with a whirlpool tub.
- The two secondary bedrooms share a skylighted full bath.

Plan K-667-N

Bedrooms: 3	Baths: 2
Living Area:	
Main floor	1,645 sq. ft.
Total Living Area:	**1,645 sq. ft.**
Standard basement	1,675 sq. ft.
Garage and storage	476 sq. ft.
Exterior Wall Framing:	2x4 or 2x6

Foundation Options:
Standard basement
Slab
(Typical foundation & framing conversion diagram available—see order form.)

BLUEPRINT PRICE CODE:	B

INTERIOR VIEW

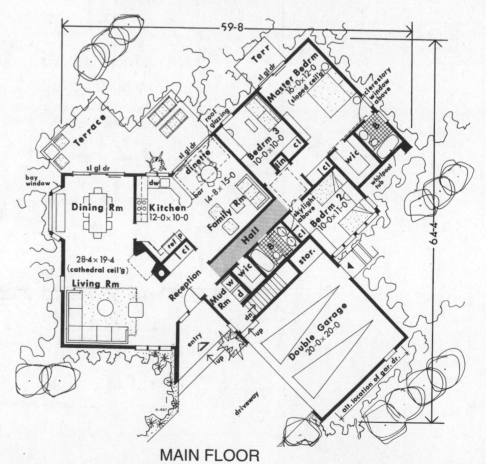

MAIN FLOOR

Plan K-667-N

PRICES AND DETAILS
ON PAGES 12-15

Compact Style

- Half-round transom windows and decorative columns capture interest for this stylish and compact one-story.
- The foyer's dramatic ceiling slopes to a high 13-ft. plateau that extends into the living room and dining room.
- The spacious living room also shows off a handsome fireplace and a spectacular view of a large terrace through windows and French doors.
- The adjoining dining room features a lovely bay window and a pass-through from the kitchen.

- Bi-fold doors keep the formal rooms closed off from the informal spaces. The family room includes a functional media wall and sliding glass doors to a second terrace. The sunny dinette is easily served from the kitchen's angled serving bar.
- The sleeping wing houses three bedrooms and two baths. The master suite features a 9-ft. ceiling, a space-saving media shelf, two closets and a private whirlpool bath.
- The front-facing bedrooms boast attractive arched window arrangements under 12-ft. cathedral ceilings.

Plan AHP-9480	
Bedrooms: 3	**Baths:** 2
Living Area:	
Main floor	1,678 sq. ft.
Total Living Area:	**1,678 sq. ft.**
Standard basement	1,678 sq. ft.
Garage	440 sq. ft.
Exterior Wall Framing:	2x4 or 2x6

Foundation Options:

Standard basement
Crawlspace
Slab
(All plans can be built with your choice of foundation and framing. A generic conversion diagram is available. See order form.)

BLUEPRINT PRICE CODE:	B

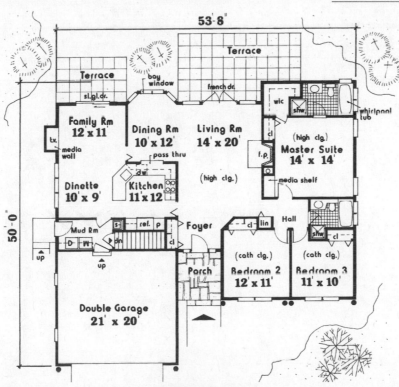

MAIN FLOOR

Smart Farmhouse

- This smart-looking farmhouse boasts a front wrapping porch, overlooked from the dining and living rooms.
- The two-story-high foyer reveals a decorative plant shelf and entry columns that accent and define these formal spaces.
- The informal living areas merge at the rear of the home and look out over the adjoining patio. The large family room shows off a big fireplace and shares a handy pass-through serving counter with the kitchen and the breakfast nook.
- A handy main-floor laundry closet is located off the kitchen.
- A nice-sized master bedroom with a TV niche and a private bath shares the upper floor with two additional bedrooms and a second bath.

Plan AG-9102

Bedrooms: 3	Baths: 2½
Living Area:	
Upper floor	769 sq. ft.
Main floor	910 sq. ft.
Total Living Area:	**1,679 sq. ft.**
Standard basement	910 sq. ft.
Garage	480 sq. ft.
Exterior Wall Framing:	2x6

Foundation Options:

Standard basement

(All plans can be built with your choice of foundation and framing. A generic conversion diagram is available. See order form.)

BLUEPRINT PRICE CODE:	B

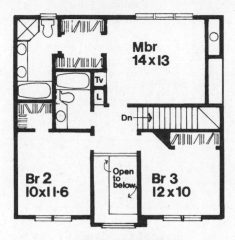

UPPER FLOOR

Mbr 14 x 13
Tv
L
Br 2 10x11·6
Open to below
Br 3 12 x 10
Dn

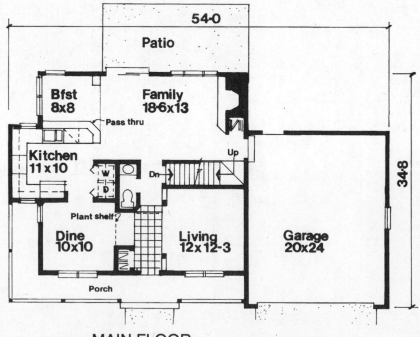

MAIN FLOOR

54-0
34·8
Patio
Bfst 8x8
Family 18·6x13
Pass thru
Kitchen 11 x 10
Up
W D
Dn
Plant shelf
Dine 10x10
Living 12x12-3
Garage 20x24
Porch

Plan AG-9102

PRICES AND DETAILS ON PAGES 12-15

Angular Fireplace Warms Kitchen And Great Room

Total living area: 1,683 sq. ft.
(Not counting garage)

Blueprint Price Code B

Plan Q-1683-1A

TO ORDER THIS BLUEPRINT,
CALL TOLL-FREE 1-800-820-1283

PRICES AND DETAILS
ON PAGES 12-15

103

Appealing, Angled Ranch

- This unique, angled ranch boasts a striking interior, which is highlighted by a dramatic domed ceiling at its center.
- The gabled entryway opens to a spacious pentagonal living area. A handsome fireplace, lots of glass and an adjoining backyard terrace are showcased, in addition to the 14-ft.-high domed ceiling.
- The dining room can be extended into the nearby den by opening the folding doors. The den features a 14-ft. sloped ceiling, an exciting solar bay and terrace access.
- A casual eating area and a nice-sized kitchen expand to the front of the home, ending at a windowed sink.
- The nearby mudroom area includes laundry facilities and an optional powder room.
- The sleeping wing offers four bedrooms, including an oversized master suite with a private terrace and a skylighted bath with dual sinks and a whirlpool tub. The secondary bedrooms share another full bath.

Plan K-669-N

Bedrooms: 4	Baths: 2-2½
Living Area:	
Main floor	1,728 sq. ft.
Total Living Area:	**1,728 sq. ft.**
Standard basement	1,545 sq. ft.
Garage and storage	468 sq. ft.
Exterior Wall Framing:	2x4 or 2x6

Foundation Options:

Standard basement

Slab

(All plans can be built with your choice of foundation and framing. A generic conversion diagram is available. See order form.)

BLUEPRINT PRICE CODE:	B

VIEW INTO DINING ROOM AND LIVING ROOM

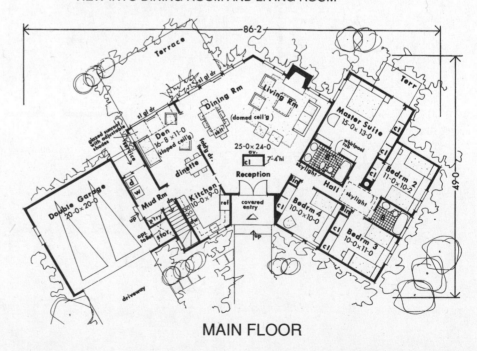

MAIN FLOOR

 TO ORDER THIS BLUEPRINT, CALL TOLL-FREE 1-800-820-1283 Plan K-669-N *PRICES AND DETAILS ON PAGES 12-15*

Breathtaking Open Space

- Soaring ceilings and an open floor plan add breathtaking volume to this charming country-style home.
- The inviting covered-porch entrance opens into the spacious living room, which boasts a spectacular 21-ft.-high cathedral ceiling. Two overhead dormers fill the area with natural light, while a fireplace adds warmth.
- Also under the cathedral ceiling, the kitchen and bayed breakfast room share an eating bar. Skylights brighten the convenient laundry room and the computer room, which provides access to a covered rear porch.
- The secluded master bedroom offers private access to another covered porch. The skylighted master bath has a walk-in closet and a 10-ft. sloped ceiling above a whirlpool tub.
- Optional upper-floor areas provide future expansion space for the needs of a growing family.

Plan J-9302

Bedrooms: 3	Baths: 2
Living Area:	
Main floor	1,745 sq. ft.
Total Living Area:	**1,745 sq. ft.**
Upper floor (future area)	500 sq. ft.
Future area above garage	241 sq. ft.
Standard basement	1,745 sq. ft.
Garage and storage	559 sq. ft.
Exterior Wall Framing:	2x4

Foundation Options:

Standard basement

Crawlspace

Slab

(All plans can be built with your choice of foundation and framing. A generic conversion diagram is available. See order form.)

BLUEPRINT PRICE CODE: B

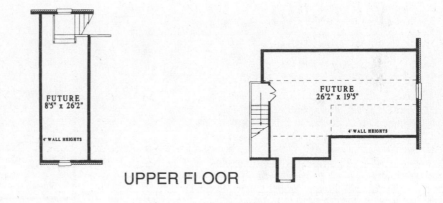

UPPER FLOOR

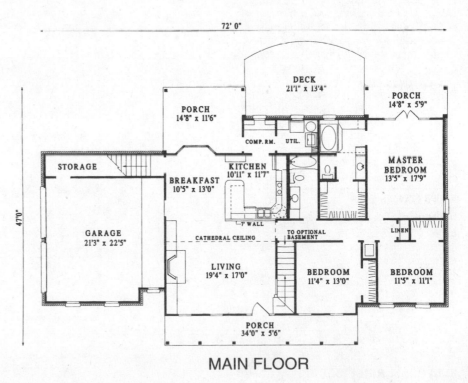

MAIN FLOOR

Open and Airy Design

- The open and airy design of this compact, affordable home makes the most of its space.
- Inside, the entry's 23½-ft. vaulted ceiling soars to the upper floor. Two decorative wood rails set off the entry from the living room. A corner fireplace topped by a wood mantel anchors the room, and French doors lead to the backyard.
- The good-sized dining room extends to the kitchen, where a handy island maximizes workspace, and a bright window adds light. Plenty of room is available for cooking and dining.
- Across the home, the secluded master bedroom is a great adult retreat. The private master bath boasts two separate vanities and a walk-in closet with convenient built-in shelves.
- At the top of the open staircase, a railed sitting area with a 16-ft. vaulted ceiling is ideal for a computer nook.
- Two spacious bedrooms are serviced by a centrally located hall bath.
- Plans for a detached two-car garage are also included in the blueprints.

Plan LS-94046-E

Bedrooms: 3	Baths: 2
Living Area:	
Upper floor	561 sq. ft.
Main floor	1,190 sq. ft.
Total Living Area:	**1,751 sq. ft.**
Standard basement	1,145 sq. ft.
Exterior Wall Framing:	2x6

Foundation Options:

Standard basement

(All plans can be built with your choice of foundation and framing. A generic conversion diagram is available. See order form.)

BLUEPRINT PRICE CODE: B

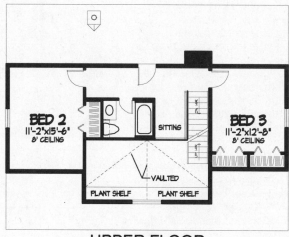

UPPER FLOOR

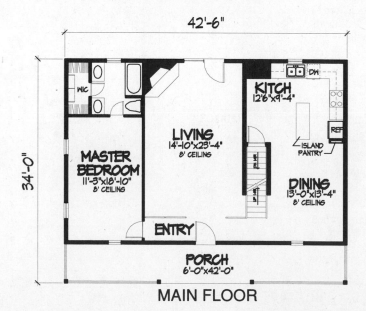

MAIN FLOOR

   Plan LS-94046-E   **PRICES AND DETAILS ON PAGES 12-15**

Style and Affordability

- This attractive family home offers affordability with style and openness.
- A brick planter accents the inviting covered porch. Inside, the sidelighted entry flows into the bright and spacious living room, with its 16½-ft. sloped ceiling and heat-circulating fireplace. Next to the fireplace, a wood bin is located beneath TV and stereo shelves.
- The sizable dining room opens to a backyard patio through French doors. The efficient U-shaped kitchen shares a serving counter with the dining room, for easy entertaining.
- On the upper floor, a railed balcony overlooks the entry and the living room.
- The bright master bedroom boasts a private bath, a walk-in closet and a handy linen closet.
- Two nice secondary bedrooms share a full bath with a large linen closet. A hallway closet provides additional storage space.

Plans H-3741-1 & -1A

Bedrooms: 3	Baths: 2½
Living Area:	
Upper floor	900 sq. ft.
Main floor	853 sq. ft.
Total Living Area:	**1,753 sq. ft.**
Standard basement	853 sq. ft.
Garage	520 sq. ft.
Exterior Wall Framing:	2x6
Foundation Options:	**Plan #**
Standard basement	H-3741-1
Crawlspace	H-3741-1A

(All plans can be built with your choice of foundation and framing. A generic conversion diagram is available. See order form.)

BLUEPRINT PRICE CODE:	**B**

UPPER FLOOR

MAIN FLOOR

BASEMENT STAIRWAY LOCATION

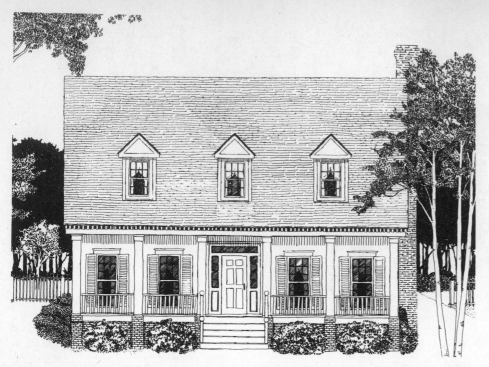

Plantation-Style Cottage

- The timeless appearance and simplicity of this charming cottage gives it overwhelming popularity.
- The energy-saving porch and functional floor plan make this home a practical choice.
- A versatile Great Room with fireplace and a view to the front porch lie before a combination kitchen/breakfast area with bay window.
- A highly desired feature found in this home is a first floor master bedroom; the attached bath also offers a second access.
- Two added bedrooms and a shared full bath compose the second level.

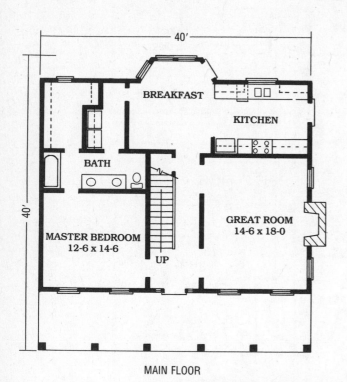

MAIN FLOOR

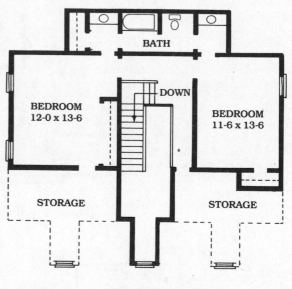

UPPER FLOOR

Plan V-1758	
Bedrooms: 3	**Baths:** 2
Space:	
Upper floor:	629 sq. ft.
Main floor:	1,129 sq. ft.
Total living area:	1,758 sq. ft.
Exterior Wall Framing:	2x6

Ceiling Heights:	
Upper floor:	8'
Main floor:	9'

Foundation options:
Crawlspace.
(Foundation & framing conversion diagram available — see order form.)

Blueprint Price Code: B

TO ORDER THIS BLUEPRINT, CALL TOLL-FREE 1-800-820-1283

Plan V-1758

PRICES AND DETAILS ON PAGES 12-15

Rustic, Vaulted Living

- A rustic yet contemporary look is achieved with the combination of diagonal and vertical siding, a steep roofline and lots of glass.
- The interior is enhanced by vaulted ceilings in the living room and in the study and sleeping room on the upper level.
- The focal point of the floor plan is the two-story-high living room, which

shows off a handsome woodstove and a dramatic window wall. An expansive deck wraps around the living room to a side entry.

- Adjoining the living room are the dining room and kitchen. A combination cooktop and breakfast bar is perfect for snacks or casual dining. An oversized window sits above the sink.
- A convenient laundry closet and full bath are centrally located and serve the two main-floor bedrooms.
- A larger bedroom shares the upper level with a study that overlooks the living room below.

Plan LMB-3702

Bedrooms: 3	**Baths:** 2
Living Area:	
Upper floor	500 sq. ft.
Main floor	1,306 sq. ft.
Total Living Area:	**1,806 sq. ft.**
Exterior Wall Framing:	2x4

Foundation Options:
Crawlspace
(Typical foundation & framing conversion diagram available—see order form.)

BLUEPRINT PRICE CODE:	B

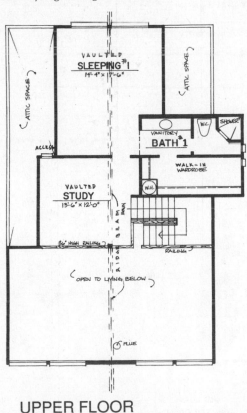

UPPER FLOOR

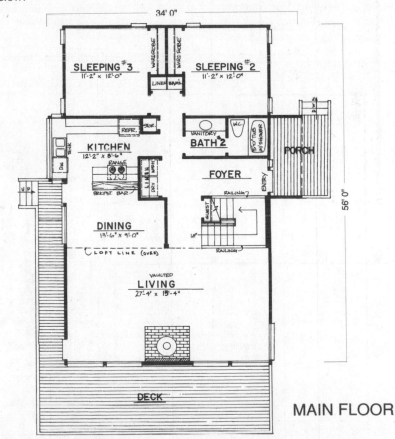

MAIN FLOOR

Breezy Beauty

- A nostalgic covered front porch, a backyard deck and a sprawling screened porch combine to make this beautiful one-story home a breezy delight.
- The front entry opens into the Great Room, which is crowned by a soaring 12-ft.-high cathedral ceiling. A handsome fireplace is flanked by built-in bookshelves and cabinets.
- The large, bayed dining room offers a 9-ft. tray ceiling and deck access through French doors.

- The adjoining kitchen boasts plenty of counter space and a handy built-in recipe desk.
- From the kitchen, a side door leads to the screened porch. A wood floor and deck access highlight this cheery room.
- A quiet hall leads past a convenient utility room to the sleeping quarters.
- The secluded master bedroom is enhanced by a spacious walk-in closet. The private master bath includes a lovely garden tub, a separate shower and dual vanities.
- Two more bedrooms with walk-in closets share a hall bath.

Plan C-8905	
Bedrooms: 3	**Baths:** 2
Living Area:	
Main floor	1,811 sq. ft.
Total Living Area:	**1,811 sq. ft.**
Screened porch	240 sq. ft.
Daylight basement	1,811 sq. ft.
Garage	484 sq. ft.
Exterior Wall Framing:	2x4
Foundation Options:	

Daylight basement
Crawlspace
(All plans can be built with your choice of foundation and framing. A generic conversion diagram is available. See order form.)

BLUEPRINT PRICE CODE: B

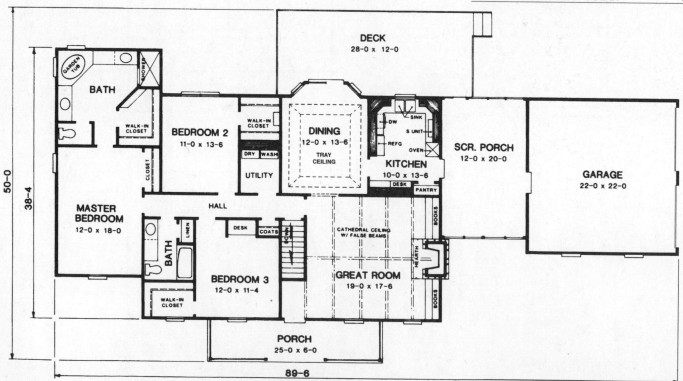

MAIN FLOOR

TO ORDER THIS BLUEPRINT, CALL TOLL-FREE 1-800-820-1283   Plan C-8905   *PRICES AND DETAILS ON PAGES 12-15*

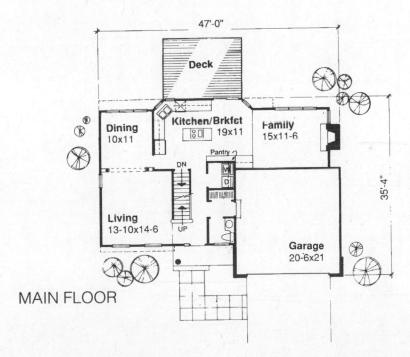

Br 4
10-4x10

Br 3
11x10

DN

Mas. Suite
14x15-6
vaulted

open to
below

Br 2
12-8x10

High Glass above

UPPER FLOOR

47'-0"

35'-4"

Deck

Dining
10x11

Kitchen/Brkfct
19x11

Family
15x11-6

Pantry

DN

Living
13-10x14-6

UP

Garage
20-6x21

MAIN FLOOR

Pleasing Combination

- This plan offers a pleasing combination of traditional and contemporary features.
- A bold column introduces the covered front entry. The vaulted entry hall leads to the formal living and dining rooms on the left, separated from each other by a half-wall with wood columns.
- The kitchen, breakfast nook and family room combine to create one huge space for everyday living or casual entertaining.
- The bayed kitchen/breakfast area features an island cooktop and a pantry closet with an adjacent built-in desk. The spacious family room is highlighted by a fireplace on one wall and lots of windows on the other.
- The upstairs master suite offers a vaulted ceiling showcased by a magnificent Palladian window. A large walk-in closet separates the sleeping area from the private master bath.
- The three remaining bedrooms share another full bath.

Plan B-90019

Bedrooms: 4	Baths: 2 ½
Space:	
Upper floor	833 sq. ft.
Main floor	987 sq. ft.
Total Living Area	**1,820 sq. ft.**
Basement	987 sq. ft.
Garage	430 sq. ft.
Exterior Wall Framing	2x4
Foundation options:	
Standard Basement	
(Foundation & framing conversion diagram available—see order form.)	
Blueprint Price Code	B

TO ORDER THIS BLUEPRINT,
CALL TOLL-FREE 1-800-820-1283

Plan B-90019

PRICES AND DETAILS
ON PAGES 12-15

111

Open Invitation

- The wide front porch of this friendly country farmhouse presents an open invitation to all who visit.
- Highlighted by a round-topped transom, the home's entrance opens directly into the spacious living room, which features a warm fireplace flanked by windows.
- The adjoining dining area is enhanced by a lovely bay window and is easily serviced by the updated kitchen's angled snack bar.
- A bright sun room off the kitchen provides a great space for informal meals or relaxation. Access to a covered backyard porch is nearby.
- The good-sized master bedroom is secluded from the other sleeping areas. The lavish master bath includes a garden tub, a separate shower, a dual-sink vanity and a walk-in closet.
- Two more bedrooms share a second full bath. A laundry/utility room is nearby.
- An additional 1,007 sq. ft. of living space can be made available by finishing the upper floor.
- All ceilings are 9 ft. high for added spaciousness.

Plan J-91078

Bedrooms: 3	Baths: 2
Living Area:	
Main floor	1,846 sq. ft.
Total Living Area:	**1,846 sq. ft.**
Future upper floor	1,007 sq. ft.
Standard basement	1,846 sq. ft.
Garage	484 sq. ft.
Exterior Wall Framing:	2x6

Foundation Options:

Standard basement
Crawlspace
Slab

(All plans can be built with your choice of foundation and framing. A generic conversion diagram is available. See order form.)

BLUEPRINT PRICE CODE:	B

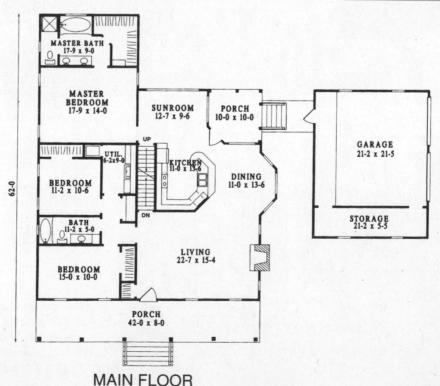

MAIN FLOOR

Plan J-91078

Spirited Split

- A lovely front porch, expressed timber and ascending exterior stairs create an anticipation that is well rewarded inside this three-bedroom split-level.
- The vaulted living room off the foyer has a handsome fireplace and front window; it joins the formal dining room with wet bar.
- Also vaulted are the kitchen and breakfast room, with pantry and entrance to the wrapping rear deck.
- Up several steps is the elegant vaulted master bedroom and private skylit bath with plant shelf above the tub and walk-in closet; two additional bedrooms and a second bath are also included.
- The lower level offers a half bath, laundry room and a bonus area with bar.

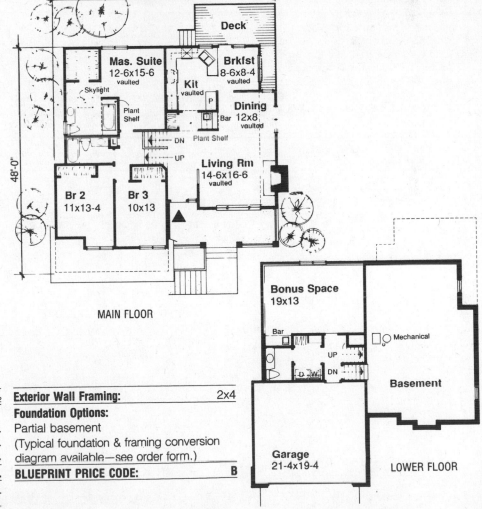

MAIN FLOOR

LOWER FLOOR

Plan B-89032		Exterior Wall Framing:	2x4
Bedrooms: 3	**Baths:** 2½	**Foundation Options:**	
Living Area:		Partial basement	
Main floor	1,424 sq. ft.	(Typical foundation & framing conversion	
Lower floor	150 sq. ft.	diagram available—see order form.)	
Bonus space	273 sq. ft.		
Total Living Area:	**1,847 sq. ft.**	**BLUEPRINT PRICE CODE:**	**B**
Partial basement	575 sq. ft.		
Garage	412 sq. ft.		

TO ORDER THIS BLUEPRINT,
CALL TOLL-FREE 1-800-820-1283

Plan B-89032

PRICES AND DETAILS
ON PAGES 12-15

113

A Real Charmer

- A tranquil railed porch makes this country one-story a real charmer.
- The main entry opens directly into the Great Room, which serves as the home's focal point. A 14-ft. cathedral ceiling soars above, while a fireplace and a built-in cabinet for games make the space a fun gathering spot.
- Beautiful French doors expand the Great Room to a peaceful covered porch at the rear of the home. Open the doors and let in the fresh summer air!
- A bayed breakfast nook unfolds from the kitchen, where the family cook will love the long island snack bar and the pantry. The carport is located nearby to save steps when you unload groceries.
- Across the home, the master bedroom features a walk-in closet with built-in shelves. A 10-ft. cathedral ceiling tops the master bath, which boasts a private toilet, a second walk-in closet and a separate tub and shower.
- A skylighted hall bath services the two secondary bedrooms.

Plan J-9508

Bedrooms: 3	Baths: 2½
Living Area:	
Main floor	1,875 sq. ft.
Total Living Area:	**1,875 sq. ft.**
Standard basement	1,875 sq. ft.
Carport	418 sq. ft.
Storage	114 sq. ft.
Exterior Wall Framing:	2x4

Foundation Options:

Standard basement
Crawlspace
Slab

(All plans can be built with your choice of foundation and framing. A generic conversion diagram is available. See order form.)

BLUEPRINT PRICE CODE:	B

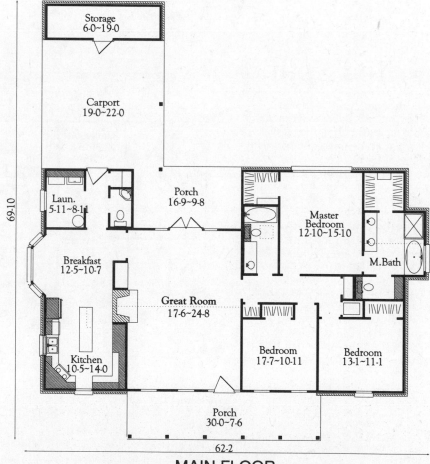

MAIN FLOOR

BASEMENT STAIRWAY LOCATION

TO ORDER THIS BLUEPRINT, CALL TOLL-FREE 1-800-820-1283

Plan J-9508

PRICES AND DETAILS ON PAGES 12-15

Country-Style Comfort

- From the charming front porch to the spacious rear deck, this country-style design offers comfortable living both inside and out.
- The angled design breaks up the lines of the house, as does the shed roof above the porch. Inside, the spaces are well defined yet flow together smoothly.
- The foyer opens to the formal living spaces, which include a living room with a cathedral ceiling and a dining room with a built-in china hutch. Lovely paned windows line the wall overlooking the porch.
- The efficient U-shaped kitchen lies between the bayed dinette and the large family room with a fireplace. Sliding glass doors in the family room open to the rear deck.
- A half-bath, a nice-sized coat closet and a laundry area are just off the entrance to the two-car garage.
- The bedroom wing features an impressive master suite with lots of closet space and a private bath with a whirlpool tub. The two front-facing bedrooms share a hall bath.

Plan HFL-1580-JE

Bedrooms: 3	Baths: 2½

Living Area:	
Main floor	1,918 sq. ft.
Total Living Area:	**1,918 sq. ft.**
Standard basement	1,984 sq. ft.
Garage	585 sq. ft.

Exterior Wall Framing: 2x6

Foundation Options:
Standard basement
Slab
(Typical foundation & framing conversion diagram available—see order form.)

BLUEPRINT PRICE CODE: B

94'-7½"

38'-1½"

DECK

heat-circulating fireplace

whirlpool tub

W.I.C.

LAV.

D'NTE 8'-6 x 13'

K 9' x 13'

FAM. R 17' x 13'

shr.

MBR 15' x 13'

D W LAUN

dish cab.

STOR.

TWO CAR GAR. 21'-8 x 27'

D. R. 10'-4 x 15'

L. R. 16'-6 x 13'-4'
cathedral ceiling

F

LIN

BR 10' x 10'

BR 10' x 13'-4'

PORCH

MAIN FLOOR

Spacious, Open Plan

- **This spacious, open plan gains a heightened sense of space from the entry with a long view of the deck and rear yard through the Great Room.**
- **The formal living area of the Great Room has a showpiece interior fireplace with built-in bookcases on either side.**
- **The island kitchen serves both the formal dining area and the sunny breakfast bay.**
- **The master suite is separate from the secondary bedrooms for privacy. It features dual walk-in closets, a sitting bay and a spacious master bath.**

Plan DD-1895

Bedrooms: 3	Baths: 2
Space:	
Total living area:	1,964 sq. ft.
Garage:	395 sq. ft.
Exterior Wall Framing:	2x4
Ceiling Heights:	9'

Foundation options:
Standard basement
Crawlspace
Slab
(Foundation & framing conversion diagram available — see order form.)

Blueprint Price Code:	B

MAIN FLOOR

BKFST.

DECK

M. BEDROOM
15^4 X 17^2

KITCHEN
12^8 X 13^0

LIVING
17^0 X 26^0

M. BATH

DINING
9^8 X 13^0

UTIL.

BEDROOM 3
12^4 X 12^6

BATH 2

ENTRY

GARAGE
18^{10} X 21^0

BEDROOM 2
12^4 X 13^0

PORCH

49^{11}

58^5

TO ORDER THIS BLUEPRINT,
CALL TOLL-FREE 1-800-820-1283

Plan DD-1895

PRICES AND DETAILS
ON PAGES 12-15

Super Sense of Space

- This stylish brick home introduces a spacious, open-feeling interior with a long view into the living room and the deck and outdoors beyond.
- The huge living and dining area boasts a dramatic fireplace flanked by built-in shelving, in addition to the spectacular view of the rear yard and deck.
- The island kitchen services both the formal dining area and the sunny breakfast bay, which provides access to the deck.
- The spacious master suite is separated from the secondary bedrooms by a large private bath and twin walk-in closets. The bedroom features a lovely bayed sitting area.
- The two extra bedrooms share a second bath with dual sinks. Each of these bedrooms is equipped with generous closet space. A handy laundry closet is just steps away.
- Nine foot ceilings are found throughout the home.

Plan DD-1895-D

Bedrooms: 3	Baths: 2
Living Area:	
Main floor	1,964 sq. ft.
Total Living Area:	**1,964 sq. ft.**
Garage	412 sq. ft.
Exterior Wall Framing:	2x4
Foundation Options:	

Slab
(Typical foundation & framing conversion diagram available—see order form.)

BLUEPRINT PRICE CODE:	B

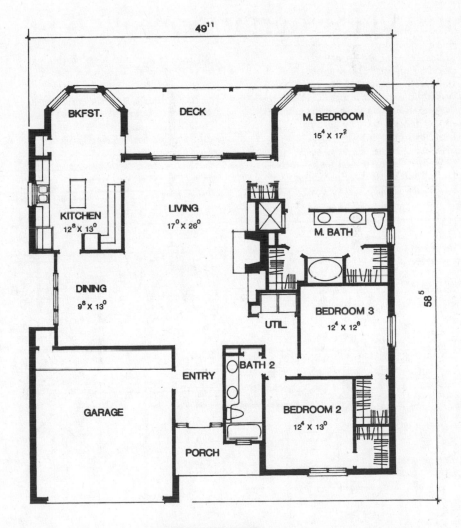

MAIN FLOOR

Nostalgic Exterior Appeal

- A lattice-trimmed front entry porch, repeated steep gables, and narrow lap siding all convey a nostalgic exterior appeal.
- The open-feeling plan offers plenty of excitement and livability for families in the 90's.
- The living room includes such dramatic features as a high-vaulted ceiling with loft overlook above, a two-story fireplace/stair tower with

built-in wet bar, and high corner glass.
- The open kitchen overlooks a snack counter and skylit dining room.
- The main floor also includes a master bedroom with access to a dramatic bath and side deck as well as a den for TV watching or overnight guests.
- The two upstairs bedrooms plus loft will give the kids plenty of private space.

UDG-90009	
Bedrooms: 3-4	**Baths:** 2

Space:	
Upper floor:	554 sq. ft.
Main floor:	1,123 sq. ft.
Total living area:	1,677 sq. ft.
Basement:	1,123 sq. ft.
Garage:	544 sq. ft.
Exterior Wall Framing:	2x4

Foundation options:
Standard Basement.
(Foundation & framing conversion diagram available — see order form.)

Blueprint Price Code:	B

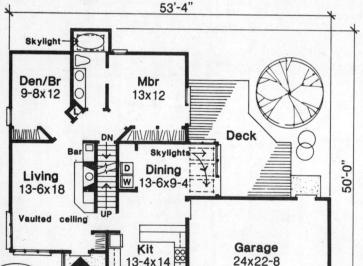

MAIN FLOOR

53'-4"

- Skylight
- Den/Br 9-8x12
- Mbr 13x12
- Bar
- DN
- Deck
- Skylights
- Dining 13-6x9-4
- D W
- Living 13-6x18
- Vaulted ceiling
- UP
- Kit 13-4x14
- Garage 24x22-8

50'-0"

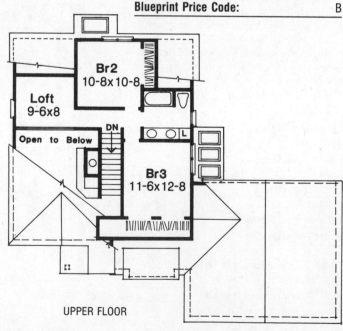

UPPER FLOOR

- Br2 10-8x10-8
- Loft 9-6x8
- Open to Below
- DN
- Br3 11-6x12-8

TO ORDER THIS BLUEPRINT, CALL TOLL-FREE 1-800-820-1283

Plan UDG-90009

PRICES AND DETAILS ON PAGES 12-15

Tasteful Charm

- Columned covered porches lend warmth and charm to the front and rear of this tasteful traditional home.
- Sidelight and transom glass brightens the entry foyer, which shares a 10-ft. ceiling with the elegant dining room.
- The dining room provides a quiet spot for formal meals, while a Palladian window arrangement adds light and flair.
- The spacious living room offers a warm fireplace and an adjacent TV cabinet. The dramatic ceiling vaults to a height of 11 ft., 8 inches. French doors give way to the skylighted rear porch, which is finished with lovely brick pavers.

Two brick steps descend to the adjoining patio, which is also beautifully paved with brick.
- The gourmet kitchen offers a built-in oven/microwave cabinet, a separate cooktop and an island snack bar with a sink. Its 10-ft. ceiling extends into the sunny breakfast nook.
- The oversized laundry room includes a handy half-bath, a wall-to-wall storage cabinet, a hanging rod, a large sink and nearby porch access.
- The secluded master bedroom boasts a 12-ft. vaulted ceiling and a large walk-in closet. In the private master bath, a glass-block divider separates the whirlpool tub from the shower stall.

Plan J-9414	
Bedrooms: 3	**Baths: 2½**
Living Area:	
Main floor	1,974 sq. ft.
Total Living Area:	**1,974 sq. ft.**
Standard basement	1,974 sq. ft.
Garage and storage	518 sq. ft.
Exterior Wall Framing:	2x4

Foundation Options:
Standard basement
Crawlspace
Slab
(All plans can be built with your choice of foundation and framing. A generic conversion diagram is available. See order form.)

BLUEPRINT PRICE CODE: B

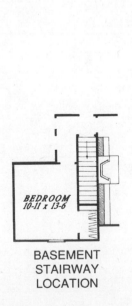

BASEMENT
STAIRWAY
LOCATION

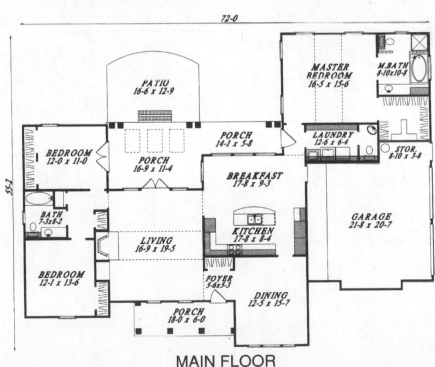

MAIN FLOOR

Rustic Country Design

- A welcoming front porch, window shutters and a bay window on the exterior of this rustic design are complemented by a comfortable, informal interior.
- A spacious country kitchen includes a bay-windowed breakfast area, center work island and abundant counter and cabinet space.
- Note the large utility room in the garage entry area.
- The large Great Room includes an impressive fireplace and another informal eating area with double doors opening to a deck, patio or screened porch. Also note the half-bath.

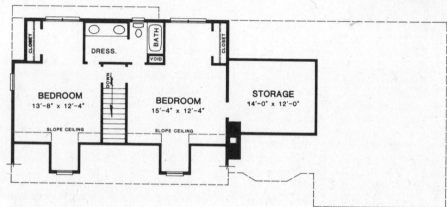

UPPER FLOOR

- The main floor master suite features a walk-in closet and compartmentalized private bath.
- Upstairs, you will find two more bedrooms, another full bath and a large storage area.

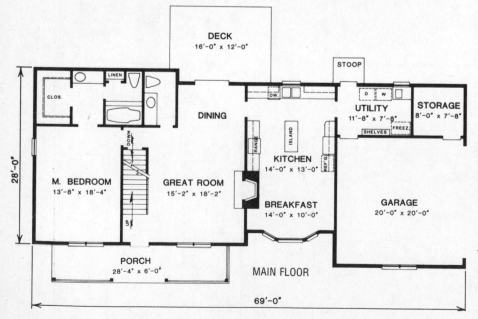

MAIN FLOOR

Plan C-8476

Bedrooms: 3	Baths: 2½

Space:

Upper floor:	720 sq. ft.
Main floor:	1,277 sq. ft.
Total living area:	**1,997 sq. ft.**
Basement:	approx. 1,200 sq. ft.
Garage:	400 sq. ft.
Storage:	(in garage) 61 sq. ft.

Exterior Wall Framing:	2x4

Foundation options:
Daylight basement.
Standard basement.
Crawlspace.
Slab.
(Foundation & framing conversion diagram available — see order form.)

Blueprint Price Code:	B

TO ORDER THIS BLUEPRINT, CALL TOLL-FREE 1-800-820-1283

Plan C-8476

PRICES AND DETAILS ON PAGES 12-15

Appealing Farmhouse

- This appealing farmhouse design features a shady and inviting front porch with decorative railings.
- Inside, 14-ft. vaulted ceilings expand the living and dining rooms.
- This large area is brightened by bay windows and warmed by a unique two-way fireplace. Sliding glass doors lead to a sunny backyard patio.
- The functional kitchen includes a pantry closet, plenty of cabinet space and a serving bar to the dining room.
- The master bedroom boasts a mirrored dressing area, a private bath and abundant closet space.
- Two additional bedrooms share another full bath. The third bedroom includes a cozy window seat.

Plan NW-521

Bedrooms: 3	Baths: 2
Living Area:	
Main floor	1,187 sq. ft.
Total Living Area:	**1,187 sq. ft.**
Garage	448 sq. ft.
Exterior Wall Framing:	2x6

Foundation Options:

Crawlspace

(All plans can be built with your choice of foundation and framing. A generic conversion diagram is available. See order form.)

BLUEPRINT PRICE CODE: A

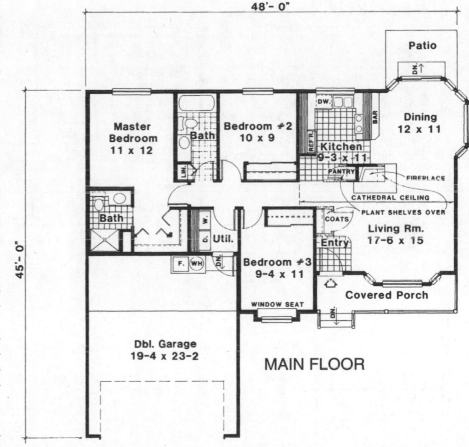

MAIN FLOOR

Love at First Sight!

- Upon seeing its covered front porch and stylish brick-accented exterior, it's easy to fall in love with this adorable home.
- Past the ornate and inviting entry, the spacious family room's dramatic window-flanked fireplace is an impressive introduction to the home's interior. A high plant shelf and a 12-ft. vaulted ceiling add to the ambience.
- The adjoining dining room is great for casual or formal occasions. The sliding glass doors that access the backyard may be built into a sunny window bay for a more dramatic effect.
- The efficient galley-style kitchen offers a pantry, an attached laundry room and a door to the garage.
- Three bedrooms occupy the sleeping wing. The master bedroom includes a roomy walk-in closet. The private master bath features a 12-ft. vaulted ceiling, a garden tub, a separate shower and a dual-sink vanity.
- A second full bath services the secondary bedrooms, one of which may be expanded by a 12-ft. vaulted ceiling.

Plan APS-1103

Bedrooms: 3	Baths: 2
Living Area:	
Main floor	1,197 sq. ft.
Total Living Area:	**1,197 sq. ft.**
Garage	380 sq. ft.
Exterior Wall Framing:	2x4

Foundation Options:

Slab

(All plans can be built with your choice of foundation and framing. A generic conversion diagram is available. See order form.)

BLUEPRINT PRICE CODE: A

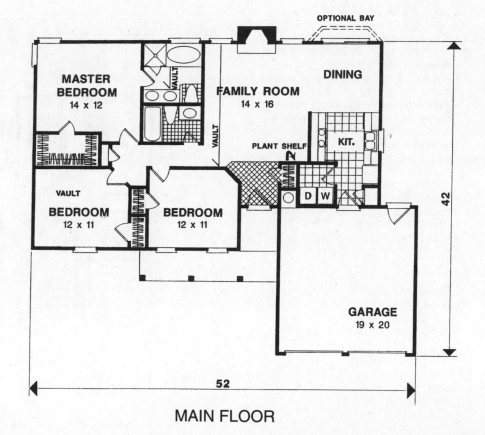

MAIN FLOOR

Plan APS-1103

Family Tradition

- This quaint home basks in tradition, with beautiful gables facing the street and vaulted family spaces inside.
- A columned front porch opens to a spacious family room, where a 16-ft. vaulted ceiling soars above a striking fireplace flanked by arched windows. The 16-ft. ceiling continues into the dining room and the kitchen.
- The sunny dining room opens to the backyard through a French door. The walk-through kitchen offers a bright angled sink, a snack bar and a large pantry closet topped by a plant shelf.
- The master suite boasts a 10½-ft. tray ceiling in the bedroom and a 13½-ft. vaulted ceiling in the lush garden bath.
- Two secondary bedrooms share another full bath. A handy laundry closet is close to the bedrooms and the garage.
- For added spaciousness, all ceilings are 9 ft. high unless otherwise specified.

Plan FB-5115-CLAI

Bedrooms: 3	Baths: 2
Living Area:	
Main floor	1,198 sq. ft.
Total Living Area:	**1,198 sq. ft.**
Daylight basement	1,198 sq. ft.
Garage	400 sq. ft.
Exterior Wall Framing:	2x4

Foundation Options:

Daylight basement

Crawlspace

(All plans can be built with your choice of foundation and framing. A generic conversion diagram is available. See order form.)

BLUEPRINT PRICE CODE:	A

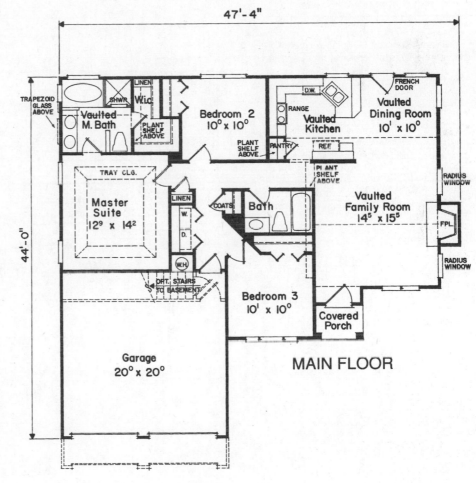

MAIN FLOOR

Economical Three-Bedroom

- A classic front porch with stately columns and gables dresses up this one-story brick home.
- The modest-sized floor plan offers three nice-sized bedrooms and a generous amount of living space.
- The large living room and breakfast area combine for a Great Room concept that overlooks a rear patio. A corner fireplace and an optional sloped or gambrel ceiling accent this activity area.
- The galley kitchen with an eating bar is open to the breakfast and living areas.
- Oriented to the rear of the home is the master bedroom, which features a personal bath with twin sinks, a walk-in closet and a windowed tub.

Plan DD-1200

Bedrooms: 3	Baths: 2
Living Area:	
Main floor	1,200 sq. ft.
Total Living Area:	**1,200 sq. ft.**
Standard basement	1,200 sq. ft.
Garage	367 sq. ft.
Exterior Wall Framing:	2x4

Foundation Options:

Standard basement

Crawlspace

Slab

(All plans can be built with your choice of foundation and framing. A generic conversion diagram is available. See order form.)

BLUEPRINT PRICE CODE: A

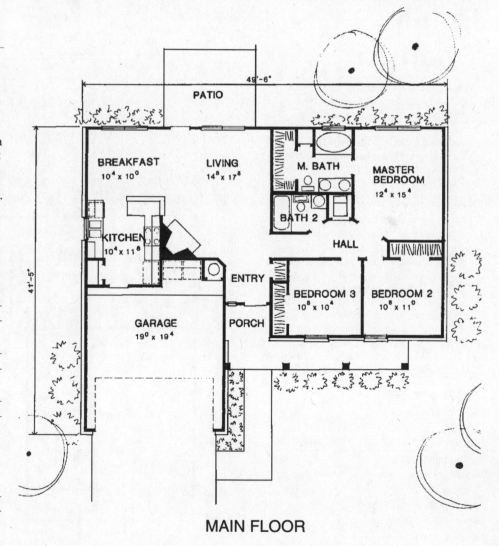

MAIN FLOOR

TO ORDER THIS BLUEPRINT,
CALL TOLL-FREE 1-800-820-1283

Plan DD-1200

PRICES AND DETAILS
ON PAGES 12-15

ELEVATION A

ELEVATION B

ELEVATION C

Striking, Sunny Master Suite

- This striking Mediterranean opens to a vaulted combination living/dining room with a view to the rear of the home and glass sliders opening to the covered patio.
- A pass-thru and eating bar separate the Great Room from the kitchen, which offers plenty of space, plus an attached breakfast area.
- Convenient laundry facilities lie close to the master bedroom and bath.
- The elegantly vaulted master suite offers his and her closets and a lovely bay window; the bath has private toilet.
- The secondary bedrooms also display vaulted ceilings.
- NOTE: All three elevation choices and plan options are included in the plans.

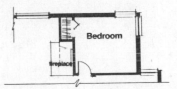

OPTION "A" W/ FIREPLACE

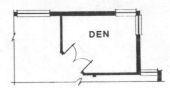

OPTION "B" W/ DEN

OPTION "C" W/ WET BAR

MASTER BATH W/ TUB OPTION

Plan HDS-90-821

Bedrooms: 3	Baths: 2

Space:

Total living area:	1,280 sq. ft.
Garage:	approx. 360 sq. ft.

Exterior Wall Framing:	concrete block

Foundation options:
Slab.
(Foundation & framing conversion diagram available — see order form.)

Blueprint Price Code:	A

MAIN FLOOR

TO ORDER THIS BLUEPRINT,
CALL TOLL-FREE 1-800-820-1283

Plan HDS-90-821

PRICES AND DETAILS
ON PAGES 12-15

125

Cozy Home for Retirees or New Families

Total living area: 1,283 sq. ft.
(Not counting basement or garage)

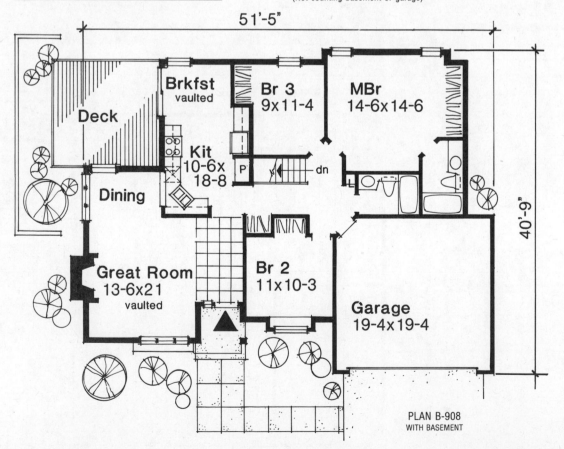

51'-5"

40'-9"

Deck

Brkfst
vaulted

Kit
10-6x
18-8

Dining

Great Room
13-6x21
vaulted

Br 3
9x11-4

MBr
14-6x14-6

P

dn

Br 2
11x10-3

Garage
19-4x19-4

PLAN B-908
WITH BASEMENT

Blueprint Price Code A
Plan B-908

PRICES AND DETAILS
ON PAGES 12-15

Stunning Stucco Home

- Paned and shuttered windows accented with arches give this home a stunning look.
- The interior design maximizes square footage and features many appointments usually found only in larger homes.
- The living room, breakfast nook and kitchen are grouped at the rear of the home, where they intermingle to create one huge living space.
- The corridor kitchen has a sunny view of the breakfast nook and the patio beyond. A pass-through above the sink connects the kitchen to the living room with fireplace.
- All three bedrooms are spacious and well lighted. The master bedroom suite comes complete with a large walk-in closet and an opulent bath that features a dual-sink vanity, a whirlpool tub and a separate shower.

Plan APS-1307	
Bedrooms: 3	**Baths:** 2
Space:	
Main floor	1,304 sq. ft.
Total Living Area	**1,304 sq. ft.**
Garage	520 sq. ft.
Exterior Wall Framing	2x4
Foundation options:	
Slab	
(Foundation & framing conversion diagram available—see order form.)	
Blueprint Price Code	**A**

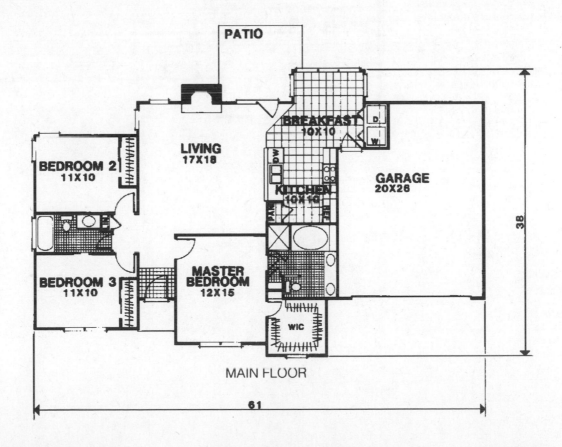

MAIN FLOOR

TO ORDER THIS BLUEPRINT,
CALL TOLL-FREE 1-800-820-1283

Plan APS-1307

PRICES AND DETAILS
ON PAGES 12-15

127

Maximum Livability

- Compact and easy to build, this appealing ranch-style home is big on charm and livability.
- The entry of the home opens to a dramatic 13-ft. vaulted living room with exposed beams, a handsome fireplace and access to a backyard patio.
- Wood post dividers set off the large raised dining room, which is brightened by a stunning window wall.
- The adjoining kitchen offers a spacious snack bar and easy access to the utility room and the two-car garage. A nice storage area is also included.
- Three bedrooms and two baths occupy the sleeping wing. One of the baths is private to the master suite, which features a walk-in closet and a dressing area with a sit-down make-up table. The two remaining bedrooms also have walk-in closets.

Plan E-1305

Bedrooms: 3	Baths: 2
Living Area:	
Main floor	1,346 sq. ft.
Total Living Area:	**1,346 sq. ft.**
Garage	441 sq. ft.
Storage	44 sq. ft.
Exterior Wall Framing:	2x4

Foundation Options:

Crawlspace
Slab
(All plans can be built with your choice of foundation and framing. A generic conversion diagram is available. See order form.)

BLUEPRINT PRICE CODE: A

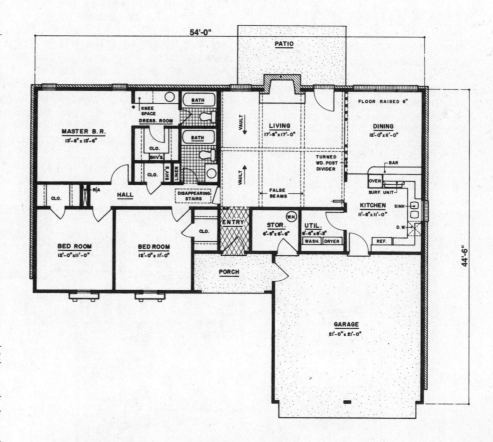

MAIN FLOOR

TO ORDER THIS BLUEPRINT, CALL TOLL-FREE 1-800-820-1283

Plan E-1305

PRICES AND DETAILS ON PAGES 12-15

Raised One-Story Design

- This clever plan raises the one-story ranch design to new heights.
- An open floor plan punctuated with high ceilings maximizes the home's square footage.
- The open living area consists of a vaulted living room with a fireplace, a dining room with a bay window and an efficient galley-style kitchen with a two-sided serving bar.
- A pantry closet, a laundry room and a nifty storage area are close to the kitchen, just off the garage entrance.
- Not to be overlooked, the outstanding master suite features a tray ceiling and a vaulted bath with a garden tub, a separate shower, a dual-sink vanity and a walk-in closet.
- Two more bedrooms, one of which has a vaulted ceiling, share a hall bath.

Plan FB-5052-LENO

Bedrooms: 3	Baths: 2
Living Area:	
Main floor	1,346 sq. ft.
Total Living Area:	**1,346 sq. ft.**
Standard basement	1,346 sq. ft.
Garage	390 sq. ft.
Exterior Wall Framing:	2x4

Foundation Options:
Daylight basement
Crawlspace
Slab
(Typical foundation & framing conversion diagram available—see order form.

BLUEPRINT PRICE CODE: A

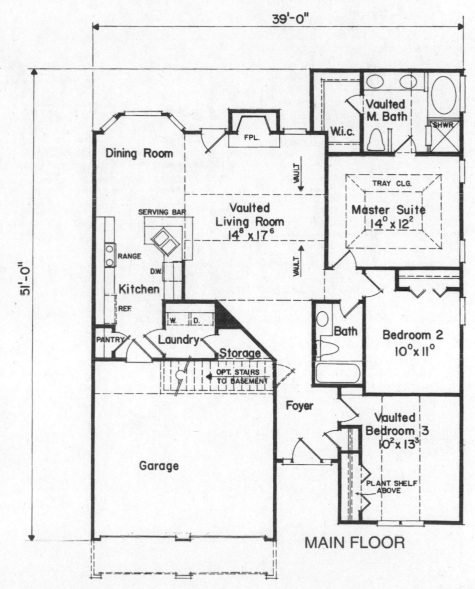

MAIN FLOOR

TO ORDER THIS BLUEPRINT,
CALL TOLL-FREE 1-800-820-1283

Plan FB-5052-LENO

PRICES AND DETAILS
ON PAGES 12-15

129

Easy-Living One-Story

- Low-maintenance brick adds style and durability to this easy-living one-story.
- The friendly porch welcomes guests inside. The entry offers a view through the living room to the backyard.
- With its massive brick fireplace, rustic beams and high 13-ft. cathedral ceiling, the living room is cozy, yet dramatic! A French door alongside the fireplace provides access to a nice patio.
- The living room is set off from the dining room by decorative wood posts. The bright dining room is also distinguished by its raised floor.
- The U-shaped kitchen is equipped with a convenient snack bar, plenty of counter space and a sunny windowed sink. Easy access to the laundry room and to the two-car garage is also a plus.
- Walk-in closets are included in each of the three bedrooms. The master suite also boasts a private bath and a separate dressing area with knee space.

Plan E-1307

Bedrooms: 3	Baths: 2
Living Area:	
Main floor	1,346 sq. ft.
Total Living Area:	**1,346 sq. ft.**
Garage	441 sq. ft.
Storage	44 sq. ft.
Exterior Wall Framing:	2x4

Foundation Options:

Crawlspace

Slab

(All plans can be built with your choice of foundation and framing. A generic conversion diagram is available. See order form.)

BLUEPRINT PRICE CODE: A

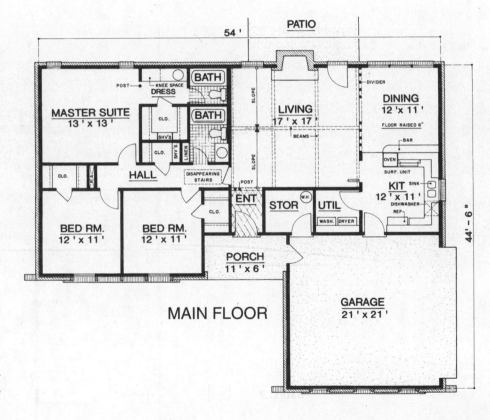

MAIN FLOOR

Plan E-1307

Feature-Filled Cottage-Style

- With its high ceilings, space-saving floor plan and luxurious amenities, this appealing cottage-style home makes the most of its size.
- Meant to impress, the 14-ft.-high covered front entry porch is bathed in light from an overhead dormer window.
- Inside, the dormer also filters light into the 14-ft.-high foyer and the spacious living room.
- The living room is expanded by a 14-ft. cathedral ceiling and warmed by a fireplace. Access to the backyard is provided by a French door.
- The bright, elegant dining room is accented by a bay window and a 10-ft. octagonal tray ceiling.
- The large island kitchen is easily accessible from the dining area and the convenient laundry area.
- The master suite is enhanced by a 10-ft. tray ceiling, a luxurious private bath and a roomy walk-in closet.

Plan OH-175

Bedrooms: 3	Baths: 2
Living Area:	
Main floor	1,352 sq. ft.
Total Living Area:	**1,352 sq. ft.**
Standard basement	1,352 sq. ft.
Garage	441 sq. ft.
Exterior Wall Framing:	2 x 4

Foundation Options:

Standard basement

(All plans can be built with your choice of foundation and framing. A generic conversion diagram is available. See order form.)

BLUEPRINT PRICE CODE:	A

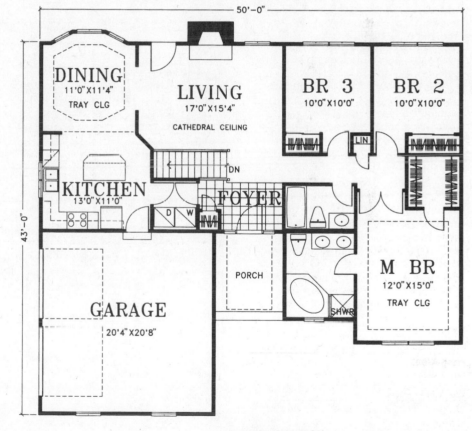

MAIN FLOOR

TO ORDER THIS BLUEPRINT,
CALL TOLL-FREE 1-800-820-1283

Plan OH-175

PRICES AND DETAILS
ON PAGES 12-15

131

Exciting Great Room Featured

- A brick and wood exterior accented by multiple gables and ornate windows gives this smart-looking one-story home lots of curb appeal.
- The amenity-filled interior is just as exciting. The 17-ft. vaulted foyer leads immediately into the spacious Great Room that also features a 17-ft.-high vaulted ceiling and a handsome fireplace flanked by windows.
- The adjoining dining room flows nicely into the breakfast area and the kitchen. The impressive kitchen offers an angled serving bar and a convenient pantry, while the sunny breakfast area has a French door to the backyard.
- The master suite boasts a 10-ft. tray ceiling and a walk-in closet with a plant shelf. The vaulted master bath features a garden tub and a dual-sink vanity.
- The two remaining bedrooms are serviced by another full bath.

Plan FB-1359

Bedrooms: 3	Baths: 2
Living Area:	
Main floor	1,359 sq. ft.
Total Living Area:	**1,359 sq. ft.**
Garage	407 sq. ft.
Exterior Wall Framing:	2x4

Foundation Options:

Crawlspace

Slab

(All plans can be built with your choice of foundation and framing. A generic conversion diagram is available. See order form.)

BLUEPRINT PRICE CODE: A

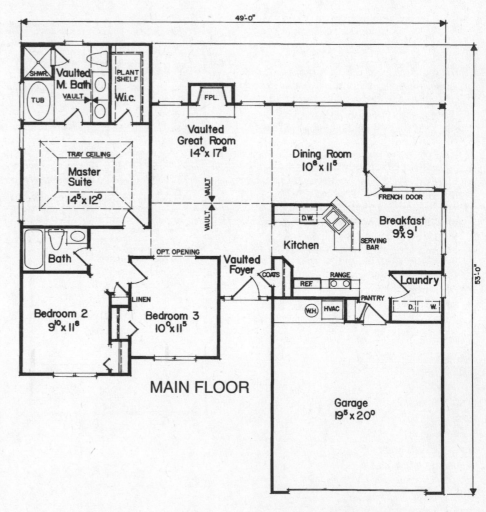

MAIN FLOOR

Plan FB-1359

PRICES AND DETAILS ON PAGES 12-15

Compact Home Big on Style

- While compact in size, this stylish one-story offers lots of room and little wasted space.
- Staggered rooflines, brick accents and beautiful arched windows smarten the exterior.
- The interior offers a large central living room with a 10-ft. ceiling, a warming fireplace flanked by windows and an adjoining patio.
- The spacious breakfast area merges with the living room and the walk-through kitchen. The formal dining room is located on the opposite end of the kitchen.
- Separated from the other two bedrooms, the master suite is both private and spacious. It offers its own garden bath with twin vanities and walk-in closets, plus a separate tub and shower.

DD-1296

Bedrooms: 3	**Baths:** 2

Space:

Main floor	1,364 sq. ft.
Total Living Area	**1,364 sq. ft.**
Standard basement	1,364 sq. ft.
Garage	443 sq. ft.
Exterior Wall Framing	**2x4**

Foundation options:
Standard Basement
Crawlspace
Slab
(Foundation & framing conversion diagram available—see order form.)

Blueprint Price Code	**A**

All in One!

- This plan puts today's most luxurious home-design features into one attractive, economical package.
- The covered front porch and the gabled roofline, accented by an arched window and a round louver vent, give the exterior a homey yet stylish appeal.
- Just inside the front door, the ceiling rises to 11 ft., offering an impressive greeting. The spacious living room is flooded with light through a central skylight and a pair of French doors that frame the smart fireplace.
- The living room flows into the nice-sized dining room, also with an 11-ft. ceiling. The adjoining kitchen offers a handy laundry closet, lots of counter space and a sunny dinette that opens to an expansive backyard terrace.
- The bedroom wing includes a wonderful master suite with a sizable sleeping room and an adjacent dressing area with two closets. Glass blocks above the dual-sink vanity in the master bath let in light yet maintain privacy. A whirlpool tub and a separate shower complete the suite.
- The larger of the two remaining bedrooms boasts an 11-ft.-high ceiling and an arched window.

Plan HFL-1680-FL

Bedrooms: 3	Baths: 2
Living Area:	
Main floor	1,367 sq. ft.
Total Living Area:	**1,367 sq. ft.**
Standard basement	1,367 sq. ft.
Garage	431 sq. ft.
Exterior Wall Framing:	2x6

Foundation Options:

Standard basement

(All plans can be built with your choice of foundation and framing. A generic conversion diagram is available. See order form.)

BLUEPRINT PRICE CODE: A

VIEW INTO LIVING ROOM

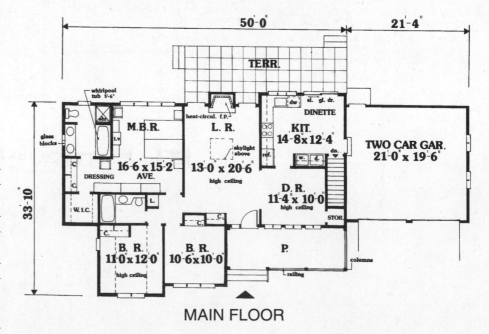

MAIN FLOOR

TO ORDER THIS BLUEPRINT, CALL TOLL-FREE 1-800-820-1283

Plan HFL-1680-FL

PRICES AND DETAILS ON PAGES 12-15

Open Great Room Design

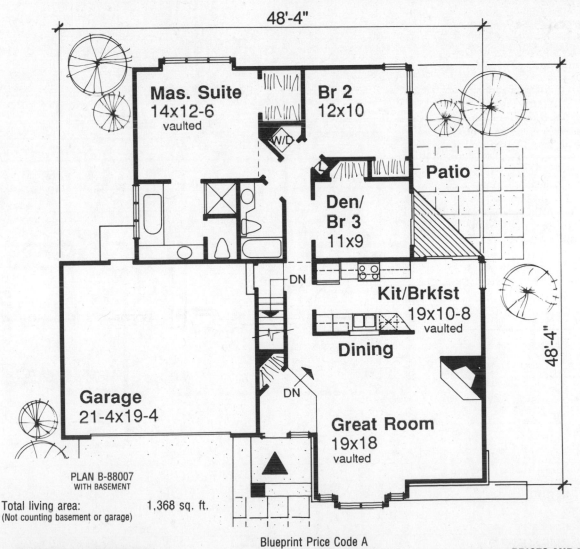

48'-4"

Mas. Suite
14x12-6
vaulted

Br 2
12x10

W/D

Patio

Den/ Br 3
11x9

DN

Kit/Brkfst
19x10-8
vaulted

Dining

DN

Garage
21-4x19-4

Great Room
19x18
vaulted

48'-4"

PLAN B-88007
WITH BASEMENT

Total living area: 1,368 sq. ft.
(Not counting basement or garage)

Blueprint Price Code A

Plan B-88007

Easy Living

- This cozy one-story design makes the most of its square footage by neatly incorporating features usually found only in much larger homes.
- Off the covered porch is a spacious living room with a dramatic corner fireplace, a ceiling that slopes to 13 ft., 6 in. and a long view to the backyard patio.
- The living room unfolds to a lovely dining room with a patio door.
- The adjoining kitchen features a snack bar for convenient serving and quick meals. The efficient, U-shaped kitchen also offers a pantry and a broom closet, plus a nearby utility/storage room.
- The gorgeous master suite is positioned for privacy. The bright bedroom has a ceiling that slopes to 11 ft. and a large front window arrangement. The master bath features dual sinks.
- The secondary bedrooms are located at the opposite end of the home and share a convenient hall bath.

Plan E-1311

Bedrooms: 3	Baths: 2
Living Area:	
Main floor	1,380 sq. ft.
Total Living Area:	**1,380 sq. ft.**
Garage	440 sq. ft.
Utility and storage	84 sq. ft.
Exterior Wall Framing:	**2x6**

Foundation Options:

Crawlspace
Slab

(All plans can be built with your choice of foundation and framing. A generic conversion diagram is available. See order form.)

BLUEPRINT PRICE CODE: A

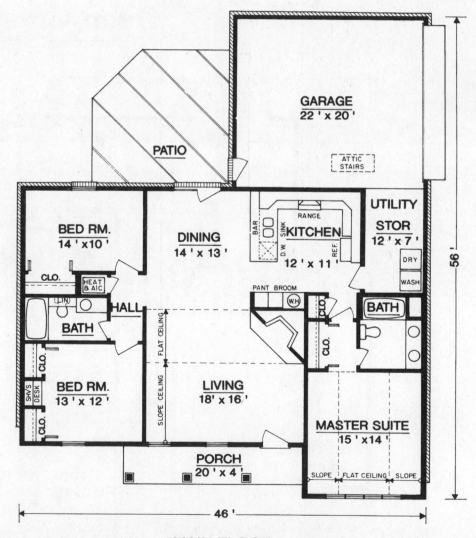

MAIN FLOOR

TO ORDER THIS BLUEPRINT, CALL TOLL-FREE 1-800-820-1283

Plan E-1311

PRICES AND DETAILS ON PAGES 12-15

Distinctive Inside and Out

- A decorative columned entry, shuttered windows and a facade of stucco and stone offer a distinct look to this economical one-story home.
- The focal point of the interior is the huge, central family room. The room is enhanced by a dramatic corner fireplace, a 15-ft.-high vaulted ceiling and a neat serving bar that extends from the kitchen and includes a wet bar.
- A decorative plant shelf adorns the entrance to the adjoining breakfast room, which features a lovely bay window. The kitchen offers a pantry and a pass-through to the family room.
- The formal dining room is easy to reach from both the kitchen and the family room, and is set off with columned arches and a raised ceiling.
- The secluded master suite boasts a vaulted private bath with dual sinks, an oval garden tub, a separate toilet room and a large walk-in closet.
- Two more bedrooms share a second bath at the other end of the home.

Plan FB-5001-SAVA

Bedrooms: 3	Baths: 2
Living Area:	
Main floor	1,429 sq. ft.
Total Living Area:	**1,429 sq. ft.**
Daylight basement	1,429 sq. ft.
Garage and storage	436 sq. ft.
Exterior Wall Framing:	2x4
Foundation Options:	
Daylight basement	
Crawlspace	
Slab	

(All plans can be built with your choice of foundation and framing. A generic conversion diagram is available. See order form.)

BLUEPRINT PRICE CODE:	A

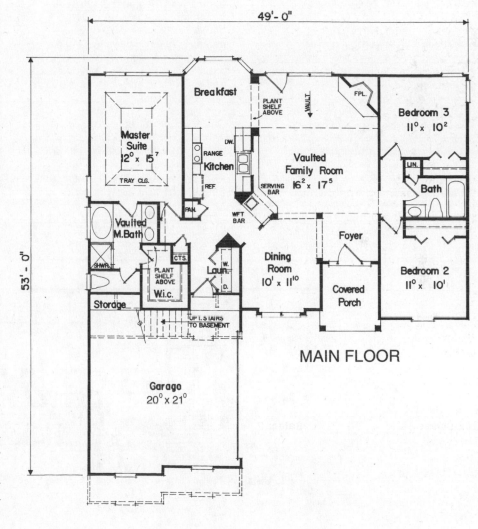

MAIN FLOOR

European Flair

- Arched window arrangements, striking stone and metal roofing above the garage give this home a European flair.
- To the left of the tiled foyer, the living room features a 10-ft. vaulted ceiling and a warm fireplace. A tall window bathes the entire room in sunlight.
- The adjacent dining room includes a pass-through to the kitchen and access to a lovely deck or screen porch.
- An inviting bayed breakfast nook is a great spot for a leisurely cup of coffee. The nook shares a 10½-ft. vaulted

ceiling with the gourmet kitchen, which includes a pantry closet.
- In the master suite, a 10-ft. vaulted ceiling creates an open feel. Two walk-in closets and a private bath with a dual-sink vanity and a separate tub and shower are added conveniences.
- A secondary bedroom nearby is serviced by a full hall bath.
- Double doors introduce a quiet den with an extra door for easy bathroom access. The den, which could also serve as a guest room or an informal gathering area, features a ceiling that jumps to 10 ft. at the window.

Plan B-94024	
Bedrooms: 2+	**Baths:** 2
Living Area:	
Main floor	1,431 sq. ft.
Total Living Area:	**1,431 sq. ft.**
Standard basement	1,431 sq. ft.
Garage	380 sq. ft.
Exterior Wall Framing:	2x6
Foundation Options:	
Standard basement	

(All plans can be built with your choice of foundation and framing. A generic conversion diagram is available. See order form.)

| **BLUEPRINT PRICE CODE:** | A |

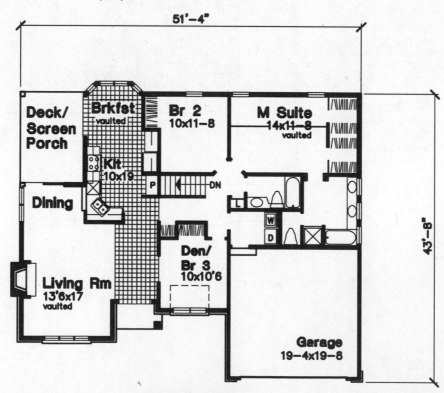

MAIN FLOOR

Plan B-94024

PRICES AND DETAILS ON PAGES 12-15

Rustic Ranch-Style Design

- This ranch-style home offers a rustic facade that is warm and inviting. The railed front porch and stone accents are especially appealing.
- The interior is warm as well, with the focal point being the attractive living room. Features here include an eye-catching fireplace, patio access and a dramatic 14-ft. sloped ceiling with exposed beams.
- The open dining room lies off the foyer and adjoins the efficient U-shaped kitchen, which includes a pantry and a broom closet.
- The master suite features a large walk-in closet and a roomy master bath.
- At the other end of the home, two secondary bedrooms with abundant closet space share another full bath.

Plan E-1410

Bedrooms: 3	Baths: 2
Living Area:	
Main floor	1,418 sq. ft.
Total Living Area:	**1,418 sq. ft.**
Garage	484 sq. ft.
Storage	38 sq. ft.
Exterior Wall Framing:	2x4

Foundation Options:

Crawlspace

Slab

(All plans can be built with your choice of foundation and framing. A generic conversion diagram is available. See order form.)

BLUEPRINT PRICE CODE:　　　　　　　　A

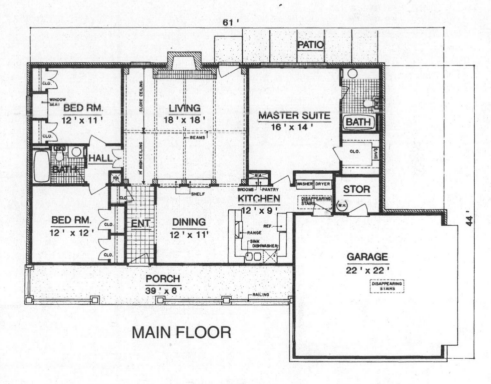

MAIN FLOOR

Cozy Three-Bedroom with Solar Features

In this design, a large stone fireplace doubles as a heat-storing thermal mass when sunlight passes through tall living room windows.

The surrounding floor can be surfaced with tile to enhance heat storage.

Living-family room boasts cathedral ceilings; built-in cabinet serves as room divider to dining room. The master bedroom has sliding glass doors to front wood deck.

PLAN C-1454
WITHOUT BASEMENT
(Specify Crawlspace or Slab Foundation)

Total living area: 1,454 sq. ft.
(Excluding carport)

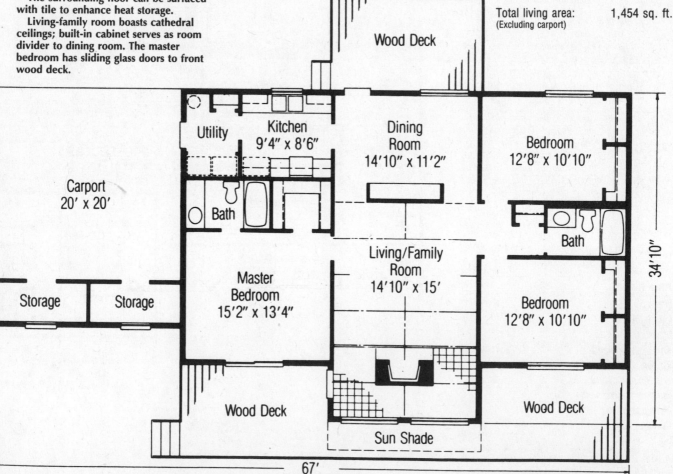

Blueprint Price Code A
Plan C-1454

**TO ORDER THIS BLUEPRINT,
CALL TOLL-FREE 1-800-820-1283**

**PRICES AND DETAILS
ON PAGES 12-15**

Victorian Form

- This beautiful home flaunts true-to-form Victorian styling in a modest one-story.
- A delightful, covered front porch and a stunning, sidelighted entry give way to the welcoming foyer.
- The foyer flows into the Great Room, which is warmed by a corner fireplace and topped by a 10-ft. stepped ceiling.
- Sliding French doors open to the backyard from both the Great Room and the adjoining formal dining room.
- On the other side of the open kitchen, a turreted breakfast room overlooks the front porch with cheery windows under an incredible 16-ft. ceiling!
- The restful master suite is graced by a charming window seat and crowned by a 10-ft. stepped ceiling. A dressing area leads to the master bath, which offers a separate tub and shower.
- To the right of the foyer, two more bedrooms share a hall bath. One bedroom features an impressive 11-ft. vaulted ceiling.
- Unless otherwise specified, all rooms have 9-ft. ceilings.

Plan AX-94319

Bedrooms: 3	Baths: 2
Living Area:	
Main floor	1,466 sq. ft.
Total Living Area:	**1,466 sq. ft.**
Standard basement	1,498 sq. ft.
Garage, storage and utility	483 sq. ft.
Exterior Wall Framing:	2x4

Foundation Options:

Standard basement
Crawlspace
Slab
(All plans can be built with your choice of foundation and framing. A generic conversion diagram is available. See order form.)

BLUEPRINT PRICE CODE: A

VIEW INTO BREAKFAST ROOM

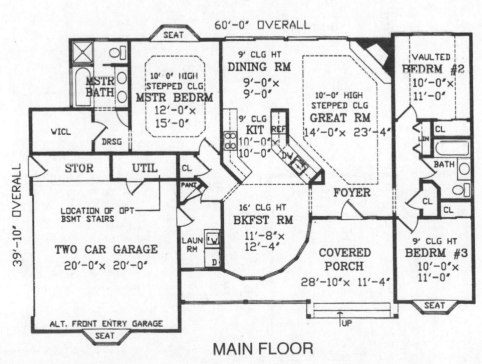

MAIN FLOOR

Fantastic Patio Home

- This design gives you a choice of three different exterior treatments, allowing you to create a home that blends with its surroundings. The blueprints include details for finishing the exterior with stucco (shown), brick or wood siding.
- The interior is geared for indoor/outdoor living, with all of the main rooms featuring lots of glass and views to the secluded patio.
- Tall windows flank the fireplace in the living room, and a French door opens to the large patio. The dining room has a large picture window viewing out to the patio and backyard. Vaulted ceilings further enhance the bright, airy look of the open living and dining rooms.
- The bayed breakfast room is a natural extension of the kitchen and has a French door to the patio. Note the handy laundry closet in the kitchen and the easy access to the garage.
- The master bedroom suite enjoys a quiet corner of the house, with private access to the patio. The fantastic master bath, entered through double doors, includes a vaulted ceiling, a garden tub and a separate shower.

PATIO

MASTER BEDROOM 16X12

LIVING 17X14

BREAKFAST

DINING 10X10

KITCHEN 10x9

D W

VAULTED CEILING

VAULTED CEILING

LINEN

BEDROOM 3 STUDY 10X11

BEDROOM 2 11X12

GARAGE 22 x20

55

43

MAIN FLOOR

Plan APS-1404	
Bedrooms: 2-3	Baths: 2
Space:	
Main floor	1,477 sq. ft.
Total Living Area	**1,477 sq. ft.**
Garage	440 sq. ft.
Exterior Wall Framing	2x4
Foundation options:	
Slab	
(Foundation & framing conversion diagram available—see order form.)	
Blueprint Price Code	A

TO ORDER THIS BLUEPRINT, CALL TOLL-FREE 1-800-820-1283

Plan APS-1404

PRICES AND DETAILS ON PAGES 12-15

Refined One-Story

- A symmetrical roofline and a stucco facade with corner quoins and keystone accents add a refined look to this elegant one-story.
- The eye-catching entry leads into a surprisingly spacious interior, beginning with a family room that features an 11-ft., 8-in.-high ceiling and a handsome window-flanked fireplace.
- The kitchen showcases an angled serving bar that faces the sunny breakfast room. A French door between the breakfast room and the formal dining room opens to a covered patio for more dining and entertaining space.
- The fantastic master suite features an elegant 10-ft. tray ceiling. The superb private bath boasts a 13-ft. vaulted ceiling, an overhead plant shelf, a garden tub and a walk-in closet.
- The two front-facing bedrooms share a hall bath that includes a vanity with knee space.

Plan FB-1531

Bedrooms: 3	Baths: 2

Living Area:

Main floor	1,531 sq. ft.
Total Living Area:	**1,531 sq. ft.**
Garage	440 sq. ft.
Exterior Wall Framing:	2x4

Foundation Options:

Crawlspace

Slab

(All plans can be built with your choice of foundation and framing. A generic conversion diagram is available. See order form.)

BLUEPRINT PRICE CODE: B

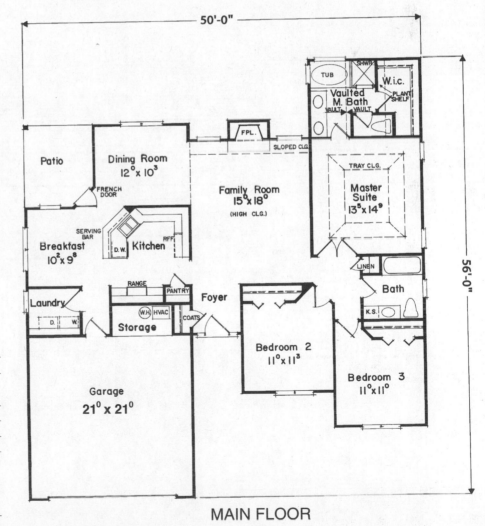

MAIN FLOOR

Solarium Adds Extra Touch of Luxury

PLAN P-6560-4A
WITHOUT BASEMENT
(CRAWLSPACE FOUNDATION)

Main floor: 1,399 sq. ft.
Solarium: 148 sq. ft.

Total living area: 1,547 sq. ft.
(Not counting garage)

TO ORDER THIS BLUEPRINT,
CALL TOLL-FREE 1-800-820-1283

Blueprint Price Code B
Plan P-6560-4A

PRICES AND DETAILS
ON PAGES 12-15

Universal Appeal

- As they observe its elegant window treatments and timeless brick exterior, passersby and guests will marvel at this appealing home.
- The central Great Room will be a surefire hit with young and old alike. For adult gatherings, there is plenty of room to mingle and converse. And what child wouldn't love to sneak an hors d'oeuvre from the breakfast bar and set up camp in front of the crackling fireplace?
- School lunches may be prepared more efficiently on the kitchen's island. Keep your snacks and sandwich bags in the handy pantry!
- If the outdoors calls to you on spring mornings, skip the bayed dining area and enjoy your tea and toast on the shaded backyard patio.
- Privacy and pampering are foremost in the master bedroom, with patio access a quick step away. In the master bath, an eye-pleasing plant shelf overlooks dual walk-in closets and twin vanities with knee space for the woman of the house.

Plan KD-1549

Bedrooms: 3	Baths: 2
Living Area:	
Main floor	1,549 sq. ft.
Total Living Area:	**1,549 sq. ft.**
Garage and storage	472 sq. ft.
Exterior Wall Framing:	2x4

Foundation Options:

Slab
(All plans can be built with your choice of foundation and framing. A generic conversion diagram is available. See order form.)

BLUEPRINT PRICE CODE: B

MAIN FLOOR

One-Story with Impact

- Striking gables, a brick facade and an elegant sidelighted entry give this one-story plenty of impact.
- The impressive interior spaces begin with an 11-ft., 8-in. raised ceiling in the foyer. To the left of the foyer, decorative columns and a large picture window grace the dining room.
- The wonderful living spaces center around a huge family room, which features a 14-ft.-high vaulted ceiling and another pair of columns that separate it from the hall. A stunning fireplace is framed by a window and a beautiful French door.
- The open kitchen and breakfast area features a built-in desk, a pantry closet and a pass-through above the sink.
- An elegant 10-ft. tray ceiling is featured in the master suite, which also boasts a 13-ft. vaulted bath with a garden spa tub, a separate shower, a big walk-in closet and an attractive plant shelf.

Plan FB-1553

Bedrooms: 3	Baths: 2
Living Area:	
Main floor	1,553 sq. ft.
Total Living Area:	**1,553 sq. ft.**
Daylight basement	1,553 sq. ft.
Garage	410 sq. ft.
Exterior Wall Framing:	2x4

Foundation Options:

Daylight basement
Crawlspace
Slab

(All plans can be built with your choice of foundation and framing. A generic conversion diagram is available. See order form.)

BLUEPRINT PRICE CODE: B

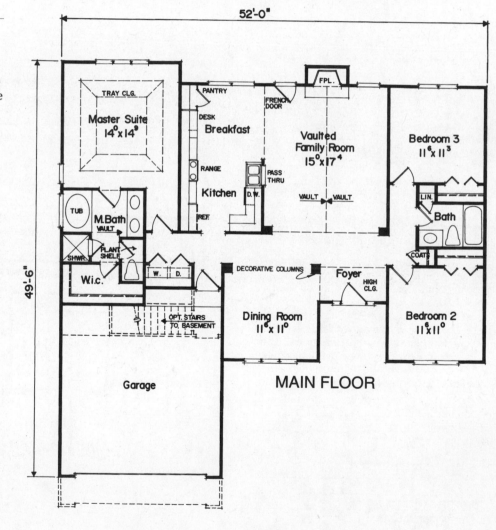

MAIN FLOOR

Plan FB-1553

PRICES AND DETAILS ON PAGES 12-15

Country Highlights

- This nice home has country highlights, with shuttered windows, lap siding and a quaint covered porch.
- The foyer flows into the spacious living room, which offers a 9-ft.-high ceiling, a warm fireplace and tall windows that give views to the front porch. French doors open from the adjoining dining room to a backyard terrace.
- The kitchen features a sunny dinette that accesses the terrace, plus an angled pass-through to the dining room. A nifty mudroom with laundry facilities accesses the garage and the terrace.
- The master bedroom boasts a large walk-in closet and a private bath with a dual-sink vanity, a whirlpool tub and a separate shower.
- Across the home, two secondary bedrooms share another full bath.
- Dormered windows brighten the unfinished upper floor, which provides for future expansion possibilities.

Plan HFL-1700-SR

Bedrooms: 3+	Baths: 2
Living Area:	
Main floor	1,567 sq. ft.
Total Living Area:	**1,567 sq. ft.**
Upper floor (unfinished)	338 sq. ft.
Standard basement	1,567 sq. ft.
Garage	504 sq. ft.
Exterior Wall Framing:	2x6
Foundation Options:	

Standard basement

Slab

(All plans can be built with your choice of foundation and framing. A generic conversion diagram is available. See order form.)

BLUEPRINT PRICE CODE:	B

VIEW INTO LIVING ROOM

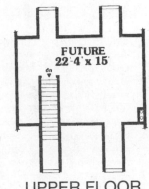

UPPER FLOOR

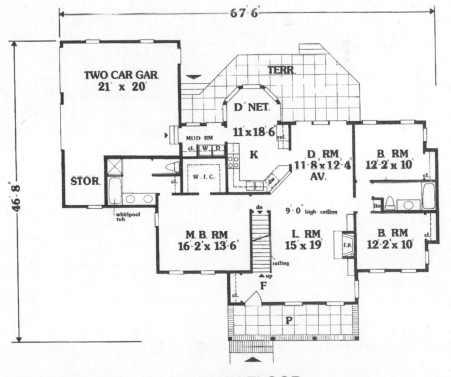

MAIN FLOOR

Elegant Touch

- A stunning exterior of brick, siding and copper flashing adds an elegant touch to this feature-filled one-story home.
- The recessed sidelighted entry opens directly into the bright and airy family room, which boasts a 12-ft. ceiling and a striking window-flanked fireplace.
- The adjacent formal dining room features a 9-ft. tray ceiling and includes a French door to a backyard patio.
- Designed with the gourmet in mind, the spacious kitchen offers a pantry, an angled eating bar and a sunny breakfast area. A French door accesses a covered back porch.
- Enhanced by a 14-ft. vaulted ceiling and decorative plant shelves, the master suite unfolds to a sitting area and a roomy walk-in closet. The vaulted master bath showcases a garden tub, a separate shower and a functional dual-sink vanity with knee space.
- On the opposite side of the home, two additional bedrooms are serviced by a second full bath.
- A laundry room is conveniently located between the entry and the garage.

Plan APS-1516

Bedrooms: 3	Baths: 2
Living Area:	
Main floor	1,593 sq. ft.
Total Living Area:	**1,593 sq. ft.**
Garage	482 sq. ft.
Exterior Wall Framing:	2x4

Foundation Options:
Slab
(All plans can be built with your choice of foundation and framing. A generic conversion diagram is available. See order form.)

BLUEPRINT PRICE CODE:	**B**

MAIN FLOOR

Plan APS-1516

PRICES AND DETAILS ON PAGES 12-15

Stately but Affordable

- Stately columns set off transom windows and support an inviting porch in this well-planned design.
- French doors give classic charm to the central Great Room, which boasts a large fireplace.
- The formal dining room features access to a covered rear porch.

- The unique kitchen arrangement offers a bright, bayed breakfast nook. The peninsula counter allows the cook to view the outdoors while preparing meals or cleaning up.
- A perfect master suite is positioned for peace and quiet. It boasts backyard views, a walk-in closet and a private bath with a garden tub, a separate shower and a dual-sink vanity.
- The two remaining bedrooms feature porch views and walk-in closets, and share a compartmentalized bath.

Plan V-1595	
Bedrooms: 3	**Baths:** 2
Living Area:	
Main floor	1,595 sq. ft.
Total Living Area:	**1,595 sq. ft.**
Garage	473 sq. ft.
Exterior Wall Framing:	2x6

Foundation Options:

Crawlspace
(All plans can be built with your choice of foundation and framing. A generic conversion diagram is available. See order form.)

BLUEPRINT PRICE CODE:	**B**

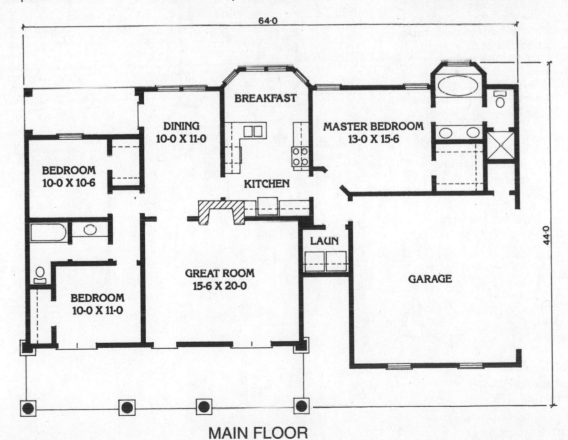

MAIN FLOOR

TO ORDER THIS BLUEPRINT,
CALL TOLL-FREE 1-800-820-1283

Plan V-1595

PRICES AND DETAILS
ON PAGES 12-15

149

Delightful Backyard Views

- This home embraces easy living with its huge backyard deck, which may be accessed from three areas of the home.
- The sidelighted entry opens to the spacious vaulted living room, where a fireplace is centered between windows.
- The adjoining dining room is adorned with decorative columns, and sliding glass doors access the expansive deck.
- The angled kitchen has a corner sink, plenty of counter space and a sunny breakfast nook that opens to the deck.
- The vaulted master suite boasts a bright sitting area with private deck access. The skylighted master bath features a large walk-in closet, a dual-sink vanity, a spa tub and a private toilet.
- Another full bath serves the two additional bedrooms. One of the bedrooms could serve as a den and boasts a high-ceilinged area that showcases a half-round transom.
- A two-car garage and a bright laundry room round out the floor plan.

Plan B-87127

Bedrooms: 2+	Baths: 2
Living Area:	
Main floor	1,630 sq. ft.
Total Living Area:	**1,630 sq. ft.**
Standard basement	1,630 sq. ft.
Garage	448 sq. ft.
Exterior Wall Framing:	2x4

Foundation Options:

Standard basement

(All plans can be built with your choice of foundation and framing. A generic conversion diagram is available. See order form.)

BLUEPRINT PRICE CODE: B

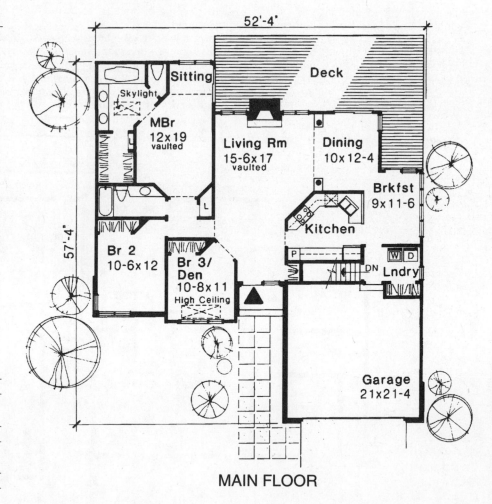

MAIN FLOOR

Plan B-87127

PRICES AND DETAILS ON PAGES 12-15

Luxurious Master Suite

- A classic brick finish and ornate window accents add to the exterior beauty of this impressive home.
- The vaulted foyer leads immediately into the formal dining room, accented by decorative columns and plant shelves, plus a dramatic window wall.
- The expansive, vaulted Great Room features a built-in cabinet, a fireplace and dual doors to the backyard.
- The kitchen offers a serving bar, a bayed breakfast room, a full pantry and a handy pass-through window to the Great Room.
- The secluded master suite boasts an ornate tray ceiling, a walk-in closet and a vaulted bath with a corner garden tub, a plant shelf and a dual-sink vanity with knee space.
- Two additional bedrooms, one with a vaulted ceiling, share a full bath.

Plan FB-5021-TORO

Bedrooms: 3	Baths: 2
Living Area:	
Main floor	1,630 sq. ft.
Total Living Area:	**1,630 sq. ft.**
Daylight basement	1,630 sq. ft.
Garage	395 sq. ft.
Exterior Wall Framing:	2x4

Foundation Options:
Daylight basement
Crawlspace
Slab
(Typical foundation & framing conversion diagram available–see order form.)

BLUEPRINT PRICE CODE:	B

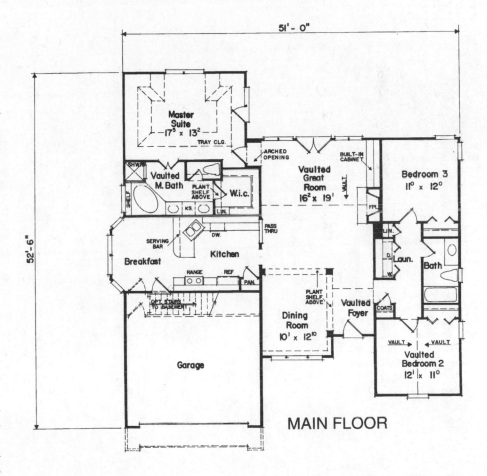

MAIN FLOOR

*TO ORDER THIS BLUEPRINT,
CALL TOLL-FREE 1-800-820-1283*

Plan FB-5021-TORO

*PRICES AND DETAILS
ON PAGES 12-15*

151

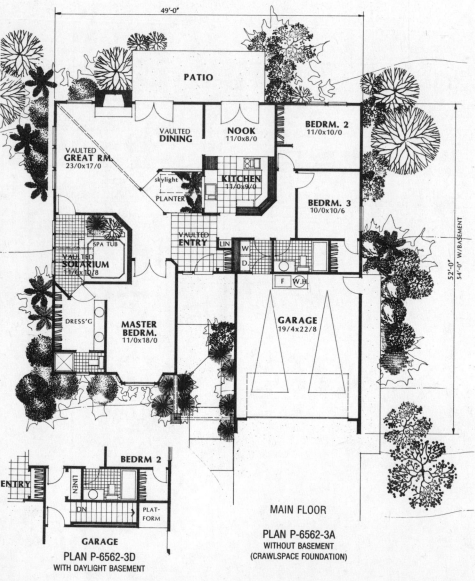

PATIO

VAULTED
DINING

NOOK
11/0x8/0

BEDRM. 2
11/0x10/0

VAULTED
GREAT RM.
23/0x17/0

skylight

PLANTER

KITCHEN
11/0x9/0

BEDRM. 3
10/0x10/6

VAULTED
ENTRY

LIN

W D

SPA TUB

VAULTED
SOLARIUM
11/0x10/8

DRESS'G

MASTER
BEDRM.
11/0x18/0

GARAGE
19/4x22/8

F W.H

49'-0"

52'-0"
54'-0" W/BASEMENT

ENTRY

LINEN

BEDRM 2

DN

PLAT-
FORM

GARAGE

PLAN P-6562-3D
WITH DAYLIGHT BASEMENT

MAIN FLOOR

PLAN P-6562-3A
WITHOUT BASEMENT
(CRAWLSPACE FOUNDATION)

Master Suite Adjoins Spa Solarium

- This elegant mid-sized design includes all the amenities needed for gracious living.
- Especially note the luxurious spa tub located in the solarium conveniently between the master suite and the Great Room.
- The large, vaulted Great Room and dining room combine to create plenty of space for entertaining and family living alike.

Plans P-6562-3A & P-6562-3D	
Bedrooms: 3	**Baths:** 2

Space:

Main floor (non-basement version):	1,639 sq. ft.
Main floor (basement version):	1,699 sq. ft.
(Both figures include 123 sq. ft. solarium.)	
Basement:	1,699 sq. ft.
Garage:	438 sq. ft.

Exterior Wall Framing:	2x4

Foundation options:
Daylight basement (P-6562-3D).
Crawlspace (P-6562-3A).
(Foundation & framing conversion diagram available — see order form.)

Blueprint Price Code:	B

TO ORDER THIS BLUEPRINT,
CALL TOLL-FREE 1-800-820-1283

Plans P-6562-3A & -3D

PRICES AND DETAILS
ON PAGES 12-15

Fine Dining

- This fine stucco home showcases a huge round-top window arrangement, which augments the central dining room with its 14½-ft. ceiling.
- A cute covered porch opens to the bright foyer, where a 13-ft.-high ceiling extends past a decorative column to the airy Great Room.
- The sunny dining room merges with the Great Room, which features a warm

fireplace, a kitchen pass-through and a French door to the backyard.
- The kitchen boasts a pantry closet, a nice serving bar and an angled sink. The vaulted breakfast nook with an optional bay hosts casual meals.
- The secluded master suite has a tray ceiling and a vaulted bath with a dual-sink vanity, a large garden tub and a separate shower. Across the home, two secondary bedrooms share another full bath.

Plan FB-5351-GENE

Bedrooms: 3	Baths: 2
Living Area:	
Main floor	1,670 sq. ft.
Total Living Area:	**1,670 sq. ft.**
Daylight basement	1,670 sq. ft.
Garage	400 sq. ft.
Exterior Wall Framing:	2x4

Foundation Options:

Daylight basement
Crawlspace
(All plans can be built with your choice of foundation and framing. A generic conversion diagram is available. See order form.)

BLUEPRINT PRICE CODE:	B

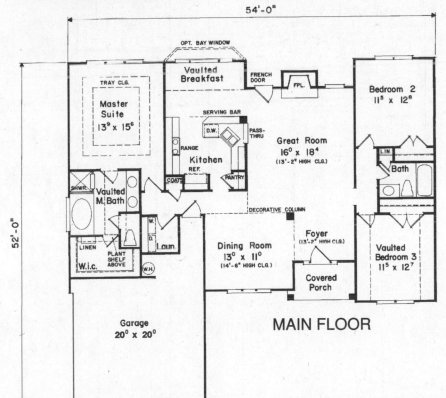

MAIN FLOOR

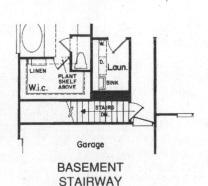

BASEMENT STAIRWAY LOCATION

Smashing Master Suite!

- Corniced gables accented with arched louvers and a covered front porch with striking columns take this one-story design beyond the ordinary.
- The vaulted ceiling in the foyer rises to join the 19-ft. vaulted ceiling in the family room. A central fireplace heats the casual areas and is framed by a window and a French door.
- An angled serving bar/snack counter connects the family room to the sunny dining room and kitchen. The adjoining breakfast room has easy access to the garage, the optional basement and the laundry room with a plant shelf.
- The master suite is simply smashing, with a 10-ft. tray ceiling and private access to the backyard. The master bath has an 11½-ft. vaulted ceiling and all the amenities, while the 13-ft.-high vaulted sitting area offers an optional fireplace.

Plan FB-1671

Bedrooms: 3	Baths: 2

Living Area:	
Main floor	1,671 sq. ft.
Total Living Area:	**1,671 sq. ft.**
Daylight basement	1,671 sq. ft.
Garage	240 sq. ft.
Exterior Wall Framing:	2x4

Foundation Options:

Daylight basement
Crawlspace

(All plans can be built with your choice of foundation and framing. A generic conversion diagram is available. See order form.)

BLUEPRINT PRICE CODE: B

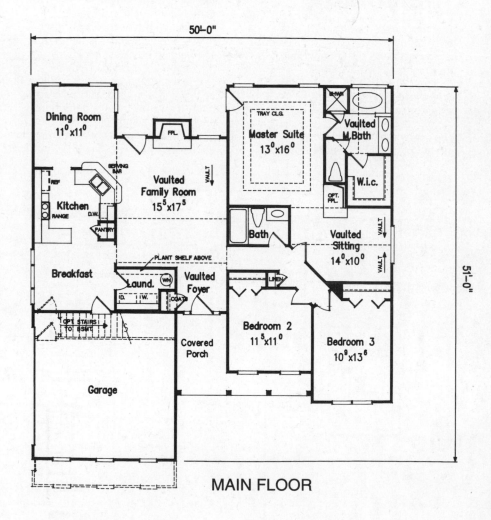

MAIN FLOOR

Plan FB-1671

PRICES AND DETAILS ON PAGES 12-15

Shady Porches, Sunny Patio

- Designed with stylish country looks, this attractive one-story also has shady porches and a sunny patio for relaxed indoor/outdoor living.
- The inviting foyer flows into the spacious living room, which is warmed by a handsome fireplace.
- The adjoining dining room has a door to a screened-in porch, which opens to the

backyard and serves as a breezeway to the nearby garage
- The U-shaped kitchen has a pantry closet and plenty of counter space. Around the corner, a space-efficient laundry/utility room exits to a big backyard patio.
- The master bedroom is brightened by windows on two sides and includes a wardrobe closet. The compartment-alized master bath offers a separate dressing area and a walk-in closet.
- Another full bath serves two additional good-sized bedrooms.

Plan C-7557	
Bedrooms: 3	**Baths:** 2
Living Area:	
Main floor	1,688 sq. ft.
Total Living Area:	**1,688 sq. ft.**
Standard basement	1,688 sq. ft.
Garage	400 sq. ft.
Exterior Wall Framing:	2x4
Foundation Options:	
Standard basement	
Crawlspace	
Slab	

(All plans can be built with your choice of foundation and framing. A generic conversion diagram is available. See order form.)

BLUEPRINT PRICE CODE: B

PATIO
18-0 x 10-0

GARAGE
20-0 x 20-0

SCREENED PORCH
12-0 x 20-6

DINING ROOM
12-0 x 13-4

KITCHEN
10 x 13

UTILITY

D
W

BEDROOM
11-0 x 13-4

CLOSET

CLOSET

DRESS

BATH

CLOSET

PAN

LIVING ROOM
15-6 x 17-8

DOWN

CLOSET

BEDROOM
12-0 x 18-0

LINEN

COAT

BEDROOM
12-0 x 11-4

DRESSING

BATH

FOYER

PORCH
26 x 6

32-0

88-8

MAIN FLOOR

Large, Stylish Spaces

• This stylish brick home greets guests with a beautiful entry court that leads to the recessed front porch.

• Beyond the porch, the bright entry flows into the Great Room, which features an 11-ft. sloped ceiling. This airy space also offers a fireplace, a sunny dining area and sliding glass doors to a backyard patio.

• The kitchen has a walk-in pantry, an open serving counter above the sink and convenient access to the laundry facilities and the garage.

• Isolated from the secondary bedrooms, the master suite boasts a 9-ft. tray ceiling, an oversized walk-in closet and an exquisite bath with two distinct sink areas, a corner garden tub and a separate shower.

• The third bedroom, which features lovely double doors and a front-facing bay window, would also make a perfect home office.

Plan SDG-91188

Bedrooms: 2+	Baths: 2
Living Area:	
Main floor	1,704 sq. ft.
Total Living Area:	**1,704 sq. ft.**
Garage	484 sq. ft.
Exterior Wall Framing:	2x4

Foundation Options:

Slab
(All plans can be built with your choice of foundation and framing. A generic conversion diagram is available. See order form.)

BLUEPRINT PRICE CODE: B

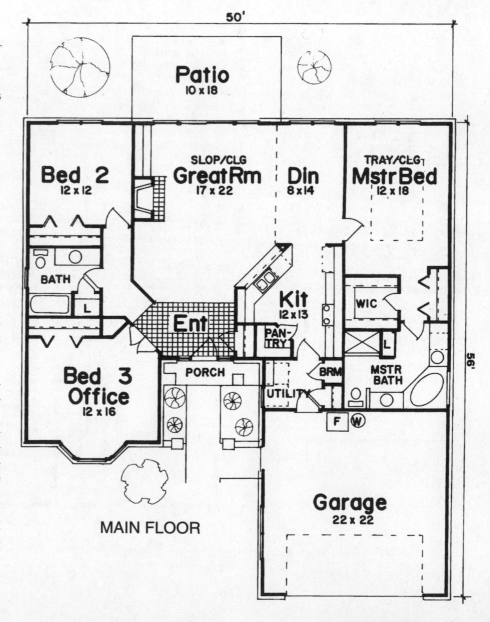

MAIN FLOOR

Plan SDG-91188

French Charm

- The exterior of this charming French home displays great details, including attractive keystones, neat quoins and huge arched window arrangements.
- Inside the home, a high plant ledge adorns the tiled foyer, which boasts a dramatic 13-ft. ceiling.
- To the left, the elegant formal dining room extends to the huge living room, which boasts a warm fireplace and neat built-in bookshelves above functional cabinets. A striking 10-ft. ceiling soars above both rooms.
- A convenient serving bar links the gourmet kitchen to the sunny bayed breakfast nook. The adjacent utility room includes a handy pantry closet.
- Across the home, a tiled foyer features access to a covered porch and the luxurious master suite. The master suite boasts a sloped 10-ft. ceiling, a window seat and a lush private bath, which is highlighted by a marble tub set into a boxed-out window.
- Two more bedrooms share a hall bath. One bedroom features a sloped 10-ft. ceiling and a nice built-in desk.

Plan RD-1714

Bedrooms: 3	Baths: 2
Living Area:	
Main floor	1,714 sq. ft.
Total Living Area:	**1,714 sq. ft.**
Garage and storage	470 sq. ft.
Exterior Wall Framing:	2x4

Foundation Options:

Crawlspace

Slab

(All plans can be built with your choice of foundation and framing. A generic conversion diagram is available. See order form.)

BLUEPRINT PRICE CODE: B

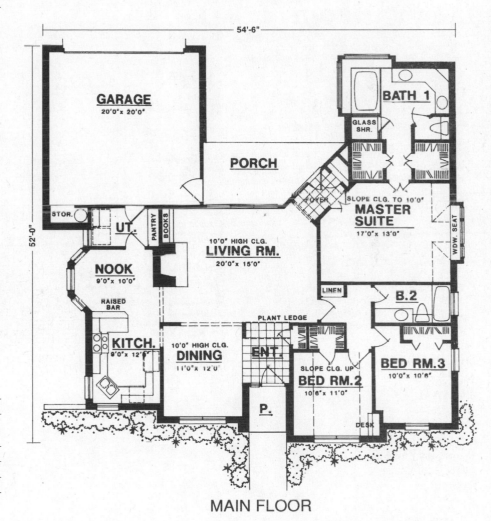

MAIN FLOOR

TO ORDER THIS BLUEPRINT,
CALL TOLL-FREE 1-800-820-1283

Plan RD-1714

PRICES AND DETAILS
ON PAGES 12-15

157

Dramatic Dining Room

- The highlight of this lovely one-story design is its dramatic dining room, which boasts a 14-ft.-high ceiling and a soaring window wall.
- The airy foyer ushers guests through a 14-ft.-high arched opening and into the 18-ft. vaulted Great Room, which is warmed by an inviting fireplace.
- The kitchen features a large pantry, a serving bar and a handy pass-through to the Great Room. The bright breakfast area offers a convenient laundry closet and outdoor access.
- The two secondary bedrooms share a compartmentalized bath.
- The removed master suite features a 14-ft. tray ceiling, overhead plant shelves and an adjoining 13½-ft. vaulted sitting room. An exciting garden tub is found in the luxurious master bath.

Plan FB-5008-ALLE

Bedrooms: 3	Baths: 2
Living Area:	
Main floor	1,715 sq. ft.
Total Living Area:	**1,715 sq. ft.**
Daylight basement	1,715 sq. ft.
Garage	400 sq. ft.
Exterior Wall Framing:	2x4

Foundation Options:

Daylight basement

Crawlspace

Slab

(All plans can be built with your choice of foundation and framing. A generic conversion diagram is available. See order form.)

BLUEPRINT PRICE CODE: B

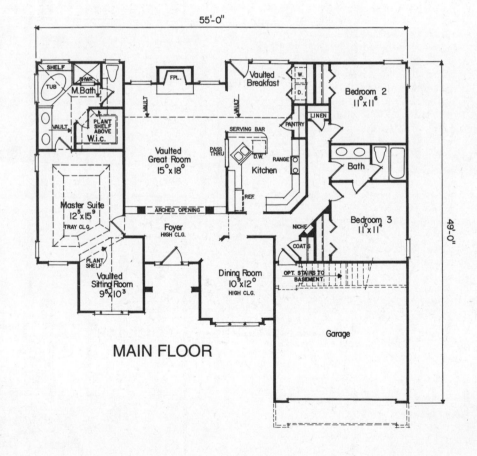

MAIN FLOOR

Plan FB-5008-ALLE

PRICES AND DETAILS ON PAGES 12-15

One-Story Design Features
Deluxe Master Bedroom and Bath

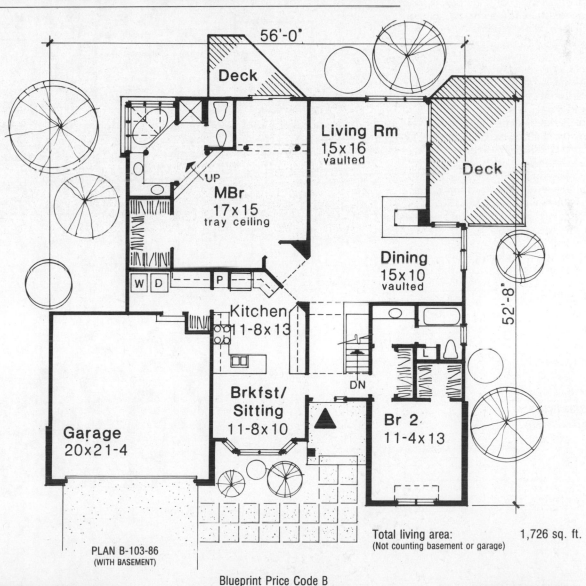

56'-0"

Deck

Living Rm
15 x 16
vaulted

Deck

UP

MBr
17 x 15
tray ceiling

Dining
15 x 10
vaulted

W D   P

Kitchen
11-8 x 13

DN

Brkfst/
Sitting
11-8 x 10

Br 2
11-4 x 13

Garage
20 x 21-4

52'-8"

PLAN B-103-86
(WITH BASEMENT)

Total living area: 1,726 sq. ft.
(Not counting basement or garage)

TO ORDER THIS BLUEPRINT,
CALL TOLL-FREE 1-800-820-1283

Blueprint Price Code B
Plan B-103-86

PRICES AND DETAILS
ON PAGES 12-15

159

Enticing Interior

- Filled with elegant features, this modern country home's exciting floor plan is as impressive as it is innovative.
- Past the inviting columned porch, the entrance gallery flows into the spacious living room/dining room area.
- Boasting a 14-ft.-high sloped ceiling, the living room is enhanced by a semi-circular window bay and includes a handsome fireplace. The adjoining dining room offers sliding glass doors to a backyard terrace.
- The skylighted kitchen features an eating bar that serves the sunny bayed dinette. A convenient half-bath and a laundry/mudroom are nearby.
- Brightened by a bay window, the luxurious master bedroom shows off his-and-hers walk-in closets. The master bath showcases a whirlpool garden tub under a glass sunroof.
- Two additional bedrooms share a skylighted hallway bath.

Plan K-685-DA

Bedrooms: 3	**Baths:** 2½
Living Area:	
Main floor	1,760 sq. ft.
Total Living Area:	**1,760 sq. ft.**
Standard basement	1,700 sq. ft.
Garage	482 sq. ft.
Exterior Wall Framing:	2x4 or 2x6

Foundation Options:

Standard basement
Slab
(All plans can be built with your choice of foundation and framing. A generic conversion diagram is available. See order form.)

BLUEPRINT PRICE CODE:	**B**

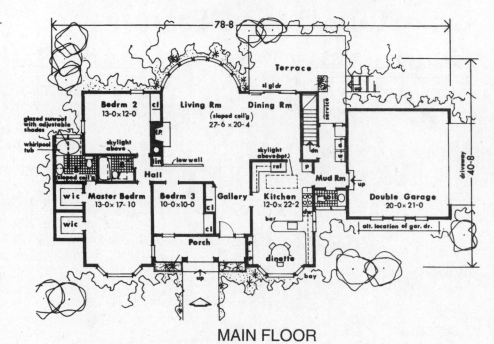

MAIN FLOOR

VIEW INTO LIVING AND DINING ROOMS

TO ORDER THIS BLUEPRINT, CALL TOLL-FREE 1-800-820-1283 Plan K-685-DA *PRICES AND DETAILS ON PAGES 12-15*

Charming Traditional

- The attractive facade of this traditional home features decorative fretwork and louvers in the gables, plus eye-catching window and door treatments.
- The entry area features a commanding view of the living room, which boasts a 12½-ft. ceiling and a corner fireplace. A rear porch and patio are visible through French doors.
- The bayed dining room shares an eating bar with the U-shaped kitchen. The nearby utility room includes a pantry and laundry facilities.
- The quiet master suite includes a big walk-in closet and a private bath with a dual-sink vanity.
- On the other side of the home, double doors close off the two secondary bedrooms from the living areas. A full bath services this wing.

Plan E-1428

Bedrooms: 3	Baths: 2
Living Area:	
Main floor	1,415 sq. ft.
Total Living Area:	**1,415 sq. ft.**
Garage	484 sq. ft.
Storage	60 sq. ft.
Exterior Wall Framing:	2x6

Foundation Options:

Crawlspace
Slab

(All plans can be built with your choice of foundation and framing. A generic conversion diagram is available. See order form.)

BLUEPRINT PRICE CODE: **A**

MAIN FLOOR

Wide Angles
Add Style

- The comfortably-sized living areas of this gorgeous home are stylishly enhanced by wide, interesting angles.
- Past the covered front porch, the sidelighted front door brightens the living room just ahead.
- The spacious living room is warmed by a dramatic corner fireplace and opens to an angled, covered back porch.
- A stunning bayed dining room merges with the kitchen and its functional angled snack bar. Laundry facilities and access to the garage are nearby.
- The master suite is removed from the secondary bedrooms and features double doors to a deluxe private bath with an angled spa tub, a dual-sink vanity and a large walk-in closet.
- Another full bath serves the two additional bedrooms at the opposite end of the home.

Plan E-1426

Bedrooms: 3	Baths: 2
Living Area:	
Main floor	1,420 sq. ft.
Total Living Area:	**1,420 sq. ft.**
Garage and storage	540 sq. ft.
Exterior Wall Framing:	2x6

Foundation Options:

Crawlspace
Slab
(All plans can be built with your choice of foundation and framing. A generic conversion diagram is available. See order form.)

BLUEPRINT PRICE CODE: **A**

MAIN FLOOR

TO ORDER THIS BLUEPRINT, CALL TOLL-FREE 1-800-820-1283   Plan E-1426   *PRICES AND DETAILS ON PAGES 12-15*

Photo by Mark Englund/HomeStyles

Style and Economy

- This attractive one-story home successfully combines a modest square footage with stylish extras such as vaulted ceilings, a fireplace and a relaxing deck.
- The sidelighted entry opens to the spacious living room, which is brightened by a Palladian window arrangement.
- The living room shares a 15-ft. vaulted ceiling and a high plant shelf with the adjoining dining room. A handsome fireplace adds warmth and ambience to the entire area.
- Sliding glass doors open from the dining room to a good-sized deck, a perfect spot for outdoor meals.
- The efficient galley-style kitchen is open to the dining room for easy serving. A pantry closet is a nice feature.
- The quiet master bedroom boasts an 11-ft. vaulted ceiling and a nice private bath. A second bath serves the other two bedrooms, one of which could function as a den or a home office.

Plan B-87106

Bedrooms: 2+	Baths: 2
Living Area:	
Main floor	1,252 sq. ft.
Total Living Area:	**1,252 sq. ft.**
Standard basement	1,252 sq. ft.
Garage	400 sq. ft.
Exterior Wall Framing:	2x4

Foundation Options:

Standard basement

(All plans can be built with your choice of foundation and framing. A generic conversion diagram is available. See order form.)

BLUEPRINT PRICE CODE:	**A**

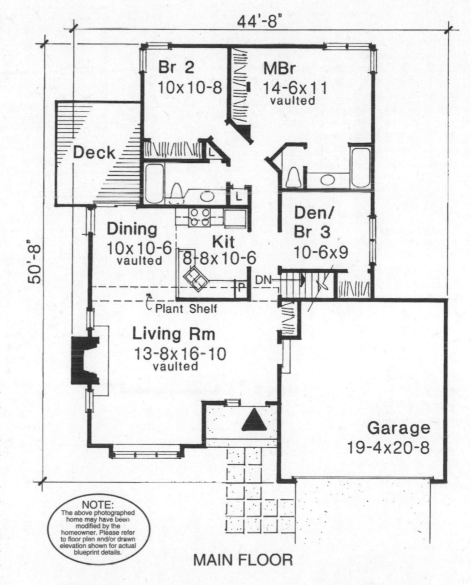

MAIN FLOOR

TO ORDER THIS BLUEPRINT,
CALL TOLL-FREE 1-800-820-1283

Plan B-87106

PRICES AND DETAILS
ON PAGES 12-15

163

Garden Home

- This thoroughly modern plan exhibits beautiful traditional touches in its exterior design.
- A garden area leads visitors to a side door with a vaulted entry.
- A delightful kitchen/nook area is just to the right of the entry, and includes a convenient snack bar, a pantry and a nearby laundry room. The bayed breakfast nook overlooks the front yard.
- The living and dining areas share a 12½-ft.-high vaulted ceiling, making an impressive space for entertaining and family living. The stone fireplace and patio view add to the dramatic atmosphere.
- The master suite boasts a large closet and a private bath.
- Two more bedrooms share another bath off the hall.

Plans P-6598-2A & -2D

Bedrooms: 3	Baths: 2
Living Area:	
Main floor (with crawlspace)	1,375 sq. ft.
Main floor (with basement)	1,470 sq. ft.
Total Living Area:	**1,375/1,470 sq. ft.**
Daylight basement	1,470 sq. ft.
Garage	435 sq. ft.
Exterior Wall Framing:	2x4
Foundation Options:	**Plan #**
Daylight basement	P-6598-2D
Crawlspace	P-6598-2A

(All plans can be built with your choice of foundation and framing. A generic conversion diagram is available. See order form.)

BLUEPRINT PRICE CODE: A

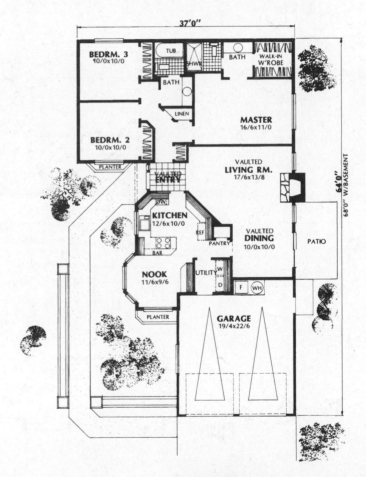

MAIN FLOOR

BASEMENT STAIRWAY LOCATION

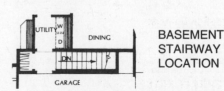

Sleek One-Story

- Steep, sleek rooflines and a trio of French doors with half-round transoms give this one-story a look of distinction.
- The covered front porch opens to the spacious living room, where a central fireplace cleverly incorporates a wet bar, bookshelves and a coat closet.
- Behind the fireplace, the adjoining dining room offers views to the backyard through an arched window arrangement. The two rooms are expanded by 11-ft. ceilings and a covered back porch.
- A snack bar connects the dining room to the U-shaped kitchen, which offers a pantry closet and large windows over the sink. Laundry facilities are nearby.
- The secluded master suite features a large walk-in closet and a private bath. Across the home, the secondary bedrooms each have a walk-in closet and share another full bath.

Plan E-1427

Bedrooms: 3	Baths: 2
Living Area:	
Main floor	1,444 sq. ft.
Total Living Area:	**1,444 sq. ft.**
Garage and storage	540 sq. ft.
Exterior Wall Framing:	2x4

Foundation Options:

Crawlspace

Slab

(All plans can be built with your choice of foundation and framing. A generic conversion diagram is available. See order form.)

BLUEPRINT PRICE CODE: A

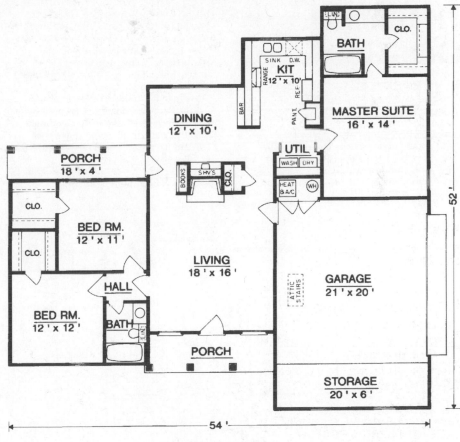

MAIN FLOOR

TO ORDER THIS BLUEPRINT,
CALL TOLL-FREE 1-800-820-1283

Plan E-1427

PRICES AND DETAILS
ON PAGES 12-15

165

Traditional One-Story Cottage

Shuttered windows, covered porch trimmed with Colonial style posts and fascia, small window panes that match the paneling of the garage doors, clapboard siding with corner board trim, and other Colonial touches combine to imbue this cottage with Early American charm.

An attractive and functional entrance hall with convenient closet space acts as a buffer between the casual and formal activity areas. At the rear of the house, the kitchen with dining space has sliding glass doors leading to a rear garden terrace.

Designed for family living, the plan features three bedrooms and two full baths, one of which serves the master bedroom privately. You will also note the master bedroom has an oversized walk-in closet. The central walkway that serves the bedroom wing is flanked on both sides by numerous storage and linen closets. Both bathrooms have built-in vanities.

Another interesting feature is the play room located at the rear of the attached garage. A utility room of generous proportions is also found in both versions of the plan. The plan with a basement provides for a family room that measures 17' x 11'. A convenient access to the garage connects with the hallway leading to the family room. A corner fireplace with a raised hearth opening is featured in both plans.

Overall width of the home measures 60' and the greatest depth including front and rear projections is 40'.

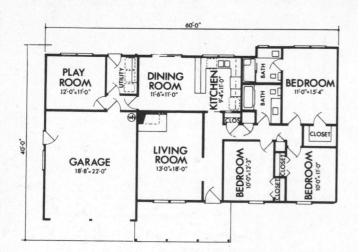

PLAN H-3707-1A
WITHOUT BASEMENT
(CRAWLSPACE FOUNDATION)

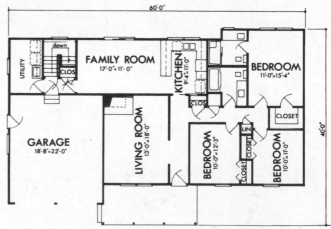

PLAN H-3707-1
WITH BASEMENT

Total living area: 1,486 sq. ft.
(Not counting garage)

Blueprint Price Code A

166   *TO ORDER THIS BLUEPRINT,*
CALL TOLL-FREE 1-800-820-1283   Plans H-3707-1 & -1A   *PRICES AND DETAILS*
ON PAGES 12-15

Rustic Comfort

- Rustic charm highlights the exterior of this design, while the interior is filled with all the latest comforts.
- The wide, covered porch opens to a roomy entry, where two 7-ft.-high openings with decorative railings view into the dining room.
- Straight ahead lies the sunken living room, which features a 16-ft.-high vaulted ceiling with exposed beams. The fireplace is faced with floor-to-ceiling fieldstone, adding to the rustic look. A rear door opens to a large patio with twin plant areas.

- The large U-shaped kitchen has such nice extras as a china niche with glass shelves. Other bonuses include the adjacent sewing/hobby room, the oversized utility room and the storage area and built-in workbench in the side-entry garage.
- The secluded master suite hosts a sunken sleeping area with built-in bookshelves. One step up is a cozy sitting area that is outlined by brick columns and a railed room divider. Double doors open to the deluxe bath, which offers a niche with glass shelves.
- Double doors conceal two more bedrooms and a full bath.

Plan E-1607

Bedrooms: 3	**Baths:** 2

Living Area:

Main floor	1,600 sq. ft.
Total Living Area:	**1,600 sq. ft.**
Standard basement	1,600 sq. ft.
Garage	484 sq. ft.
Storage	132 sq. ft.
Exterior Wall Framing:	2x6

Foundation Options:

Standard basement
Crawlspace
Slab
(All plans can be built with your choice of foundation and framing. A generic conversion diagram is available. See order form.)

BLUEPRINT PRICE CODE: B

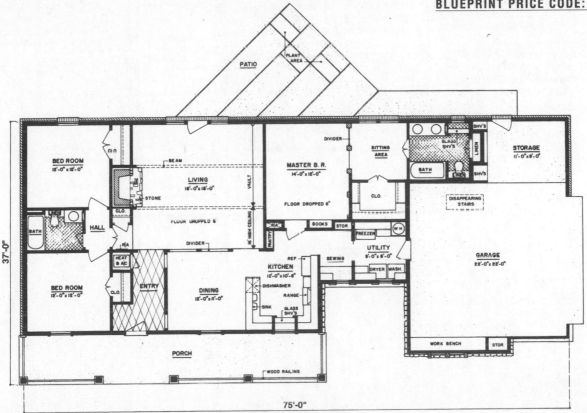

MAIN FLOOR

Luxury in a Small Package

- The elegant exterior of this design sets the tone for the luxurious spaces within.
- The foyer opens to the centrally located living room, which features a 15-ft. cathedral ceiling, a two-way fireplace and access to a lovely rear terrace.
- The unusual kitchen design includes an angled snack bar that lies between the bayed breakfast den and the formal dining room. Sliding glass doors open to another terrace.
- The master suite is a dream come true, with its romantic fireplace, built-in desk and 9-ft.-high tray ceiling. The private bath includes a whirlpool tub and a dual-sink vanity.
- Another full bath serves the remaining two bedrooms, one of which boasts a cathedral ceiling and a tall arched window.

Plan AHP-9300

Bedrooms: 3	Baths: 2
Living Area:	
Main floor	1,513 sq. ft.
Total Living Area:	**1,513 sq. ft.**
Standard basement	1,360 sq. ft.
Garage	400 sq. ft.
Exterior Wall Framing:	2x4 or 2x6

Foundation Options:

Standard basement

Crawlspace

Slab

(All plans can be built with your choice of foundation and framing. A generic conversion diagram is available. See order form.)

BLUEPRINT PRICE CODE:	B

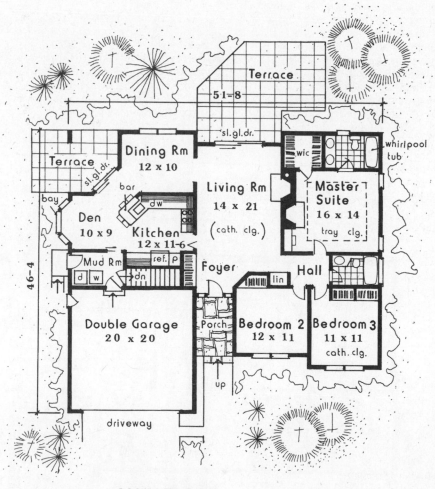

MAIN FLOOR

Plan AHP-9300

PRICES AND DETAILS ON PAGES 12-15

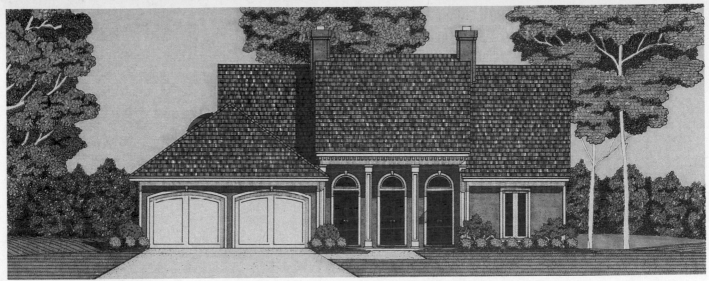

Distinctive and Elegant

- A distinctive look is captured in the exterior of this elegant one-story. Half-round transoms grace the three glass doors that open to the columned, covered front porch.

- The spacious living room at the center of the homer commands attention, with its 15-ft. ceiling and inviting fireplace. A glass door flanked by windows opens to a skylighted porch, which is also accessible from the secondary bedroom at the back of the home.

- The unique dining room overlooks the two backyard porches and boasts an elegant octagonal design, shaped by columns and cased openings.

- A 14-ft. sloped, skylighted ceiling adds drama to the gourmet kitchen, which also showcases an angled cooktop bar and a windowed sink. Laundry facilities and storage space are nearby.

- The luxurious master suite is secluded at the rear of the home, with private access to the porch. The sumptuous master bath features an oval spa tub, a separate shower, dual vanities and a huge walk-in closet.

Plan E-1628

Bedrooms: 3	Baths: 2
Living Area:	
Main floor	1,655 sq. ft.
Total Living Area:	**1,655 sq. ft.**
Garage and storage	549 sq. ft.
Exterior Wall Framing:	2x6

Foundation Options:

Crawlspace

Slab

(All plans can be built with your choice of foundation and framing. A generic conversion diagram is available. See order form.)

BLUEPRINT PRICE CODE: B

MAIN FLOOR

Free-Flowing Floor Plan

- A fluid floor plan with open indoor/outdoor living spaces characterizes this exciting luxury home.
- The stylish columned porch opens to a spacious living room and dining room expanse that overlooks the outdoor spaces. The breathtaking view also includes a dramatic corner fireplace.
- The dining area opens to a bright kitchen with an angled eating bar. The overall spaciousness of the living areas is increased with high 12-ft. ceilings.
- A sunny, informal eating area adjoins the kitchen, and an angled set of doors opens to a convenient main-floor laundry room near the garage entrance.
- The vaulted master bedroom has a walk-in closet and a sumptuous bath with an oval tub.
- A separate wing houses two additional bedrooms and another full bath.
- Attic space is accessible from stairs in the garage and in the bedroom wing.

REAR VIEW

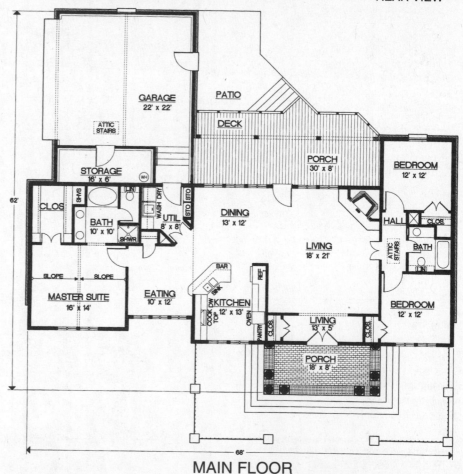

MAIN FLOOR

Plan E-1710

Bedrooms: 3	Baths: 2
Living Area:	
Main floor	1,792 sq. ft.
Total Living Area:	**1,792 sq. ft.**
Standard basement	1,792 sq. ft.
Garage	484 sq. ft.
Storage	96 sq. ft.
Exterior Wall Framing:	2x6

Foundation Options:

Standard basement
Crawlspace
Slab

(All plans can be built with your choice of foundation and framing. A generic conversion diagram is available. See order form.)

BLUEPRINT PRICE CODE:	B

TO ORDER THIS BLUEPRINT, CALL TOLL-FREE 1-800-820-1283

Plan E-1710

PRICES AND DETAILS ON PAGES 12-15

Extra Sparkle

- A lovely front porch with a cameo front door, decorative posts, bay windows and dormers give this country-style home extra sparkle.
- The Great Room is at the center of the floor plan, where it merges with the dining room and the screened porch. The Great Room features a 10-ft. tray ceiling, a fireplace, a built-in wet bar and a wall of windows to the patio.
- The eat-in kitchen has a half-wall that keeps it open to the Great Room and hallway. The dining room offers a half-wall facing the foyer and a bay window overlooking the front porch.
- The delectable master suite is isolated from the other bedrooms and includes a charming bay window, a 10-ft. tray ceiling and a luxurious private bath.
- The two smaller bedrooms are off the main foyer and separated by a full bath.
- A mudroom with a washer and dryer is accessible from the two-car garage.

Plan AX-91312

Bedrooms: 3	Baths: 2
Space:	
Main floor	1,595 sq. ft.
Total Living Area	**1,595 sq. ft.**
Screened Porch	178 sq. ft.
Basement	1,595 sq. ft.
Garage, Storage and Utility	508 sq. ft.
Exterior Wall Framing	2x4

Foundation Options:

Daylight basement

Standard basement

Slab

(All plans can be built with your choice of foundation and framing. A generic conversion diagram is available. See order form.)

Blueprint Price Code	B

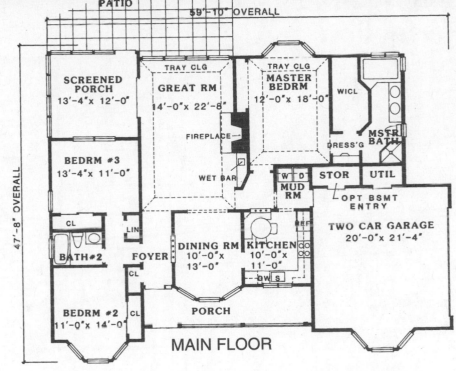

MAIN FLOOR

VIEW INTO GREAT ROOM

Planned to Perfection

- This attractive and stylish home offers an interior design that is planned to perfection.
- The covered entry and vaulted foyer create an impressive welcome.
- The vaulted Great Room features a corner fireplace, a wet bar and lots of windows. The adjoining dining room offers a bay window and access to a covered patio.
- The gourmet kitchen includes an island cooktop, a garden window above the sink and a built-in desk. The attached nook is surrounded by windows that overlook a delightful planter.
- The master suite boasts a tray ceiling that rises to 9½ ft. and a peaceful reading area that accesses a private patio. The superb master bath features a garden tub and a separate shower.
- Two secondary bedrooms share a compartmentalized bath.

Plan S-4789

Bedrooms: 3	Baths: 2
Living Area:	
Main floor	1,665 sq. ft.
Total Living Area:	**1,665 sq. ft.**
Standard basement	1,665 sq. ft.
Garage	400 sq. ft.
Exterior Wall Framing:	2x6

Foundation Options:

Standard basement
Crawlspace
Slab

(All plans can be built with your choice of foundation and framing. A generic conversion diagram is available. See order form.)

BLUEPRINT PRICE CODE:	**B**

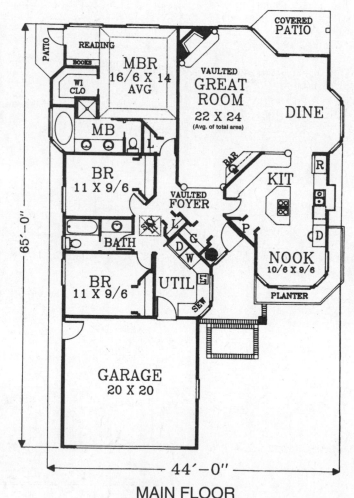

MAIN FLOOR

BASEMENT STAIRWAY LOCATION

Plan S-4789

Classic Country-Style

- At the center of this rustic country-style home is an enormous living room with a flat beamed ceiling, a massive stone fireplace and access to a patio and a covered rear porch.
- The adjoining eating area and kitchen provide plenty of room for casual dining and meal preparation. The eating area is visually enhanced by a 14-ft. sloped ceiling with false beams. The kitchen includes a snack bar, a pantry closet and a built-in spice cabinet.
- The formal dining room gets plenty of pizzazz from the stone-faced wall and arched planter facing the living room.
- The secluded master suite has it all, including a private bath, a separate dressing area and a large walk-in closet with built-in shelves.
- The two remaining bedrooms have big closets and easy access to a full bath.

Plan E-1808	
Bedrooms: 3	**Baths:** 2
Living Area:	
Main floor	1,800 sq. ft.
Total Living Area:	**1,800 sq. ft.**
Garage	605 sq. ft.
Exterior Wall Framing:	2x4
Foundation Options:	
Crawlspace	
Slab	

(All plans can be built with your choice of foundation and framing. A generic conversion diagram is available. See order form.)

BLUEPRINT PRICE CODE:	B

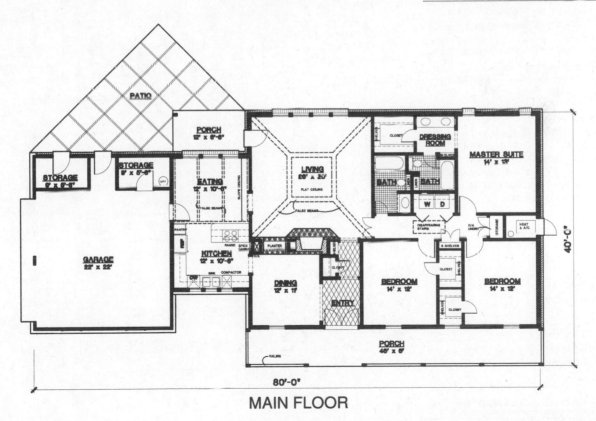

MAIN FLOOR

TO ORDER THIS BLUEPRINT,
CALL TOLL-FREE 1-800-820-1283

Plan E-1808

PRICES AND DETAILS
ON PAGES 12-15

173

Masterful Master Suite

- This gorgeous home features front and rear covered porches and a master suite so luxurious it deserves its own wing.
- The expansive entry welcomes visitors into a spacious, skylighted living room, which boasts a handsome fireplace. The adjacent formal dining room overlooks the front porch.
- Designed for efficiency, the kitchen features an angled snack bar, a bayed eating area and views of the porch. An all-purpose utility room is conveniently located off the kitchen.
- The kitchen, eating area, living room and dining room are all heightened by 12-ft. ceilings.
- The sumptuous and secluded master suite features a tub and a separate shower, a double-sink vanity, a walk-in closet with built-in shelves and a compartmentalized toilet.
- The two secondary bedrooms share a hall bath at the other end of the home. The rear bedroom offers porch access.
- The garage features built-in storage and access to unfinished attic space.

Plan E-1811

Bedrooms: 3	Baths: 2
Living Area:	
Main floor	1,800 sq. ft.
Total Living Area:	**1,800 sq. ft.**
Garage and storage	634 sq. ft.
Exterior Wall Framing:	2x6

Foundation Options:

Crawlspace
Slab
(All plans can be built with your choice of foundation and framing. A generic conversion diagram is available. See order form.)

BLUEPRINT PRICE CODE:	B

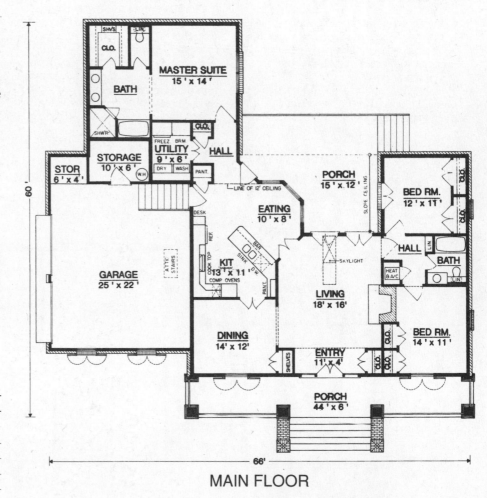

MAIN FLOOR

Plan E-1811

PRICES AND DETAILS ON PAGES 12-15

Modern Charmer

- This attractive plan combines country-style charm with a modern floor plan.
- The central foyer ushers guests past a study and on into the huge living room, which is highlighted by an 11-ft. ceiling, a corner fireplace and access to a big, covered backyard porch.
- An angled snack bar joins the living room to the bayed nook and the efficient kitchen. The formal dining room is easily reached from the kitchen and the foyer. A utility room and a half-bath are just off the garage entrance.
- The master suite, isolated for privacy, boasts a magnificent bath with a garden tub, a separate shower, double vanities and two walk-in closets.
- Two more bedrooms are located on the opposite side of the home and are separated by a hall bath.
- Ceilings in all rooms are at least 9 ft. high for added spaciousness.

REAR VIEW

Plan VL-2069

Bedrooms: 3	Baths: 2½
Living Area:	
Main floor	2,069 sq. ft.
Total Living Area:	**2,069 sq. ft.**
Garage	460 sq. ft.
Exterior Wall Framing:	2x4

Foundation Options:

Crawlspace

Slab

(All plans can be built with your choice of foundation and framing. A generic conversion diagram is available. See order form.)

BLUEPRINT PRICE CODE: C

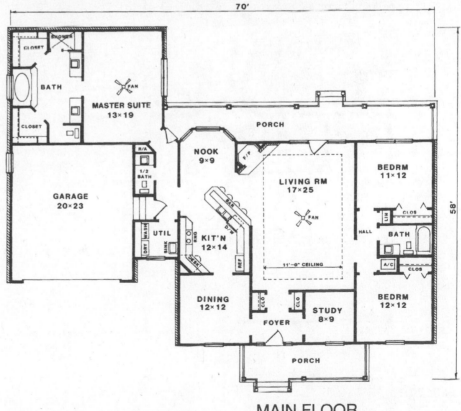

MAIN FLOOR

Rustic Welcome

- This rustic design boasts an appealing exterior with a covered front porch that offers guests a friendly welcome.
- Inside, the centrally located Great Room features an 11-ft., 8-in. cathedral ceiling with exposed wood beams. A massive fireplace separates the living area from the large dining room, which offers access to a nice backyard patio.
- The galley-style kitchen flows between the formal dining room and the bayed

breakfast room, which offers a handy pantry and access to laundry facilities.
- The master suite features a walk-in closet and a compartmentalized bath.
- Across the Great Room, two additional bedrooms have extra closet space and share a second full bath.
- The side-entry garage gives the front of the home an extra-appealing and uncluttered look.
- The optional daylight basement offers expanded living space. The stairway (not shown) would be located along the wall between the dining room and the back bedroom.

Plan C-8460

Bedrooms: 3	Baths: 2
Living Area:	
Main floor	1,670 sq. ft.
Total Living Area:	**1,670 sq. ft.**
Daylight basement	1,600 sq. ft.
Garage	427 sq. ft.
Exterior Wall Framing:	2x4

Foundation Options:
Daylight basement
Crawlspace
Slab
(All plans can be built with your choice of foundation and framing. A generic conversion diagram is available. See order form.)

BLUEPRINT PRICE CODE: B

MAIN FLOOR

PATIO 14'-0" x 10'-0"

STORAGE 8'-4" x 7'-6"

UTILITY 8'-2" x 7'-6"

BREAKFAST 10'-0" x 9'-6"

KITCHEN 9'-8" x 8'-8"

DINING RM. 19'-8" x 11'-2"

BEDROOM 12'-10" x 12'-0"

PAN.

DRESS.

BATH

CL

LIN

BATH

GARAGE 21'-2" x 20'-2"

M. BEDROOM 15'-8" x 13'-10"

CATHEDRAL CLG.

GREAT RM. 19'-8" x 18'-2"

BEDROOM 13'-0" x 11'-0"

PORCH 21'-0" x 6'-0"

30'-0"

73'-8"

TO ORDER THIS BLUEPRINT, CALL TOLL-FREE 1-800-820-1283

Plan C-8460

PRICES AND DETAILS ON PAGES 12-15

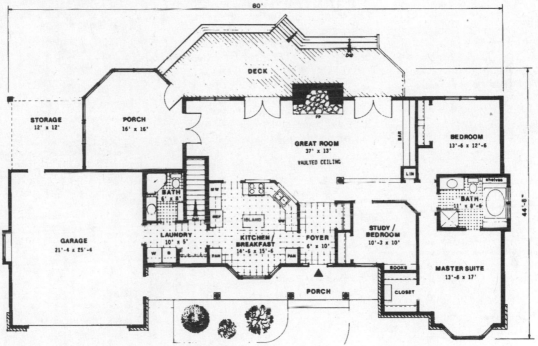

Spectacular Great Room Overlooks Rear Deck

- An inviting covered porch welcomes you inside this stylish ranch.
- Inside, your attention is drawn to a spectacular Great Room; nearly 500 square feet of relaxing, activity or entertaining space is offered, as is a stone fireplace flanked by French doors that open to a large, rear deck, an attached three-season porch and built-in bar.
- A bayed informal eating area, work island and dual pantries highlight the modern kitchen, also with nearby laundry room and bath.
- A bayed master suite, a second bedroom and a study or third bedroom complete the floor plan.

Plan CPS-1156

Bedrooms: 2-3	Baths: 2
Space:	
Main floor	1,770 sq. ft.
Total Living Area	**1,770 sq. ft.**
Basement	1,770 sq. ft.
Garage	540 sq. ft.
Exterior Wall Framing	2x6

Foundation options:

Standard Basement

(Foundation & framing conversion diagram available—see order form.)

Blueprint Price Code	B

Rustic, Relaxed Living

- The screened porch of this rustic home offers a cool place to dine on warm summer days. The covered front porch provides an inviting welcome and a place for pure relaxation.
- With its warm fireplace and surrounding windows, the home's spacious living room is ideal for unwinding indoors. The living room unfolds to a nice-sized dining area that overlooks a backyard patio and opens to the screened porch.
- The U-shaped kitchen is centrally located and features a nice windowed sink. A handy pantry and a laundry room adjoin to the right.
- Three large bedrooms make up the home's sleeping wing. The master bedroom boasts a roomy private bath with a step-up spa tub, a separate shower and two walk-in closets.
- The secondary bedrooms share a compartmentalized hall bath.

Plan C-8650

Bedrooms: 3	Baths: 2
Living Area:	
Main floor	1,773 sq. ft.
Total Living Area:	**1,773 sq. ft.**
Daylight basement	1,773 sq. ft.
Garage	441 sq. ft.
Exterior Wall Framing:	2x4

Foundation Options:
Daylight basement
Crawlspace
Slab
(All plans can be built with your choice of foundation and framing. A generic conversion diagram is available. See order form.)

BLUEPRINT PRICE CODE:	B

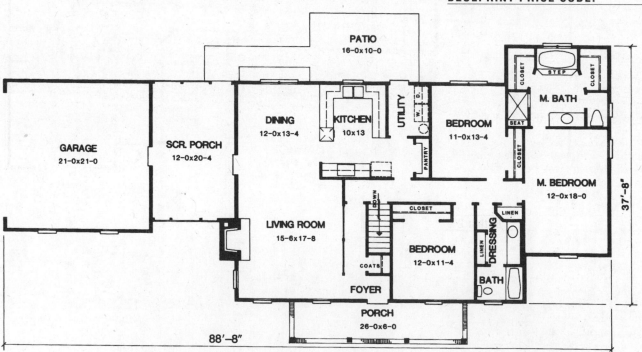

MAIN FLOOR

TO ORDER THIS BLUEPRINT, CALL TOLL-FREE 1-800-820-1283   Plan C-8650   *PRICES AND DETAILS ON PAGES 12-15*

Country Charm, Cottage Look

- An interesting combination of stone and stucco gives a charming cottage look to this attactive country home.
- Off the inviting sidelighted entry, the formal dining room is defined by striking columns.
- The dining room expands into the living room, which boasts a fireplace and built-in shelves. A French door provides access to a cute backyard patio.
- The galley-style kitchen unfolds to a sunny morning room.
- All of the living areas are expanded by 10-ft. ceilings.
- The master bedroom features a 10-ft. ceiling and a nice bayed sitting area. The luxurious master bath boasts an exciting garden tub and a glass-block shower, as well as a big walk-in closet and a dressing area with two sinks.
- Across the home, two additional bedrooms with walk-in closets and private dressing areas share a tidy compartmentalized bath.

Plan DD-1790

Bedrooms: 3	Baths: 2½
Living Area:	
Main floor	1,790 sq. ft.
Total Living Area:	**1,790 sq. ft.**
Standard basement	1,790 sq. ft.
Garage	438 sq. ft.
Exterior Wall Framing:	2x4

Foundation Options:

Standard basement

Crawlspace

Slab

(All plans can be built with your choice of foundation and framing. A generic conversion diagram is available. See order form.)

BLUEPRINT PRICE CODE: B

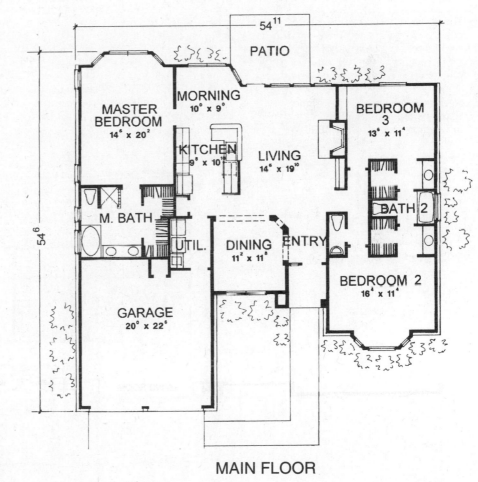

MAIN FLOOR

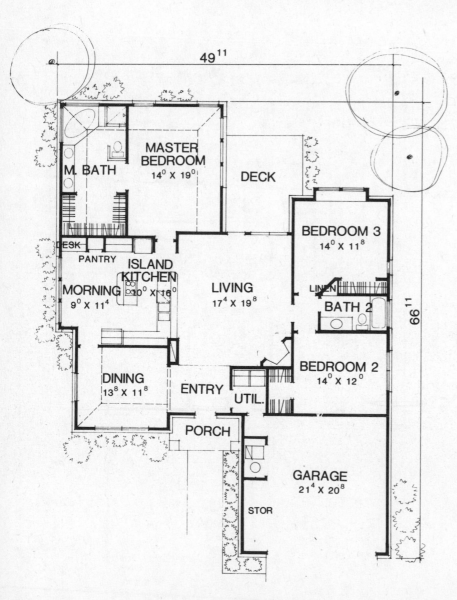

Single-Level Elegance

- A large living room with corner fireplace lies at the center of this updated ranch. The living room accesses the rear deck and yard.
- The island kitchen incorporates a morning room, built-in desk and handy pantry, and also overlooks the living room for uninterrupted conversation.
- The formal dining room features a trayed ceiling and has a view of the front yard.
- The master suite offers multiple windows overlooking the deck and rear yard. The private bath focuses on a corner luxury tub with separate shower.
- Two extra bedrooms share a second bath, and are well separated from the master suite for privacy.

Plan DD-1836-B

Bedrooms: 3	Baths: 2
Space:	
Main floor	1,836 sq. ft.
Total Living Area	**1,836 sq. ft.**
Basement	1,836 sq. ft.
Garage	441 sq. ft.
Exterior Wall Framing	**2x4**

Foundation options:
Standard Basement
Crawlspace
Slab
(Foundation & framing conversion diagram available—see order form.)

Blueprint Price Code	**B**

TO ORDER THIS BLUEPRINT, CALL TOLL-FREE 1-800-820-1283
Plan DD-1836-B
PRICES AND DETAILS ON PAGES 12-15

Delightful Great Room

- An expansive Great Room with a 10-ft. vaulted ceiling, a warm corner fireplace and an angled wet bar highlights this tastefully appointed home.
- On the exterior, decorative plants thrive in the lush wraparound planter that leads to the sheltered entry. The foyer is brightened by a sidelight and a skylight.
- To the left, the kitchen offers an island cooktop with lots room for food preparation and serving. The bayed breakfast nook is enhanced by bright windows and a 12½-ft. vaulted ceiling.
- Formal dining is hosted in the space adjoining the Great Room. Graced by a lovely bay window, the room also offers French doors to a covered patio.
- In the sleeping wing of the home, the master bedroom features a sitting area and a walk-in closet. The private master bath boasts a relaxing Jacuzzi tub.
- Two secondary bedrooms share a full bath nearby. Laundry facilities are also convenient.

Plan S-52394

Bedrooms: 3	Baths: 2
Living Area:	
Main floor	1,841 sq. ft.
Total Living Area:	**1,841 sq. ft.**
Standard basement	1,789 sq. ft.
Garage	432 sq. ft.
Exterior Wall Framing:	2x6

Foundation Options:

Standard basement
Crawlspace
Slab

(All plans can be built with your choice of foundation and framing. A generic conversion diagram is available. See order form.)

BLUEPRINT PRICE CODE: B

MAIN FLOOR

Plan S-52394

Cozy Comfort

- This comfortable one-story is small enough to be cozy, but large enough to contain luxurious amenities.
- The two-car carport offers two storage areas and is entered from the side, keeping the charming brick facade clean and uncluttered.
- A lovely French door opens to the main entry foyer, which is set off by beautiful brick columns.
- To the left, the formal dining room offers functional cabinets and shelves between some of its columns.
- Straight ahead, the spacious living room is enhanced by an energy-efficient fireplace with glass doors. Other highlights include a 12-ft. sloped ceiling, storage shelves and views of a backyard patio through tall windows.
- The well-planned kitchen features two pantries, a versatile snack bar and a sunny eating nook. The adjacent utility room provides laundry facilities and carport access.
- The secluded master suite boasts a private bath and a walk-in closet. The two front bedrooms share a hall bath.

Plan E-1819

Bedrooms: 3	Baths: 2
Living Area:	
Main floor	1,846 sq. ft.
Total Living Area:	**1,846 sq. ft.**
Carport	440 sq. ft.
Storage	120 sq. ft.
Exterior Wall Framing:	2x6

Foundation Options:

Crawlspace

Slab

(All plans can be built with your choice of foundation and framing. A generic conversion diagram is available. See order form.)

BLUEPRINT PRICE CODE: **B**

MAIN FLOOR

Plan E-1819

PRICES AND DETAILS ON PAGES 12-15

Indoor/Outdoor Delights

- A curved porch in the front and a garden sun room in the back make this home an indoor/outdoor delight.
- Inside, a roomy kitchen is open to a five-sided, glassed-in dining room that views out to the porch.
- The living room features a fireplace along a glass wall that adjoins the gloriously sunny garden room.

- Wrapped in windows, the garden room accesses the backyard as well as a large storage area in the unobtrusive, side-entry garage.
- The master suite is no less luxurious, featuring a a sumptuous master bath with a garden spa tub, a corner shower and a walk-in closet.
- Each of the two remaining bedrooms has a boxed-out window and a walk-in closet. A full bath with a corner shower and a dual-sink vanity is close by.
- A stairway leads to the attic, which provides more potential living space.

Plan DD-1852

Bedrooms: 3	Baths: 2
Living Area:	
Main floor	1,852 sq. ft.
Total Living Area:	**1,852 sq. ft.**
Standard basement	1,852 sq. ft.
Garage	528 sq. ft.
Exterior Wall Framing:	2x4

Foundation Options:
Standard basement
Crawlspace
Slab
(All plans can be built with your choice of foundation and framing. A generic conversion diagram is available. See order form.)

BLUEPRINT PRICE CODE: B

72⁶

52⁶

GARDEN ROOM
24⁰ X 10⁰

STORAGE

M. BATH
LINEN

MASTER BEDROOM
12⁴ X 15⁴

ATTIC

LIVING
20⁸ X 20⁰

GARAGE
22⁰ X 24⁰

BASEMENT

UTIL.

BEDROOM 3
11⁰ X 13⁰

BATH 2
LINEN

KITCHEN
12⁴ X 11⁴

DINING
12⁰ X 12⁰

ENTRY

BEDROOM 2
13⁰ X 11⁰

PORCH

MAIN FLOOR

TO ORDER THIS BLUEPRINT,
CALL TOLL-FREE 1-800-820-1283

Plan DD-1852

PRICES AND DETAILS
ON PAGES 12-15

183

Classic Ranch

- With decorative brick quoins, a columned porch and stylish dormers, the exterior of this classic one-story provides an interesting blend of Early American and European design.
- Flowing from the foyer, the bay-windowed dining room is enhanced by an 11½-ft.-high stepped ceiling.
- The spacious Great Room, separated from the dining room by a columned arch, features a stepped ceiling, a built-in media center and a striking fireplace. Lovely French doors lead to a big backyard patio.
- The breakfast room, which shares an eating bar with the kitchen, boasts a ceiling that slopes to 12 feet. French doors access a covered rear porch.
- The master bedroom has a 10-ft. tray ceiling, a sunny bay window and a roomy walk-in closet. The master bath features a whirlpool tub in a bayed nook and a separate shower.
- The front-facing bedroom is enhanced by a 10-ft.-high vaulted area over an arched transom window.

Plan AX-93304

Bedrooms: 3	Baths: 2

Living Area:

Main floor	1,860 sq. ft.
Total Living Area:	**1,860 sq. ft.**
Standard basement	1,860 sq. ft.
Garage/utility/storage	434 sq. ft.
Exterior Wall Framing:	2x4

Foundation Options:

Standard basement
Crawlspace
Slab

(All plans can be built with your choice of foundation and framing. A generic conversion diagram is available. See order form.)

BLUEPRINT PRICE CODE:	**B**

VIEW INTO GREAT ROOM

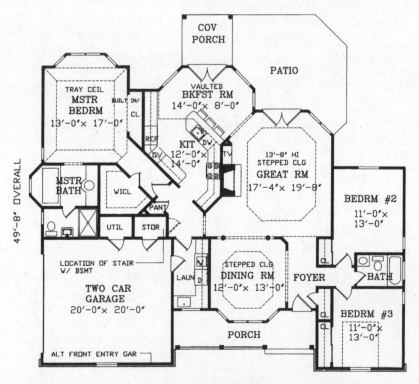

MAIN FLOOR

Plan AX-93304

PRICES AND DETAILS ON PAGES 12-15

Expansive Traditional

- Skylights, cathedral and tray ceilings and an open floor plan brighten and expand this traditional home.
- A covered front porch, a large dining room and a skylighted living room with a nice fireplace and a 12-ft. ceiling make guests feel at home instantly.
- For extended living space, the back patio is accessible from the living room through sliding glass doors.
- A cathedral ceiling presides over the efficient kitchen and the cozy eating area. A large utility room nearby offers extra freezer and storage space.
- The kitchen can be closed off from the dining room to minimize noise and remove clutter from sight.
- The luxurious master suite features a tray ceiling, a walk-in closet, double vanities, a unique skylighted quarter-round tub and a separate shower.
- Two large secondary bedrooms share a hall bath. The front bedroom features a cathedral ceiling and double closets.
- The garage is at the back of the house and features two large built-in storage areas, one accessible from the outside.

Plan E-1825

Bedrooms: 3	Baths: 2
Living Area:	
Main floor	1,865 sq. ft.
Total Living Area:	**1,865 sq. ft.**
Garage and storage	616 sq. ft.
Exterior Wall Framing:	2x6

Foundation Options:

Crawlspace

Slab

(Typical foundation & framing conversion diagram available—see order form.)

BLUEPRINT PRICE CODE:	B

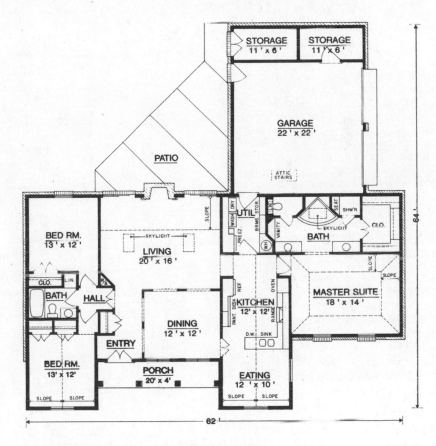

MAIN FLOOR

Upscale Charm

- Country charm and the very latest in conveniences mark this upscale home. To add extra appeal, all of the living areas are housed on one floor, yet may be expanded to the upper floor later.
- Set off from the foyer, the dining room is embraced by elegant columns. Arched windows in the dining room and in the bedroom across the hall echo the delicate detailing of the covered front porch.
- Straight ahead, the family room flaunts a wall of French doors overlooking a covered back porch and a large deck.
- A curved island snack bar smoothly connects the gourmet kitchen to the sunny breakfast area, which features a dramatic 13-ft. vaulted ceiling brightened by skylights. All other rooms have 9-ft. ceilings. A nearby computer room and a laundry/utility room with a recycling center are other amenities.
- The master bedroom's private bath includes a dual-sink vanity and a floor-to-ceiling storage unit with a built-in chest of drawers. Other extras include a step-up spa tub and a separate shower.

Plan J-92100

Bedrooms: 3+	Baths: 2
Living Area:	
Main floor	1,877 sq. ft.
Total Living Area:	**1,877 sq. ft.**
Upper floor (future areas)	1,500 sq. ft.
Standard basement	1,877 sq. ft.
Garage and storage	551 sq. ft.
Exterior Wall Framing:	2x4

Foundation Options:

Standard basement
Crawlspace
Slab

(All plans can be built with your choice of foundation and framing. A generic conversion diagram is available. See order form.)

BLUEPRINT PRICE CODE:	B

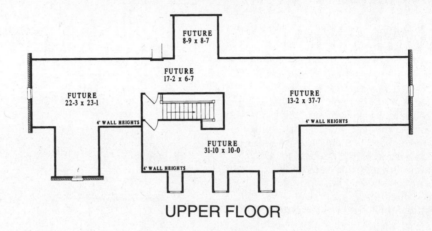

UPPER FLOOR

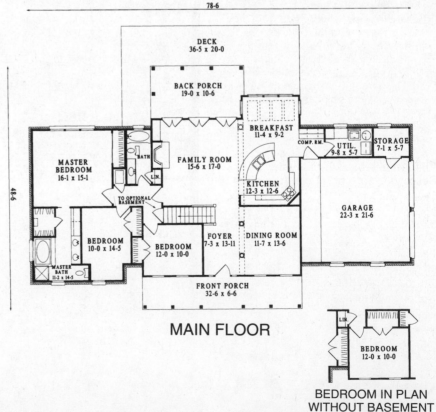

MAIN FLOOR

BEDROOM IN PLAN
WITHOUT BASEMENT

Garden Home with a View

- This clever design proves that privacy doesn't have to be compromised even in high-density urban neighborhoods. From within, views are oriented to a beautiful, lush entry courtyard and a covered rear porch.
- The exterior appearance is sheltered, but warm and welcoming.
- The innovative interior design centers on a unique kitchen, which directs traffic away from the working areas while still serving the entire home.
- The sunken family room features a 14-ft. vaulted ceiling and a warm fireplace.
- The master suite is highlighted by a sumptuous master bath with an oversized shower and a whirlpool tub, plus a large walk-in closet.
- The formal living room is designed and placed in such a way that it can become a third bedroom, a den, or an office or study room, depending on family needs and lifestyles.

Plan E-1824

Bedrooms: 2+	Baths: 2
Living Area:	
Main floor	1,891 sq. ft.
Total Living Area:	**1,891 sq. ft.**
Garage	506 sq. ft.
Storage	60 sq. ft.
Exterior Wall Framing:	2x4

Foundation Options:

Crawlspace
Slab
(All plans can be built with your choice of foundation and framing. A generic conversion diagram is available. See order form.)

BLUEPRINT PRICE CODE: B

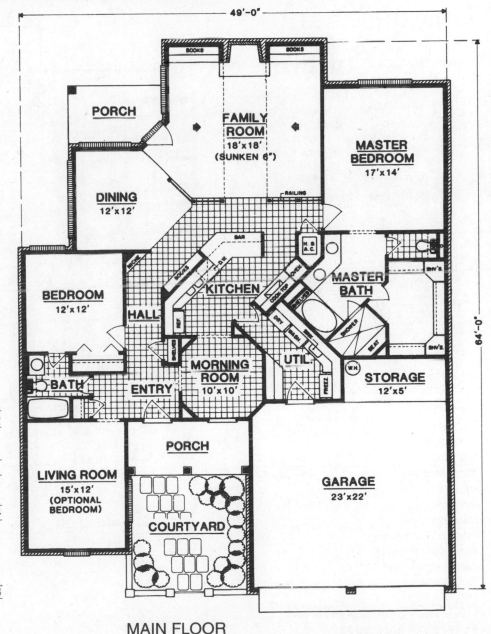

MAIN FLOOR

TO ORDER THIS BLUEPRINT,
CALL TOLL-FREE 1-800-820-1283

Plan E-1824

PRICES AND DETAILS
ON PAGES 12-15

187

Ultimate French Comfort

- Delightful interior touches coupled with a striking French facade make this home the ultimate in one-story comfort.
- In the sidelighted entry, an attractive overhead plant ledge captures the eye.
- The entry opens to the formal dining and living rooms—both of which boast 10-ft. ceilings.
- In the living room, a handy wet bar and a media center flank a handsome fireplace. Large windows frame wide backyard views. Around the corner, French doors open to a back porch.
- Adjacent to the dining room, the kitchen offers a speedy serving bar. A bayed nook lights up with morning sun.
- Double doors open to the master bedroom, with its cute window seat and TV shelf. A 10-ft. ceiling tops it off.
- Two walk-in closets with glamorous mirror doors flank the walkway to the master bath, which offers an exotic garden tub and a separate shower.
- One of the two roomy secondary bedrooms offers a walk-in closet, a built-in desk and a gorgeous window.

Plan RD-1895

Bedrooms: 3	Baths: 2
Living Area:	
Main floor	1,895 sq. ft.
Total Living Area:	**1,895 sq. ft.**
Garage and storage	485 sq. ft.
Exterior Wall Framing:	2x4

Foundation Options:

Crawlspace
Slab

(All plans can be built with your choice of foundation and framing. A generic conversion diagram is available. See order form.)

BLUEPRINT PRICE CODE: **B**

MAIN FLOOR

Plan RD-1895

PRICES AND DETAILS ON PAGES 12-15

Magnificent Great Room

- A magnificent Great Room anchors this gorgeous Mediterranean-style home.
- From the foyer, an arched entrance introduces the den, study or extra bedroom. If desired, the closet could be modified to house a wet bar.
- The formal dining room offers an excellent space for special meals.
- Straight ahead, the massive Great Room boasts a handsome fireplace. Pocket sliding glass doors open to a covered patio with skylights.
- Secluded from the rest of the home and beyond two arched entryways, the master bedroom has its own patio access. Highlights in the master bath include a walk-in closet, a raised whirlpool tub and a separate shower beneath a 14½-ft. vaulted ceiling.
- Natural light floods the breakfast nook and the adjoining kitchen, which sports a serving counter. Handy laundry facilities are just a few steps away.
- Two more good-sized bedrooms share a full bath and easy patio access.

Plan HDS-99-196

Bedrooms: 3+	Baths: 2
Living Area:	
Main floor	1,901 sq. ft.
Total Living Area:	**1,901 sq. ft.**
Garage	484 sq. ft.
Exterior Wall Framing:	8-in. concrete block

Foundation Options:

Slab
(All plans can be built with your choice of foundation and framing. A generic conversion diagram is available. See order form.)

BLUEPRINT PRICE CODE: B

MAIN FLOOR

Plan HDS-99-196

Classic Symmetry

- This traditional one-story, with its hip roof, dual dormers and matching wings, has the classic symmetry of a stately country home.
- The decorative dormers are also functional, filling the foyer and the dining room with natural light.
- The foyer and the dining room also enjoy 13-ft., 8-in. cathedral ceilings, and are separated by an arched divider and an open-railed stairwell.

- The spacious living room is enhanced by a 10-ft. tray ceiling, a fireplace and sliding glass doors to the backyard.
- The large kitchen and breakfast area is designed for today's lifestyles. The sunny breakfast area features a bay window, while the island kitchen has plenty of cabinet and counter space.
- The master suite boasts a spectacular 14-ft., 6-in. cathedral ceiling, plenty of windows and a walk-in closet. The master bath includes a spa tub and a dual-sink vanity that incorporates a sit-down grooming table.
- Two other bedrooms are convenient to a hall bath and a laundry closet.

Plan OH-177

Bedrooms: 3	Baths: 2
Living Area:	
Main floor	1,902 sq. ft.
Total Living Area:	**1,902 sq. ft.**
Standard basement	1,902 sq. ft.
Garage	457 sq. ft.
Exterior Wall Framing:	2x4

Foundation Options:

Standard basement

(All plans can be built with your choice of foundation and framing. A generic conversion diagram is available. See order form.)

BLUEPRINT PRICE CODE: B

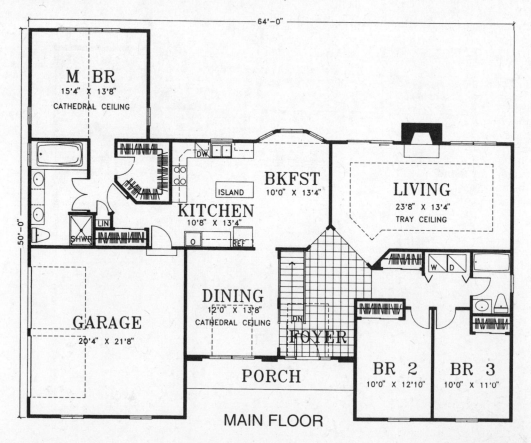

MAIN FLOOR

Plan OH-177

Morning Room with a View

- This modern-looking ranch is stylishly decorated with a pair of arched-window dormers, handsome brick trim and a covered front porch.
- Inside, the dining room is set off by columns, as it merges with the entry.
- The main living areas are oriented to the rear, where a huge central family room offers a patio view and a fireplace that may also be enjoyed from the bayed morning room and adjoining kitchen.
- The walk-through kitchen features a pantry, a snack bar to the family room and easy service to the formal dining room across the hall.
- The secluded master suite boasts a wide window seat and a private bath with a walk-in closet, a corner garden tub and a separate shower.
- Across the home, the three secondary bedrooms share another full bath. The fourth bedroom may double as a study.
- High 10-ft. ceilings are found throughout the home, except in the secondary bedrooms.

Plan DD-1962

Bedrooms: 3+	Baths: 2
Living Area:	
Main floor	1,962 sq. ft.
Total Living Area:	**1,962 sq. ft.**
Standard basement	1,962 sq. ft.
Garage	386 sq. ft.
Exterior Wall Framing:	2x4

Foundation Options:

Standard basement

Crawlspace

Slab

(All plans can be built with your choice of foundation and framing. A generic conversion diagram is available. See order form.)

BLUEPRINT PRICE CODE:	B

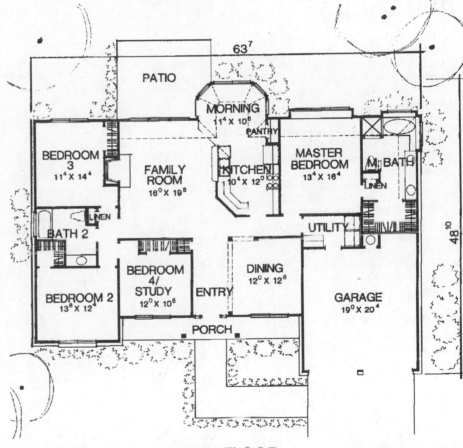

MAIN FLOOR

TO ORDER THIS BLUEPRINT,
CALL TOLL-FREE 1-800-820-1283

Plan DD-1962

PRICES AND DETAILS
ON PAGES 12-15

191

Big, Vaulted Great Room

- Behind this home's unpretentious facade lies an exciting and highly livable floor plan.
- The 16-ft.-high vaulted entry leads visitors to the impressive Great Room, where a corner fireplace rises to meet the 16-ft. exposed-beam ceiling.
- The skylighted central kitchen has a 12-ft. vaulted ceiling and a nice pantry.
- The sunny nook includes a 12-ft. ceiling, a built-in work desk and access to a large patio.
- Elegant double doors open to the dazzling master suite, which includes a skylighted dressing area wth a 12-ft. ceiling. An enormous walk-in closet and a sumptuous bath with a sunken tub are also featured.
- Two secondary bedrooms share another full bath at the opposite end of the home, near the laundry room.

Plans P-6577-3A & -3D

Bedrooms: 3	Baths: 2
Living Area:	
Main floor (crawlspace version)	1,978 sq. ft.
Main floor (basement version)	2,047 sq. ft.
Total Living Area:	**1,978/2,047 sq. ft.**
Daylight basement	1,982 sq. ft.
Garage	438 sq. ft.
Exterior Wall Framing:	2x4
Foundation Options:	**Plan #**
Daylight basement	P-6577-3D
Crawlspace	P-6577-3A

(All plans can be built with your choice of foundation and framing. A generic conversion diagram is available. See order form.)

BLUEPRINT PRICE CODE:	**B/C**

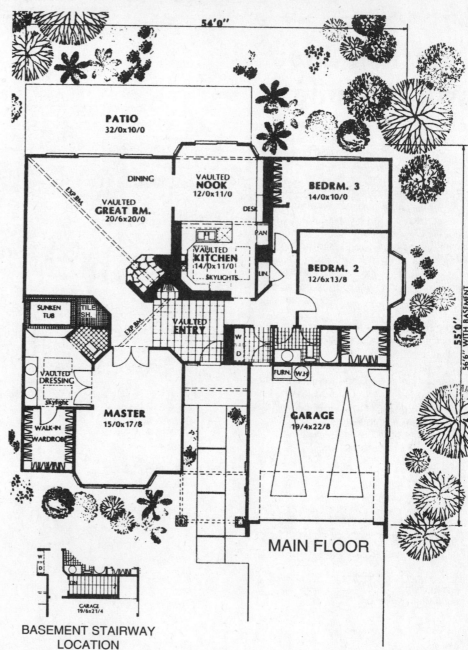

MAIN FLOOR

BASEMENT STAIRWAY LOCATION

Plans P-6577-3A & -3D
PRICES AND DETAILS ON PAGES 12-15

Spectacular Master Suite!

- The creative floor plan of this lovely rustic home includes a spacious, open activity area and a romantic master suite with spectacular angles.
- At the center of the plan, the living room, kitchen and breakfast area share a high 10-ft. ceiling. A French door in the breakfast area opens to a covered backyard porch.
- Highlighted by a nice gas fireplace, the living room includes a recessed space for a built-in entertainment center.
- The secluded master suite shows off an 8-ft., 10-in. raised ceiling and a cozy gas fireplace with a TV cabinet above.
- Double doors open into the posh master bath, which boasts a whirlpool garden tub under an 8-ft., 10-in. raised ceiling. Other highlights include a separate shower, a dual-sink vanity and a roomy walk-in closet.
- Two additional bedrooms share a second full bath.

Plan J-9406

Bedrooms: 3	Baths: 2

Living Area:

Main floor (non-bsmt. version)	1,979 sq. ft.
Main floor (basement version)	2,000 sq. ft.
Total Living Area:	**1,979/2,000 sq. ft.**
Standard basement	2,000 sq. ft.
Garage and storage	557 sq. ft.

Exterior Wall Framing: 2x4

Foundation Options:

Standard basement
Crawlspace
Slab
(All plans can be built with your choice of foundation and framing. A generic conversion diagram is available. See order form.)

BLUEPRINT PRICE CODE: B/C

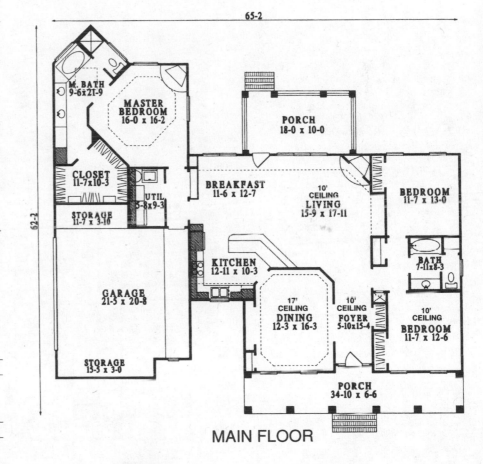

MAIN FLOOR

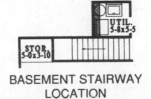

BASEMENT STAIRWAY LOCATION

Elegant Facade

- Eye-catching windows and columns add elegance to both the front and rear of this appealing ranch-style home.
- The columns of the covered front porch are repeated inside, defining the spacious gallery. The central section soars to a height of 20 ft., 4 in., basking in sunlight from a windowed dormer.
- The gorgeous Great Room features a cozy fireplace flanked by built-ins. Two sets of sliding glass doors with elliptical transoms open to a backyard terrace.
- The gourmet kitchen offers a handy snack bar, while the breakfast room expands to a columned rear porch.
- The peaceful dining room boasts a stepped ceiling that rises to 10 ft. at the stunning front window.
- The secluded master suite provides a sitting area, porch access and a private whirlpool bath with dual sinks and wardrobe closets.
- The second bedroom is brightened by an arched window arrangement under a 12½-ft.-high vaulted area.
- Ceilings are at least 9½ ft. high throughout the home.

Plan AX-4315

Bedrooms: 3	Baths: 2
Living Area:	
Main floor	2,018 sq. ft.
Total Living Area:	**2,018 sq. ft.**
Basement	2,018 sq. ft.
Garage/storage/utility	474 sq. ft.
Exterior Wall Framing:	2x4

Foundation Options:
Daylight basement
Standard basement
Crawlspace
Slab
(All plans can be built with your choice of foundation and framing. A generic conversion diagram is available. See order form.)

BLUEPRINT PRICE CODE: C

VIEW INTO GREAT ROOM

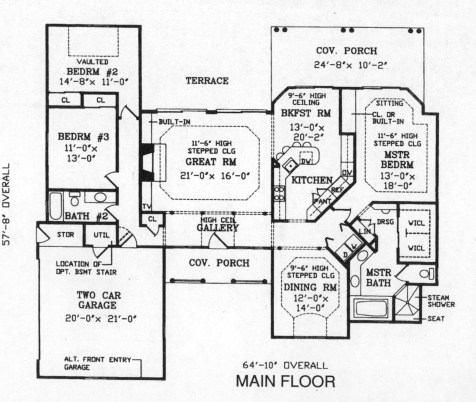

MAIN FLOOR

Memories in the Making

- You will enjoy years of memories in this peaceful country home.
- A tranquil covered porch opens into the foyer, where regal columns introduce the formal dining room. Soaring 10-ft. ceilings enhance the foyer, dining room, kitchen and breakfast nook.
- Past two closets, a 15-ft., 4-in. cathedral ceiling adds glamour to the living room. A grand fireplace flanked by French doors under beautiful quarter-round transoms will wow your guests! The

French doors open to an inviting porch that is great for afternoon get-togethers.
- The sunny breakfast bay merges with the gourmet kitchen, which includes a large pantry and an island snack bar. Bi-fold doors above the sink create a handy pass-through to the living room.
- A neat computer room nearby allows the kids to do their homework under a parent's watchful eye.
- Across the home, a stylish 10-ft. tray ceiling crowns the master suite. The skylighted master bath features a refreshing whirlpool tub.
- A hall bath services two additional bedrooms. The larger bedroom is expanded by a 10-ft. vaulted ceiling.

Plan J-9294	
Bedrooms: 3	**Baths: 2**
Living Area:	
Main floor	2,018 sq. ft.
Total Living Area:	**2,018 sq. ft.**
Standard basement	2,018 sq. ft.
Garage and storage	556 sq. ft.
Exterior Wall Framing:	2x4
Foundation Options:	
Standard basement	
Crawlspace	
Slab	

(All plans can be built with your choice of foundation and framing. A generic conversion diagram is available. See order form.)

BLUEPRINT PRICE CODE:	C

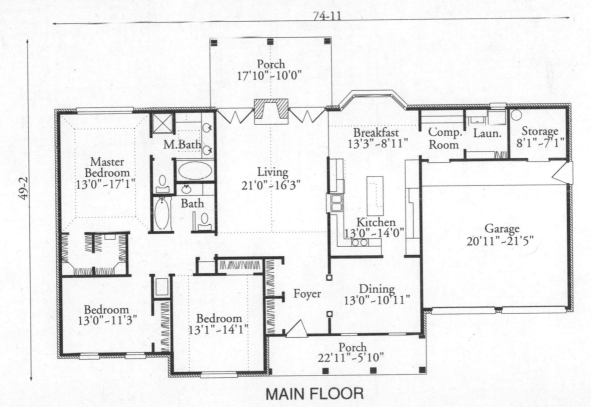

MAIN FLOOR

Deluxe
Master Bath

- Stylish decks, bay windows and a deluxe master bath are just some of the amenities found in this modern home.
- Recessed double doors open into the inviting skylighted entry, which views the backyard beyond.
- Past the entry, the spacious sunken living room offers a unique fireplace with a built-in wood bin. Sliding glass doors open from the living and dining rooms to a handsome backyard deck.
- A dramatic skywall illuminates the exciting kitchen, which also features a snack bar to the adjoining dining room.
- The fantastic master suite boasts a private backyard deck, in addition to a lavish bath that showcases a step-up spa tub, a designer shower, a dual-sink vanity and a roomy walk-in closet.
- Another full bath is convenient to the two secondary bedrooms, each with a window seat in a split bay.

Plans P-6600-4A & -4D

Bedrooms: 3	Baths: 2
Living Area:	
Main floor (crawlspace version)	2,050 sq. ft.
Main floor (basement version)	2,110 sq. ft.
Total Living Area:	**2,050/2,110 sq. ft.**
Daylight basement	2,080 sq. ft.
Garage	794 sq. ft.
Exterior Wall Framing:	**2x6**
Foundation Options:	**Plan #**
Daylight basement	P-6600-4D
Crawlspace	P-6600-4A

(All plans can be built with your choice of foundation and framing. A generic conversion diagram is available. See order form.)

BLUEPRINT PRICE CODE:	**C**

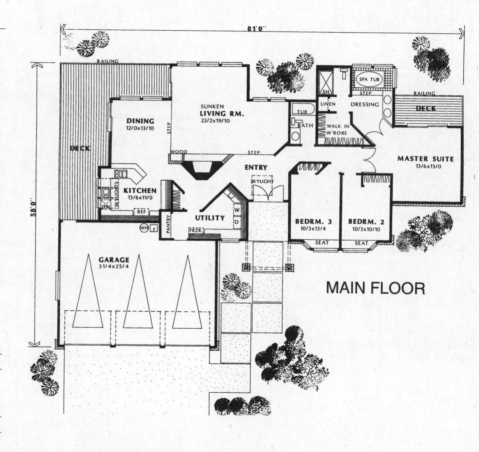

MAIN FLOOR

BASEMENT STAIRWAY LOCATION

TO ORDER THIS BLUEPRINT, CALL TOLL-FREE 1-800-820-1283
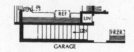
Plans P-6600-4A & -4D
PRICES AND DETAILS ON PAGES 12-15

Luxurious Ranch

- This luxurious farmhouse is introduced by a covered front porch, which opens to a sidelighted foyer.
- A spectacular central living room with an 11-ft. ceiling and a corner fireplace lies at the center of the home. A French door accesses a wide backyard porch.
- An angled eating bar joins the living room to the kitchen and bayed nook. The formal dining room is located on the opposite end of the kitchen, overlooking the front porch.
- The lavish master suite is separated from the other bedrooms and boasts a bayed sitting area and a private bath with dual vanities and a walk-in closet.
- A study, two additional bedrooms and a second full bath are located to the right of the foyer.
- Ceilings in all rooms are at least 9 ft. high for added spaciousness.

Plan VL-2085

Bedrooms: 3+	Baths: 2½
Living Area:	
Main floor	2,085 sq. ft.
Total Living Area:	**2,085 sq. ft.**
Garage	460 sq. ft.
Exterior Wall Framing:	2x4

Foundation Options:

Crawlspace

Slab

(All plans can be built with your choice of foundation and framing. A generic conversion diagram is available. See order form.)

BLUEPRINT PRICE CODE: C

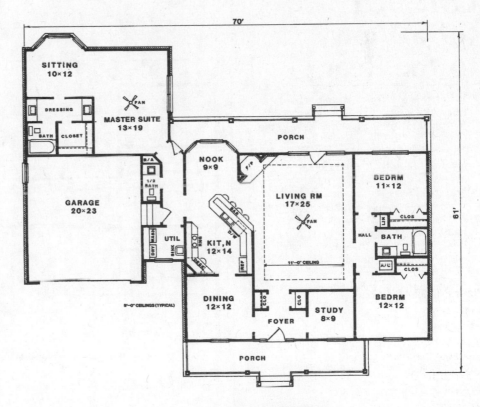

MAIN FLOOR

TO ORDER THIS BLUEPRINT,
CALL TOLL-FREE 1-800-820-1283

Plan VL-2085

PRICES AND DETAILS
ON PAGES 12-15

197

Oriented for a View to the Rear

- While this plan offers an attractive and cozy-looking front view, it is especially designed for settings with a view to the rear.
- The rooms used most frequently are located in the rear, and offer easy access to a large deck or porch.
- The spacious Great Room includes a large fireplace and windows to the rear.
- A convenient kitchen area features a laundry room on one end and a breakfast nook on the other. A large walk-in pantry connects the kitchen to the garage.
- A deluxe master suite includes a bath with separate tub and shower, plus a walk-in closet.

Plan V-2088

Bedrooms: 3	**Baths:** 2

Space:

Main floor	2,088 sq. ft.
Total Living Area	**2,088 sq. ft.**
Garage	540 sq. ft.
Exterior Wall Framing	2x6

Foundation options:

Crawlspace

(Foundation & framing conversion diagram available—see order form.)

Blueprint Price Code	C

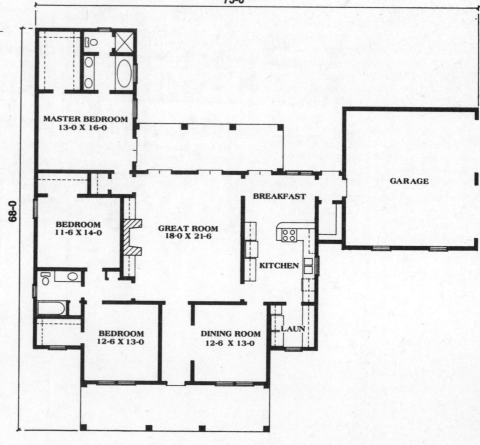

MAIN FLOOR

75-0

68-0

MASTER BEDROOM
13-0 X 16-0

BEDROOM
11-6 X 14-0

GREAT ROOM
18-0 X 21-6

BREAKFAST

KITCHEN

GARAGE

BEDROOM
12-6 X 13-0

DINING ROOM
12-6 X 13-0

LAUN

Plan V-2088

PRICES AND DETAILS ON PAGES 12-15

A Taste of Europe

- This tasteful one-story home is characterized by a European exterior and an ultra-modern interior.
- High 10-ft. ceilings grace the central living areas, from the foyer to the Great Room, and from the nook through the kitchen to the dining room.
- The inviting Great Room showcases a fireplace framed by glass that overlooks the covered back porch.
- A snack bar unites the Great Room with the bayed nook and the galley-style kitchen. A spacious utility room is just off the kitchen and accessible from the two-car garage as well.
- The secluded master suite boasts a luxurious private bath and French doors that open to the covered backyard porch.
- The master bath features a raised garden spa tub set into an intimate corner, with a separate shower nearby. A large walk-in closet and two sinks separated by a built-in makeup table are also included.
- Two additional bedrooms, a second full bath and a front study or home office make up the remainder of this up-to-date design.

Plan VL-2162	
Bedrooms: 3	**Baths:** 2
Living Area:	
Main floor	2,162 sq. ft.
Total Living Area:	**2,162 sq. ft.**
Garage	498 sq. ft.
Exterior Wall Framing:	2x4

Foundation Options:

Crawlspace
Slab
(All plans can be built with your choice of foundation and framing. A generic conversion diagram is available. See order form.)

BLUEPRINT PRICE CODE: C

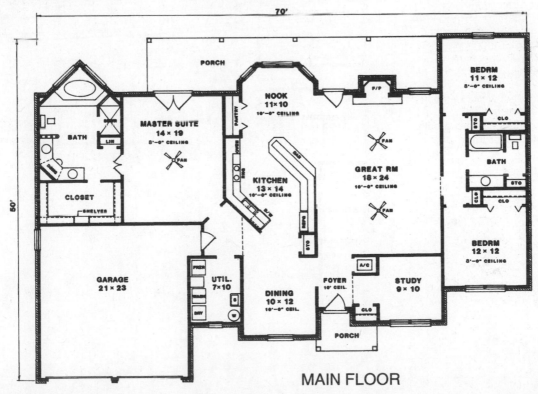

MAIN FLOOR

Classic Mix

- With its decorative dormers, corner quoins and columned porch, this classic country-style home exhibits an interesting blend of European and Early American design influences.
- The inviting entry leads into the spacious living room set off with columns. Warmed by a fireplace, the living room features built-in shelving and French doors accessing a backyard patio.
- The adjacent island kitchen easily serves the formal dining room and the sunny, bay-windowed morning nook.
- The master bedroom is secluded for privacy. The master bath has a spa tub, a dual-sink vanity, a separate shower and his-and-hers walk-in closets.
- Two additional bedrooms share a second bath. A convenient laundry area is nearby.
- Ten-foot ceilings throughout the plan give the home an open, airy feel.

Plan DD-2166-1

Bedrooms: 3+	Baths: 2
Living Area:	
Main floor	2,178 sq. ft.
Total Living Area:	**2,178 sq. ft.**
Standard basement	2,178 sq. ft.
Garage	440 sq. ft.
Exterior Wall Framing:	2x4

Foundation Options:

Standard basement
Crawlspace
Slab
(All plans can be built with your choice of foundation and framing. A generic conversion diagram is available. See order form.)

BLUEPRINT PRICE CODE: C

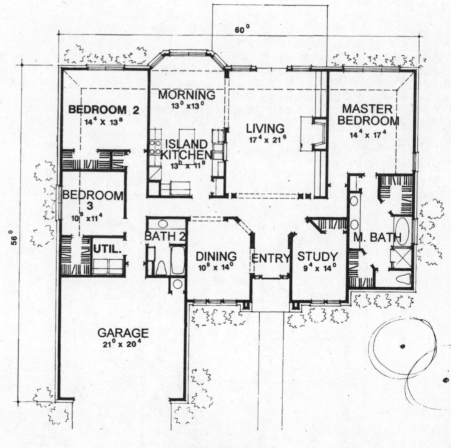

MAIN FLOOR

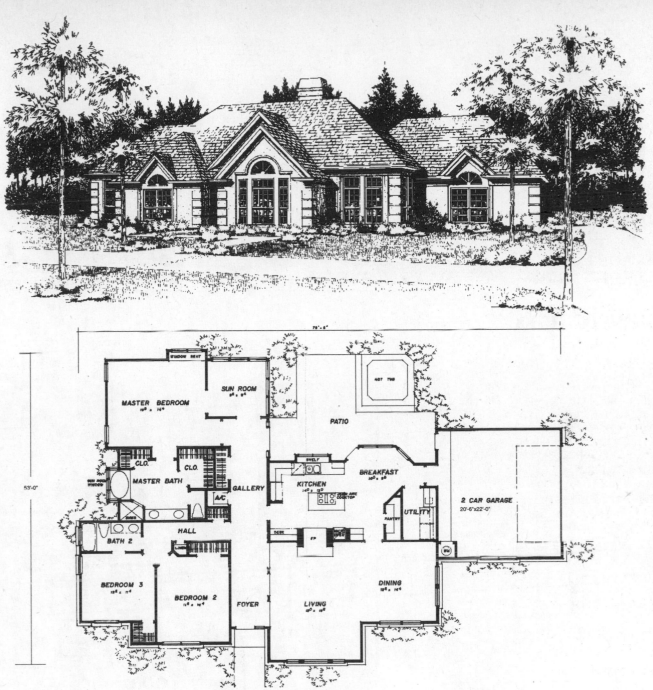

French Flair

- Quoins and semi-circular transoms give this French country home elegance and charm.
- The formal living areas at the front of the home combine for a huge entertainment center; a see-thru fireplace opens to the large island kitchen and bayed breakfast room, opposite.
- A rear patio offers a perfect spot for a hot tub.
- The foyer isolates the bedrooms; a gallery and luxury bath with garden tub and separate shower buffer the master suite and private sun room.

Plan DW-2198	
Bedrooms: 3	**Baths:** 2
Space:	
Main floor	2,198 sq. ft.
Total Living Area	**2,198 sq. ft.**
Basement	2,198 sq. ft.
Garage	451 sq. ft.
Exterior Wall Framing	2x4

Foundation options:
Standard Basement
Crawlspace
Slab
(Foundation & framing conversion diagram available—see order form.)

Blueprint Price Code	C

TO ORDER THIS BLUEPRINT,
CALL TOLL-FREE 1-800-820-1283

Plan DW-2198

PRICES AND DETAILS
ON PAGES 12-15

201

Deluxe Suite!

- Decorative corner quoins, arched windows and a sleek hip roofline give this charming home a European look.
- The inviting foyer extends its 12-ft. ceiling into the formal spaces. The airy living room is brightened by high half- and quarter-round windows.
- The adjoining formal dining room is set off with elegant columned openings and high plant shelves.
- The island kitchen features a pantry and a sunny breakfast bay. A pass-through over the sink serves the family room.
- Boasting a 17-ft. vaulted ceiling and a glass-flanked fireplace, the family room also enjoys backyard access.
- The deluxe master suite includes a private sitting room. Both the bedroom and the sitting room have an 11-ft. tray ceiling and a view of a romantic two-sided fireplace. The master bath boasts a 13½-ft. vaulted ceiling, a garden tub, a three-sided mirror and a dual-sink vanity with knee space.
- A second bath is shared by the two remaining bedrooms.
- Unless otherwise noted, all rooms have 9-ft. ceilings.

Plan FB-5154-GEOR

Bedrooms: 3	Baths: 2½
Living Area:	
Main floor	2,236 sq. ft.
Total Living Area:	**2,236 sq. ft.**
Daylight basement	2,236 sq. ft.
Garage	483 sq. ft.
Exterior Wall Framing:	2x4

Foundation Options:

Daylight basement
Crawlspace
(All plans can be built with your choice of foundation and framing. A generic conversion diagram is available. See order form.)

BLUEPRINT PRICE CODE: C

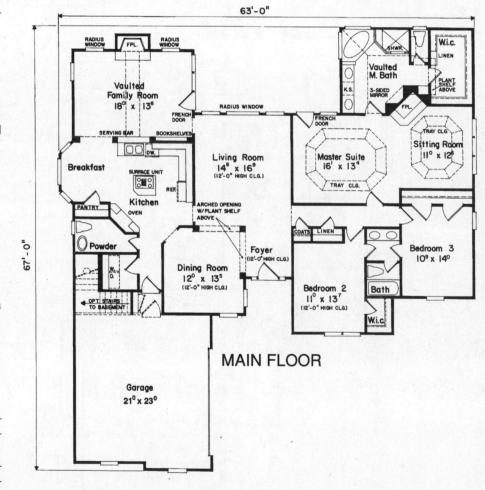

MAIN FLOOR

 TO ORDER THIS BLUEPRINT, CALL TOLL-FREE 1-800-820-1283   Plan FB-5154-GEOR   PRICES AND DETAILS ON PAGES 12-15

Homey Hacienda

- This stylish home combines visual impact with an easy-living floor plan.
- Appealing arched windows attract the eye, while the low-sloping tiled roof and deep overhangs protect the home from the sun's rays.
- The tiled front entry is flanked by the dining room and a quiet study.

- Straight ahead, the spacious sunken living room features a fireplace bordered by bright windows.
- The adjoining breakfast area has sliding glass doors to a covered rear patio. The kitchen features a snack bar and a pass-through to the living room.
- The secluded master suite offers a large walk-in closet and a private bath with a luxurious spa tub. French doors lead to the patio.
- The two remaining bedrooms enjoy private access to another full bath.

Plan Q-2298-1A	
Bedrooms: 3+	**Baths:** 2½
Living Area:	
Main floor	2,298 sq. ft.
Total Living Area:	**2,298 sq. ft.**
Garage	433 sq. ft.
Exterior Wall Framing:	2x4
Foundation Options:	
Slab	

(All plans can be built with your choice of foundation and framing. A generic conversion diagram is available. See order form.)

| **BLUEPRINT PRICE CODE:** | **C** |

MAIN FLOOR

Easy Elegance

- Beautiful details combine with many traditional elements to give this home an easy but elegant feel.
- Inside, a 14-ft. ceiling tops the entry. Two half-walls with built-in shelves and natural wood columns introduce the dining room and a quiet study. The dining room features an 11-ft. ceiling, while the study has a 9-ft. ceiling and a neat built-in desk with shelves above.
- Beyond two more wood columns, the stunning living room shows off a 10-ft. stepped ceiling.
- A butler's pantry and a step-in pantry are nestled between the dining room and the gourmet kitchen. The kitchen's high counter extends to the adjacent family room, while the sunny breakfast nook overlooks a back porch.
- The family room includes a 10-ft. stepped ceiling, a media center and French doors to the porch.
- Two secondary bedrooms nearby are serviced by a full bath.
- Across the home, a 10-ft. stepped ceiling and a sitting area highlight the master bedroom. Two walk-in closets lead to the private bath, where two vanities make life a little easier.

Plan RD-2448

Bedrooms: 3+	Baths: 3
Living Area:	
Main floor	2,448 sq. ft.
Total Living Area:	**2,448 sq. ft.**
Garage and storage	539 sq. ft.
Exterior Wall Framing:	2x4

Foundation Options:

Crawlspace
Slab
(All plans can be built with your choice of foundation and framing. A generic conversion diagram is available. See order form.)

BLUEPRINT PRICE CODE: C

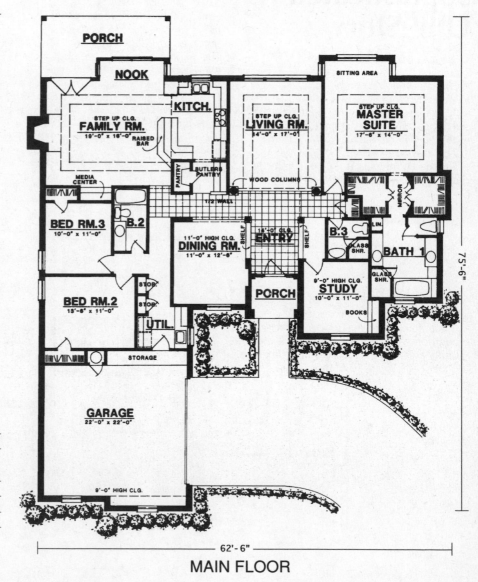

MAIN FLOOR

Sophisticated One-Story

- Beautiful windows accentuated by elegant keystones highlight the exterior of this sophisticated one-story design.
- An open floor plan is the hallmark of the interior, beginning with the foyer that provides instant views of the study as well as the dining and living rooms.
- The spacious living room boasts a fireplace with built-in bookshelves and a rear window wall that stretches into the morning room.
- The sunny morning room has a snack bar to the kitchen. The island kitchen includes a walk-in pantry, a built-in desk and easy access to the utility room and the convenient half-bath.
- The master suite features private access to a nice covered patio, plus an enormous walk-in closet and a posh bath with a spa tub and glass-block shower.
- A hall bath serves the two secondary bedrooms. These three rooms, plus the utility area, have standard 8-ft. ceilings. Other ceilings are 10 ft. high.

Plan DD-2455

Bedrooms: 3+	Baths: 2½
Living Area:	
Main floor	2,457 sq. ft.
Total Living Area:	**2,457 sq. ft.**
Standard basement	2,457 sq. ft.
Garage	585 sq. ft.
Exterior Wall Framing:	2x4

Foundation Options:

Standard basement
Crawlspace
Slab

(All plans can be built with your choice of foundation and framing. A generic conversion diagram is available. See order form.)

BLUEPRINT PRICE CODE: C

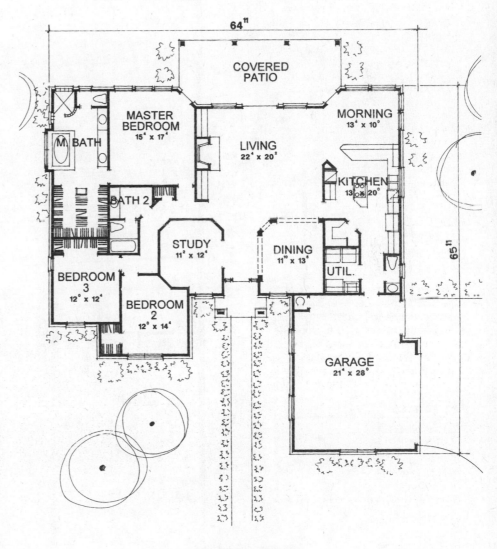

MAIN FLOOR

TO ORDER THIS BLUEPRINT,
CALL TOLL-FREE 1-800-820-1283

Plan DD-2455

PRICES AND DETAILS
ON PAGES 12-15

205

Attractive One-Story Design

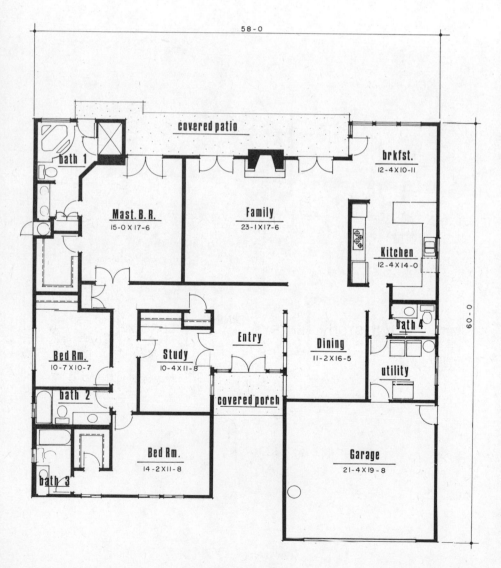

covered patio

bath 1

brkfst.
12-4 X 10-11

Mast. B.R.
15-0 X 17-6

Family
23-1 X 17-6

Kitchen
12-4 X 14-0

bath 4

Bed Rm.
10-7 X 10-7

Study
10-4 X 11-8

Entry

Dining
11-2 X 16-5

utility

bath 2

covered porch

Bed Rm.
14-2 X 11-8

bath 3

Garage
21-4 X 19-8

58-0

60-0

- **Three bedrooms** are more-or-less isolated in a quiet zone at the left, and each has a private bath.
- **Master suite** features deluxe bath with access to a covered patio.
- **Main part of the home** is designed in a Great Room concept, with the family room, dining room, breakfast nook and kitchen all flowing together.
- **A study** off the entry way can serve as a home office or sitting room off the bedroom hallway.
- **A convenient utility room** and powder room are located in the passage way from the garage to the kitchen.

Plan Q-2476-1A

Bedrooms: 3	Baths: 3½

Space:

Total living area:	2,476 sq. ft.
Garage:	420 sq. ft.

Exterior Wall Framing:	2x4

Foundation options:
Slab only.
(Foundation & framing conversion diagram available — see order form.)

Blueprint Price Code:	C

Open and Airy

- Dramatic round-topped windows and a distinctive hip roofline add character to this open and airy one-story home.
- Highlighted by a delightful arched transom window, the 12-ft.-high entry introduces the spacious interior.
- A lovely Palladian window brightens the formal dining room, which flows diagonally into the living room to create an even more open feel.
- The good-sized living room features glass doors to a covered backyard porch. A handsome corner fireplace adds warmth to the area.
- The unique kitchen includes a snack bar that serves the bay-windowed morning room. Garage access, a laundry room and a half-bath are conveniently nearby.
- The master bedroom is secluded for privacy. The master bath boasts a garden tub, a separate shower, a dual-sink vanity and a roomy walk-in closet.
- Two additional bedrooms offer private access to a shared bath.

Plan DD-2379

Bedrooms: 3+	Baths: 2½
Living Area:	
Main floor	2,479 sq. ft.
Total Living Area:	**2,479 sq. ft.**
Standard basement	2,479 sq. ft.
Garage	470 sq. ft.
Exterior Wall Framing:	2x4

Foundation Options:

Standard basement
Crawlspace
Slab

(All plans can be built with your choice of foundation and framing. A generic conversion diagram is available. See order form.)

BLUEPRINT PRICE CODE:	C

MAIN FLOOR

TO ORDER THIS BLUEPRINT,
CALL TOLL-FREE 1-800-820-1283

Plan DD-2379

PRICES AND DETAILS
ON PAGES 12-15

207

Exquisite Farmhouse

- This exquisite home is characterized by a nostalgic facade that disguises a uniquely modern floor plan.
- The covered front porch leads guests to the bright, sidelighted foyer. The foyer is flanked by the formal dining room and a quiet study as it flows to the living room.
- The spacious living room boasts an 11-ft. stepped ceiling and a handsome corner fireplace. French doors open to a covered back porch.
- The walk-through kitchen features a sunny bayed breakfast nook, a nifty work desk and an angled sink and snack counter.
- A half-bath, a laundry room and access to the two-car garage are all close by.
- The isolated master suite boasts two walk-in closets and a lavish private bath with a bayed garden tub, a separate shower and a dual-sink vanity.
- At the opposite end of the home, three additional bedrooms are serviced by two full baths.

Plan VL-2483	
Bedrooms: 4	**Baths:** 3½
Living Area:	
Main floor	2,483 sq. ft.
Total Living Area:	**2,483 sq. ft.**
Garage	504 sq. ft.
Exterior Wall Framing:	2x4
Foundation Options:	
Crawlspace	
Slab	

(All plans can be built with your choice of foundation and framing. A generic conversion diagram is available. See order form.)

BLUEPRINT PRICE CODE:	C

MAIN FLOOR

Plan VL-2483

PRICES AND DETAILS ON PAGES 12-15

Updated Creole

- This Louisiana-style raised cottage features a tin roof, shuttered windows and three pairs of French doors, all of which add to the comfort and nostalgic appeal of this Creole classic.
- The French doors enter from the cool and relaxing front porch to the formal living areas and a front bedroom.
- The central living room merges with the dining room and the kitchen's eating area. A fireplace warms the whole area while more French doors access a covered backyard porch.
- The efficient kitchen offers an angled snack bar and a bay-windowed nook that overlooks the porch and deck.
- A secluded master suite showcases a private bathroom, fit for the most demanding taste. Across the home the secondary bedrooms include abundant closet space and share a full bath.
- This full-featured, energy-efficient design also includes a large utility room and extra storage space in the garage.

Plan E-1823

Bedrooms: 3	Baths: 2
Living Area:	
Main floor	1,800 sq. ft.
Total Living Area:	**1,800 sq. ft.**
Garage	550 sq. ft.
Exterior Wall Framing:	2x6

Foundation Options:

Crawlspace

Slab

(All plans can be built with your choice of foundation and framing. A generic conversion diagram is available. See order form.)

BLUEPRINT PRICE CODE:	B

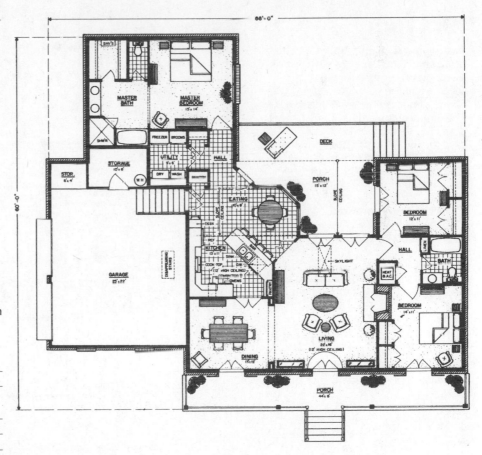

MAIN FLOOR

TO ORDER THIS BLUEPRINT,
CALL TOLL-FREE 1-800-820-1283

Plan E-1823

PRICES AND DETAILS
ON PAGES 12-15

209

Cozy Covered Porches

- Twin dormers give this raised one-story design the appearance of a two-story. Two covered porches and a deck supplement the main living areas with plenty of outdoor entertaining space.
- The large central living room features a dramatic fireplace, a 12-ft. ceiling with a skylight and access to both porch areas.
- Double doors open to a bayed eating area, which overlooks the adjoining deck and includes a sloped ceiling that rises to 12 ft. in the kitchen. An angled snack bar and a pantry are also featured.
- The elegant master suite is tucked to one side of the home and also overlooks the backyard and deck. Laundry facilities and garage access are nearby.
- Across the home, two additional bedrooms share another full bath.

Plan E-1826

Bedrooms: 3	Baths: 2
Living Area:	
Main floor	1,800 sq. ft.
Total Living Area:	**1,800 sq. ft.**
Garage	550 sq. ft.
Storage	84 sq. ft.
Exterior Wall Framing:	2x6

Foundation Options:
Crawlspace
Slab
(All plans can be built with your choice of foundation and framing. A generic conversion diagram is available. See order form.)

BLUEPRINT PRICE CODE: B

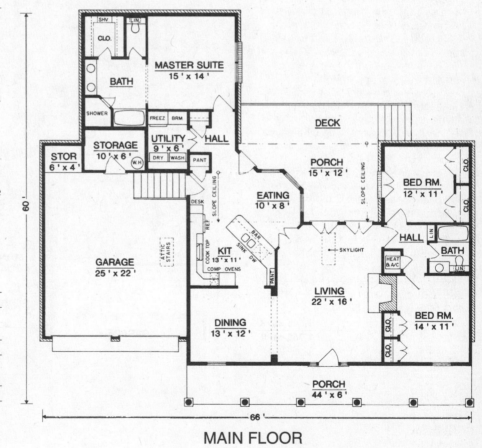

MAIN FLOOR

Plan E-1826

PRICES AND DETAILS ON PAGES 12-15

Designed for Livability

- As you enter this excitingly spacious traditional home, you see through the extensive windows to the backyard.
- This four-bedroom home was designed for the livability of the maturing family with the separation of the master suite.
- The formal dining room expands spatially to the living room while being set off by a decorative column and plant shelves.
- The bay that creates the morning room and the sitting area for the master suite also adds excitement to this plan, both inside and out.
- The master bath offers an exciting oval tub under glass and a separate shower, as well as a spacious walk-in closet and a dressing area.

Plan DD-1696

Bedrooms: 4	Baths: 2
Living Area:	
Main floor	1,748 sq. ft.
Total Living Area:	**1,748 sq. ft.**
Standard basement	1,748 sq. ft.
Garage	393 sq. ft.
Exterior Wall Framing:	2x4

Foundation Options:

Standard basement
Crawlspace
Slab
(All plans can be built with your choice of foundation and framing. A generic conversion diagram is available. See order form.)

BLUEPRINT PRICE CODE:	B

MAIN FLOOR

TO ORDER THIS BLUEPRINT,
CALL TOLL-FREE 1-800-820-1283

Plan DD-1696

PRICES AND DETAILS
ON PAGES 12-15

211

Fresh Air

- With its nostalgic look and country style, this lovely home brings a breath of fresh air into any neighborhood.
- Past the inviting wraparound porch, the foyer is brightened by an arched transom window above the front door.
- The adjoining formal dining room is defined by decorative columns and features a 9-ft., 4-in. stepped ceiling.
- The bright and airy kitchen includes a pantry, a windowed sink and a sunny breakfast area with porch access.
- Enhanced by an 11-ft stepped ceiling, the spacious Great Room is warmed by a fireplace flanked by sliding glass doors to a covered back porch.
- The lush master bedroom boasts an 11-ft. tray ceiling and a bayed sitting area. The master bath showcases a circular spa tub with a glass-block wall.
- The two remaining bedrooms are serviced by a second bath and a nearby laundry room. The protruding bedroom has a 12-ft. vaulted ceiling.
- Additional living space can be made available by finishing the upper floor.

Plan AX-93308

Bedrooms: 3+	Baths: 2
Living Area:	
Main floor	1,793 sq. ft.
Total Living Area:	**1,793 sq. ft.**
Standard basement	1,793 sq. ft.
Unfinished upper floor	779 sq. ft.
Garage and utility	471 sq. ft.
Exterior Wall Framing:	2x4

Foundation Options:
Standard basement
Crawlspace
Slab
(All plans can be built with your choice of foundation and framing. A generic conversion diagram is available. See order form.)

BLUEPRINT PRICE CODE:	B

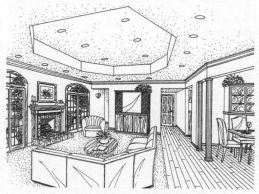

VIEW INTO GREAT ROOM

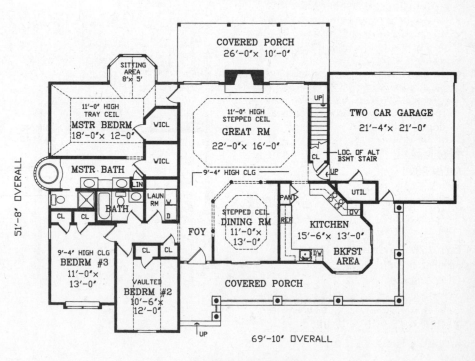

MAIN FLOOR

Plan AX-93308

PRICES AND DETAILS
ON PAGES 12-15

Showy One-Story

- Dramatic windows embellish the exterior of this showy one-story home.
- Inside, the entry provides a sweeping view of the living room, where sliding glass doors open to the backyard patio and flank a dramatic fireplace.
- Skylights accent the living room's 12-ft. sloped ceiling, while arched openings define the formal dining room.
- Double doors lead from the dining room to the kitchen and informal eating area. The kitchen features a built-in work desk and a pantry. An oversized utility room adjoins the kitchen and accesses the two-car garage.
- A 10-ft. tray ceiling adorns the master suite. The private bath is accented with a skylight above the fabulous fan-shaped marble tub. His-and-hers vanities, a separate shower and a huge walk-in closet are also featured.
- Two more bedrooms and a full bath are located at the other end of the home.
- The front-facing bedroom boasts a 12-ft. sloped ceiling.

Plan E-1830

Bedrooms: 3	Baths: 2
Living Area:	
Main floor	1,868 sq. ft.
Total Living Area:	**1,868 sq. ft.**
Garage and storage	616 sq. ft.
Exterior Wall Framing:	2x6

Foundation Options:

Crawlspace

Slab

(All plans can be built with your choice of foundation and framing. A generic conversion diagram is available. See order form.)

BLUEPRINT PRICE CODE: **B**

MAIN FLOOR

TO ORDER THIS BLUEPRINT,
CALL TOLL-FREE 1-800-820-1283

Plan E-1830

PRICES AND DETAILS
ON PAGES 12-15

213

Elegance Inside and Out

- The raised front porch of this home is finely detailed with wood columns, railings, moldings, and French doors with half-round transoms.
- The living room, dining room and entry have 12-ft.-high ceilings. Skylights illuminate the living room, which offers a fireplace and access to a roomy deck.
- The efficient kitchen permits easy service to both the dining room and the casual eating area.
- The master suite features a raised tray ceiling and an enormous skylighted bath with a walk-in closet, dual vanities and a large quarter-circle spa tub surrounded by a mirror wall.
- On the left, two secondary bedrooms are insulated from the more active areas of the home by an efficient hallway, and also share another full bath.

Plan E-1909

Bedrooms: 3	Baths: 2
Living Area:	
Main floor	1,936 sq. ft.
Total Living Area:	**1,936 sq. ft.**
Garage	484 sq. ft.
Storage	132 sq. ft.
Exterior Wall Framing:	2x6

Foundation Options:

Crawlspace

Slab

(All plans can be built with your choice of foundation and framing. A generic conversion diagram is available. See order form.)

BLUEPRINT PRICE CODE: B

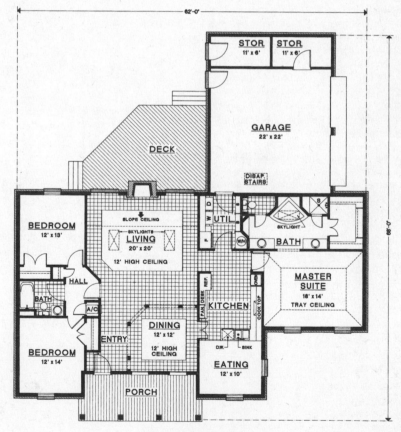

MAIN FLOOR

TO ORDER THIS BLUEPRINT, CALL TOLL-FREE 1-800-820-1283

Plan E-1909

PRICES AND DETAILS ON PAGES 12-15

A Real Original

- This home's round window, elegant entry and transom windows create an eye-catching, original look.
- Inside, high ceilings and tremendous views let the eyes wander. The foyer provides an exciting look at the expansive deck and the inviting spa through the living room's tall windows. The windows frame a handsome fireplace, while a 10-ft. ceiling adds volume and interest.
- To the right of the foyer is a cozy den or home office with its own fireplace, 10-ft. ceiling and dramatic windows.
- The spacious kitchen/breakfast area features an oversized snack bar island and opens to a large screen porch. Within easy reach are the laundry room and the entrance to the garage.
- The bright formal dining room overlooks the deck and boasts a ceiling that vaults up to 10 feet.
- The secluded master suite looks out to the deck as well, with access through a patio door. The private bath features a dynamite corner spa tub, a separate shower and a large walk-in closet.
- A second bedroom and bath complete the main floor.

Plan B-90065

Bedrooms: 2+	Baths: 2
Living Area:	
Main floor	1,889 sq. ft.
Total Living Area:	**1,889 sq. ft.**
Standard basement	1,889 sq. ft.
Garage	406 sq. ft.
Exterior Wall Framing:	2x6

Foundation Options:

Standard basement
(All plans can be built with your choice of foundation and framing. A generic conversion diagram is available. See order form.)

BLUEPRINT PRICE CODE:	**B**

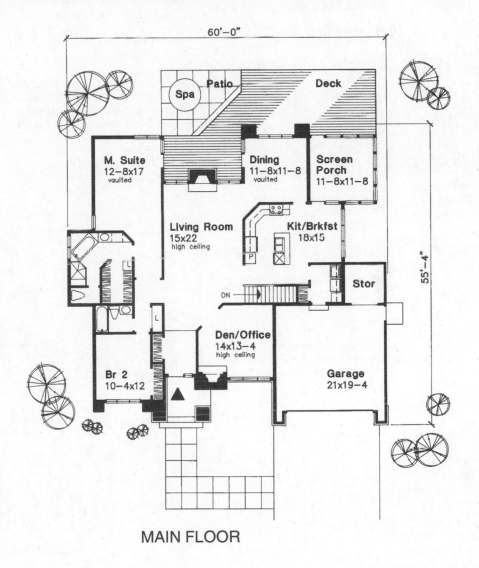

MAIN FLOOR

Plan B-90065

Photo by Mark Englund/HomeStyles

Spectacular Country Kitchen

- Repeated front-projecting gables, brick accents and a half-round window give a rustic appeal to this exciting one-story.
- Past the inviting columned entry, a plant shelf presides over the foyer.
- Straight ahead, the sunken living room boasts a 12-ft. vaulted ceiling and a warming fireplace flanked by windows.
- The adjoining dining room features a sunny bay window and is easily served by a pass-through from the kitchen.

- The spectacular country kitchen offers a second fireplace and glass doors to a backyard deck. A pantry and a built-in desk are also included. A nearby laundry room gives convenient access to the two-car garage.
- The luxurious master suite is enhanced by corner windows and a 9-ft. ceiling. The master bath has an overhead plant shelf, a walk-in closet and a separate tub and shower.
- Two more bedrooms share a roomy second bath and a hallway linen closet.
- The front-facing den off the entry could double as a home office, library or guest bedroom.

Plan B-88009	
Bedrooms: 3+	**Baths:** 2
Living Area:	
Main floor	1,993 sq. ft.
Total Living Area:	**1,993 sq. ft.**
Standard basement	1,993 sq. ft.
Garage	484 sq. ft.
Exterior Wall Framing:	2x4

Foundation Options:

Standard basement
(All plans can be built with your choice of foundation and framing. A generic conversion diagram is available. See order form.)

BLUEPRINT PRICE CODE: **B**

**NOTE:
The above photographed home may have been modified by the homeowner. Please refer to floor plan and/or drawn elevation shown for actual blueprint details.

60'-0"

48'-4"

Master Suite
16-6x12-9
High Ceiling

Plant Shelf

Living Rm
14x21-6
vaulted

Dining
13-6x10

DN

Deck

Country Kitchen
28x13

Desk

DN

DN

Plant Shelf

Lndry
D W

P

Den
11x10-3

Br 2
10x11

Br 3
10x10-6

Raised Ceiling

Garage
22x22

MAIN FLOOR

Plan B-88009

PRICES AND DETAILS *ON PAGES 12-15*

Photo by Mark Englund/HomeStyles

French Garden Design

- A creative, angular design gives this traditional French garden home an exciting, open and airy floor plan.
- Guests enter through a covered, columned porch that opens into the large, angled living and dining rooms.
- High 12-ft. ceilings highlight the living and dining area, which also features corner windows, a wet bar, a cozy fireplace and access to a huge covered backyard porch.
- The angled walk-through kitchen, also with a 12-ft.-high ceiling, offers plenty of work space and an adjoining informal eating nook that faces a delightful private courtyard. The nearby utility area has extra freezer space, a walk-in pantry and garage access.
- The home's bedrooms are housed in two separate wings. One wing boasts a luxurious master suite, which features a large walk-in closet, an angled tub and a separate shower.
- Two large bedrooms in the other wing share a hall bath. Each bedroom has a walk-in closet.

Plan E-2004

Bedrooms: 3	Baths: 2
Living Area:	
Main floor	2,023 sq. ft.
Total Living Area:	**2,023 sq. ft.**
Garage	484 sq. ft.
Storage	87 sq. ft.
Exterior Wall Framing:	2x6

Foundation Options:

Crawlspace

Slab

(All plans can be built with your choice of foundation and framing. A generic conversion diagram is available. See order form.)

BLUEPRINT PRICE CODE: C

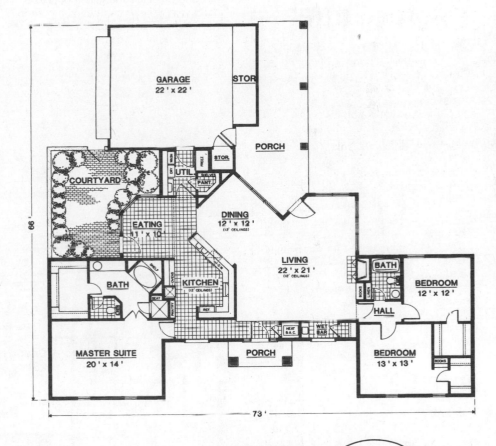

MAIN FLOOR

**NOTE: The above photographed home may have been modified by the homeowner. Please refer to floor plan and/or drawn elevation shown for actual blueprint details.

Photo courtesy of Breland & Farmer Designers, Inc.

Luxurious Master Suite

- The inviting facade of this gorgeous one-story design boasts a sheltered porch, symmetrical architecture and elegant window treatments.
- Inside, beautiful arched openings frame the living room, which features a 12-ft. ceiling, a dramatic fireplace and a wet bar that is open to the deluxe kitchen.
- The roomy kitchen is highlighted by an island cooktop, a built-in desk and a snack bar that faces the bayed eating area and the covered back porch.
- Isolated to the rear of the home, the master suite is a romantic retreat, offering an intimate sitting area and a luxurious bath. Entered through elegant double doors, the private bath showcases a skylighted corner tub, a separate shower, his-and-hers vanities, and a huge walk-in closet.
- The two remaining bedrooms have walk-in closets and share a hall bath.
- Unless otherwise specified, the home has 9-ft. ceilings throughout.

Plan E-2106

Bedrooms: 3	Baths: 2
Living Area:	
Main floor	2,177 sq. ft.
Total Living Area:	**2,177 sq. ft.**
Standard basement	2,177 sq. ft.
Garage and storage	570 sq. ft.
Exterior Wall Framing:	2x4

Foundation Options:
Standard basement
Crawlspace
Slab
(All plans can be built with your choice of foundation and framing. A generic conversion diagram is available. See order form.)

BLUEPRINT PRICE CODE: C

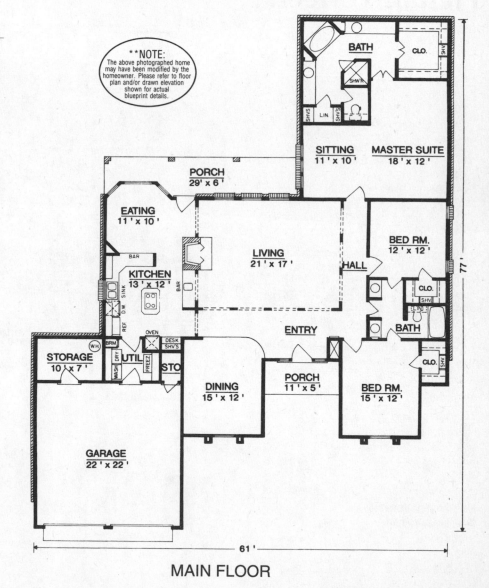

NOTE: The above photographed home may have been modified by the homeowner. Please refer to floor plan and/or drawn elevation shown for actual blueprint details.

MAIN FLOOR

TO ORDER THIS BLUEPRINT, CALL TOLL-FREE 1-800-820-1283

Plan E-2106

PRICES AND DETAILS ON PAGES 12-15

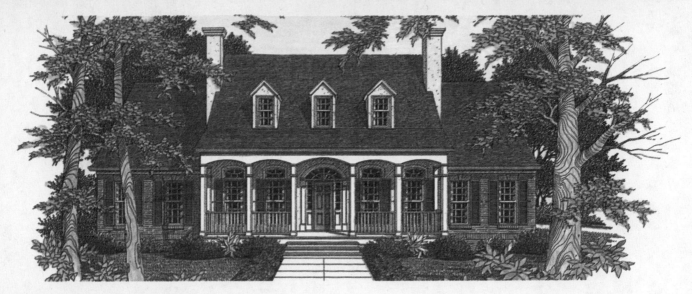

Picture-Perfect!

- With graceful arches, columns and railings, the wonderful front porch makes this home the picture of country charm. Decorative chimneys, shutters and quaint dormers add more style.
- Inside, the foyer shows off sidelights and a fantail transom. The foyer is flanked by the dining room and a bedroom, both of which boast porch views and arched transoms. All three areas are expanded by 10-ft. ceilings.
- The living room also flaunts a 10-ft. ceiling, plus a fireplace and French doors that open to a skylighted porch. The remaining rooms offer 9-ft. ceilings.
- The L-shaped kitchen has an island cooktop and a sunny breakfast nook.
- A Palladian window arrangement brightens the sitting alcove in the master suite. Other highlights include porch access and a fantastic bath with a garden tub and a separate shower.
- The upper floor is perfect for future expansion space.

Plan J-9401

Bedrooms: 3+	Baths: 2½
Living Area:	
Main floor	2,089 sq. ft.
Total Living Area:	**2,089 sq. ft.**
Upper floor (unfinished)	878 sq. ft.
Standard basement	2,089 sq. ft.
Garage and storage	530 sq. ft.
Exterior Wall Framing:	2x4

Foundation Options:

Standard basement
Crawlspace
Slab

(All plans can be built with your choice of foundation and framing. A generic conversion diagram is available. See order form.)

BLUEPRINT PRICE CODE:	C

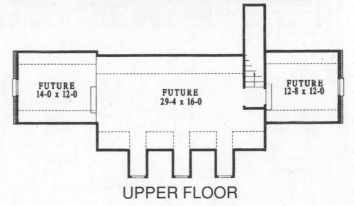

UPPER FLOOR

MAIN FLOOR

Versatile
Sun Room

- This cozy country-style home offers an inviting front porch and an interior just as welcoming.
- The spacious living room features a warming fireplace and windows that overlook the porch.
- The living room opens to a dining area, where French doors access a covered porch and a sunny patio.
- The island kitchen has a sink view, plenty of counter space, and a handy pass-through to the adjoining sun room. The bright sun room is large enough to serve as a formal dining room, a family room or a hobby room.
- The private master suite is secluded to the rear. A garden spa tub, dual walk-in closets and separate dressing areas are nice features found in the master bath.

Plan J-90014

Bedrooms: 3	Baths: 2½
Living Area:	
Main floor	2,190 sq. ft.
Total Living Area:	**2,190 sq. ft.**
Standard basement	2,190 sq. ft.
Garage	465 sq. ft.
Storage	34 sq. ft.
Exterior Wall Framing:	2x6

Foundation Options:

Standard basement

Crawlspace

Slab

(All plans can be built with your choice of foundation and framing. A generic conversion diagram is available. See order form.)

BLUEPRINT PRICE CODE: C

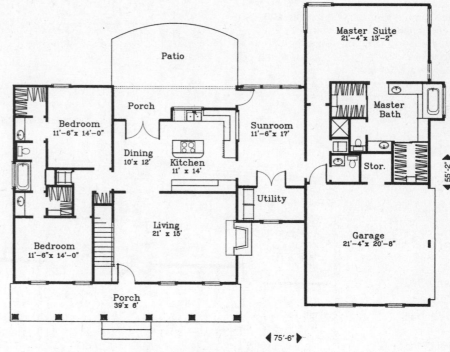

MAIN FLOOR

*TO ORDER THIS BLUEPRINT,
CALL TOLL-FREE 1-800-820-1283*

Plan J-90014

*PRICES AND DETAILS
ON PAGES 12-15*

Classic Styling

- This handsome one-story traditional would look great in town or in the country. The shuttered and paned windows, narrow lap siding and brick accents make it a classic.
- The sprawling design begins with the spacious, central living room, featuring a beamed ceiling that slopes up to 14 feet. A window wall overlooks the covered backyard porch, and an inviting fireplace includes an extra-wide hearth and built-in bookshelves.
- The galley-style kitchen features a snack bar to the sunny eating area and a raised-panel door to the dining room.
- The isolated master suite is a quiet haven offering a large walk-in closet, a dressing room and a spacious bath.
- Three more bedrooms, two with walk-in closets, and a compartmentalized bath are located at the opposite side of the home.

Plan E-2206	
Bedrooms: 4	**Baths:** 2
Living Area:	
Main floor	2,200 sq. ft.
Total Living Area:	**2,200 sq. ft.**
Standard basement	2,200 sq. ft.
Garage and storage	624 sq. ft.
Exterior Wall Framing:	2x6

Foundation Options:
Standard basement
Crawlspace
Slab
(All plans can be built with your choice of foundation and framing. A generic conversion diagram is available. See order form.)

BLUEPRINT PRICE CODE:	C

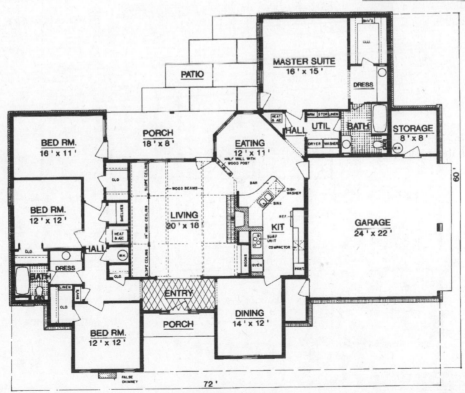

MAIN FLOOR

TO ORDER THIS BLUEPRINT,
CALL TOLL-FREE 1-800-820-1283

Plan E-2206

*PRICES AND DETAILS
ON PAGES 12-15*

221

Photo by Mark Englund/HomeStyles

Sprawling French Provincial

- This sprawling French Provincial design offers an attractive, efficient balance of living and sleeping areas.
- The family room at the center of the floor plan serves as a comfortable gathering place, complete with a handsome fireplace and an attached screened porch.
- To the right of the foyer, the formal living room overlooks the front yard and flows into the dining room.

- A U-shaped kitchen with a pantry is open to a lovely bayed breakfast area that provides views of the outdoors.
- A half-bath and a laundry room are conveniently located near the garage.
- Three bedrooms are situated at the opposite end of the home. A full bath with a separate dressing area services the two secondary bedrooms. The master bedroom offers a private bath with a cathedral ceiling and a skylighted spa tub. Ample closet space, a dual-sink vanity and a separate shower are also included.
- A stairway off the family room accesses attic storage space.

Plan C-8363

Bedrooms: 3	**Baths:** 2½
Living Area:	
Main floor	2,400 sq. ft.
Total Living Area:	**2,400 sq. ft.**
Daylight basement	2,400 sq. ft.
Garage	546 sq. ft.
Exterior Wall Framing:	2x4

Foundation Options:
Daylight basement
Crawlspace
Slab
(All plans can be built with your choice of foundation and framing. A generic conversion diagram is available. See order form.)

BLUEPRINT PRICE CODE: C

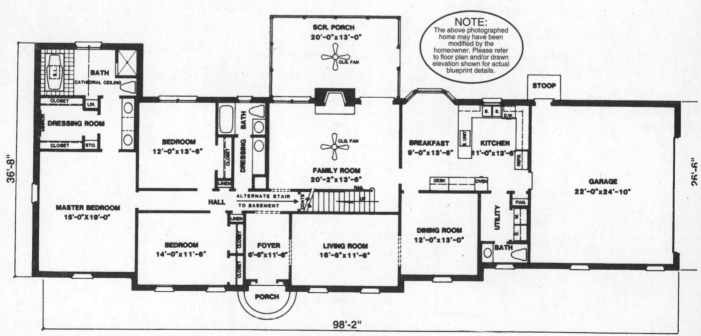

NOTE:
The above photographed home may have been modified by the homeowner. Please refer to floor plan and/or drawn elevation shown for actual blueprint details.

MAIN FLOOR

TO ORDER THIS BLUEPRINT,
CALL TOLL-FREE 1-800-820-1283

Plan C-8363

PRICES AND DETAILS
ON PAGES 12-15

High Luxury
in One Story

- Beautiful arched windows lend a luxurious feeling to the exterior of this one-story home.
- Soaring 12-ft. ceilings add volume to both the wide entry area and the central living room, which boasts a large fireplace and access to a covered porch and the patio beyond.
- Double doors separate the formal dining room from the corridor-style kitchen. Features of the kitchen include a pantry and an angled eating bar. The sunny, bayed eating area is perfect for casual family meals.
- The plush master suite has amazing amenities: a walk-in closet, a skylighted, angled whirlpool tub, a separate shower and private access to the laundry/utility room and the patio.
- Three good-sized bedrooms and a full bath are situated across the home.

Plan E-2302

Bedrooms: 4	Baths: 2
Living Area:	
Main floor	2,396 sq. ft.
Total Living Area:	**2,396 sq. ft.**
Standard basement	2,396 sq. ft.
Garage	484 sq. ft.
Exterior Wall Framing:	2x6

Foundation Options:
Standard basement
Crawlspace
Slab
(All plans can be built with your choice of foundation and framing. A generic conversion diagram is available. See order form.)

BLUEPRINT PRICE CODE: C

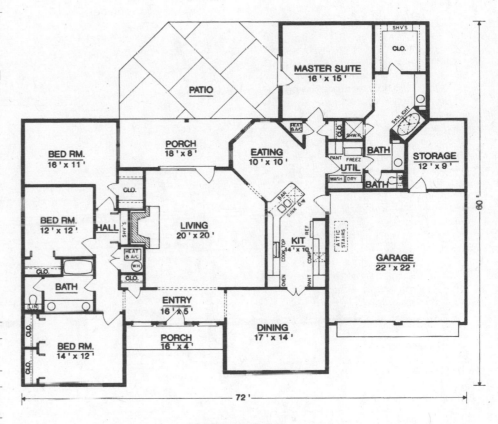

MAIN FLOOR

Wonderful Detailing

- The wonderfully detailed front porch, with its graceful arches, columns and railings, gives this home a character all its own. Dormer windows and arched transoms further accentuate the porch.
- The floor plan features a central living room with a 10-ft.-high ceiling and a fireplace framed by French doors. These doors open to a covered porch or a sun room, and a sheltered deck beyond.
- Just off the living room, the island kitchen and breakfast area provide a spacious place for family or guests. The nearby formal dining room has arched transom windows and a 10-ft. ceiling, as does the bedroom off the foyer. All of the remaining rooms have 9-ft. ceilings.
- The unusual master suite includes a window alcove, access to the porch and a fantastic bath with a garden tub.
- A huge utility room, a storage area off the garage and a 1,000-sq.-ft. attic space are other bonuses of this design.

Plan J-90019

Bedrooms: 3	Baths: 2½
Living Area:	
Main floor	2,410 sq. ft.
Total Living Area:	**2,410 sq. ft.**
Standard basement	2,410 sq. ft.
Garage	512 sq. ft.
Storage	86 sq. ft.
Exterior Wall Framing:	2x6

Foundation Options:

Standard basement
Crawlspace
Slab

(All plans can be built with your choice of foundation and framing. A generic conversion diagram is available. See order form.)

BLUEPRINT PRICE CODE:	C

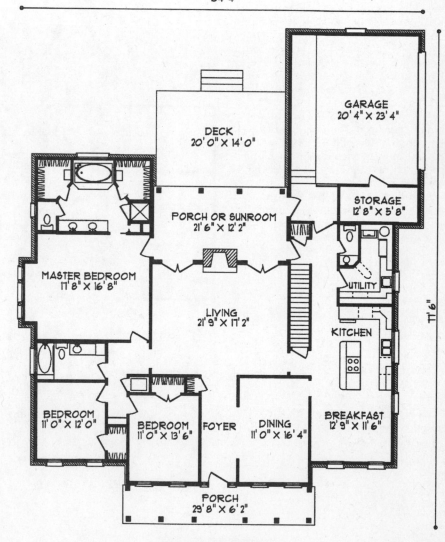

MAIN FLOOR

     Plan J-90019   *PRICES AND DETAILS ON PAGES 12-15*